THE EMPLOYER'S HANDBOOK

THE EMPLOYER'S HANDBOOK

An essential guide to employment law, personnel policies and procedures

Revised Fifth Edition

BARRY CUSHWAY

KOGAN PAGE

London and Philadelphia

This book has been endorsed by the Institute of Directors.

The endorsement is given to selected Kogan Page books which the IoD recognizes as being of specific interest to its members and providing them with up-to-date, informative and practical resources for creating business success. Kogan Page books endorsed by the IoD represent the most authoritative guidance available on a wide range of subjects including management, finance, marketing, training and HR.

The views expressed in this book are those of the author and are not necessarily the same as those of the Institute of Directors.

First published in Great Britain 2002 by Kogan Page Limited
Second edition 2004
Third edition 2005
Fourth edition 2006
Fifth edition 2007
Revised fifth edition 2008

120 Pentonville Road
London N1 9JN
United Kingdom
www.koganpage.com

525 South 4th Street, #241
Philadelphia PA 19147
USA

© Barry Cushway, 2002, 2004, 2005, 2006, 2007, 2008

Figure 17.1 reproduced by kind permission from Pearson Education Ltd.

The right of Barry Cushway to be identified as the author of this work has been asserted by him in accordance with the Copyright, Designs and Patents Act 1988.

ISBN 978 0 7494 5116 5 (hardback)
ISBN 978 0 7494 5324 4 (paperback)

British Library Cataloguing in Publication Data

A CIP record for this book is available from the British Library.

Library of Congress Cataloguing-in-Publication Data

Cushway, Barry.
    The employer's handbook : an essential guide to employment law, personnel policies, and procedures / Barry Cushway. – – Rev. 5th ed.
        p. cm.
    Includes index.
    ISBN 978-0-7494-5116-5
    1. Labor laws and legislation– –Great Britain. I. Title.
    KD3095.C87 2008
    344.4101– –dc22

                            2008011772

Typeset by JS Typesetting Ltd, Porthcawl, Wales
Printed and bound in Great Britain by Cambridge University Press

Contents

ANDERSON STRATHERN LLP – FORMIDABLE BUT FRIENDLY

The Firm

Anderson Strathern LLP is a full service law firm with its main offices in Edinburgh and Glasgow. With 45 partners and around 350 staff, we provide legal services to clients across the United Kingdom and beyond. Our business is focused on the delivery of the highest quality of legal service through specialist teams who work to develop a real understanding and interest in the business and personal objectives of our clients.

The Employment Unit

Anderson Strathern's Employment Unit has been established for over 10 years and in that time has increased from 2 lawyers to 16, attracting a succession of new clients. We have Scotland's only dedicated Discrimination Law Service, headed by Jill Bell. Our continuing growth and success was reflected in our win in the "Employment Team of the Year" category at the 2007 Cuthbert Scottish Legal Awards.

With four partners (two of whom are accredited by the Law Society of Scotland as specialists in Employment Law), a Director, three Associates and a further eight solicitors, our team has the resources and breadth of experience to deal with the full range of employment disputes. Uniquely in a firm of our size, our practice acts for both employers and employees and we are, accordingly, well able to see disputes from both sides of the traditional employer/employee divide. This gives us an insight into the way in which our opponents are likely to conduct matters and a well deserved reputation for solving problems rather than exacerbating them. In addition to transactional work and strategic advice our team is able to deliver bespoke training in Employment and Discrimination.

We believe in the client relationship. We encourage the development of client teams where lawyers really work with, rather than for, the client. We believe that that develops both client and job satisfaction and, as a result, our staff turnover is very low. We work so that the client/lawyer relationship is one that can be built up and developed over a number of years with the client knowing that whichever member of the team takes on their case will remain with them until their case is resolved.

Client List

A sample of our employment client list includes:
- Scottish and Southern Energy plc
- The Royal College of Nursing
- The University of Edinburgh
- INEOS Manufacturing Scotland Limited (formerly a part of BP)
- Glenmorangie
- Royal Zoological Society of Scotland
- East Lothian Council

NEIL MACLEAN,
DEFENDER OF CLIENTS WITH THE FEROCITY OF A THREE-HEADED ROTTWEILER, AND DAUGHTER.

ANDERSON STRATHERN
SOLICITORS

Neil takes his job seriously. Very seriously. We wouldn't have it any other way. And, let's face it, neither would you. Employment Law is a serious business and for that you need a very serious player. But Neil isn't just a lawyer. His qualities as a person: his ability to listen, reassure and sing the occasional lullaby unaccompanied make him approachable, friendly and, above all, someone you want to do business with. He's just one of the many talented and committed people at Anderson Strathern. He's just one of the many reasons why we're one of the best full-service law firms in Scotland.

FORMIDABLE BUT FRIENDLY | 0131 270 7700 | 0141 242 6060 |
www.andersonstrathern.co.uk

BANKING | CONSENT, BUILD & INFRASTRUCTURE | CHARITIES | COMMERCIAL REAL ESTATE | CONSTRUCTION & PROJECTS | CORPORATE | DISCRIMINATION | DISPUTE RESOLUTION | EDUCATION | **EMPLOYMENT** | FAMILY | HEALTH & SOCIAL CARE | INSURANCE SECTOR | IP/IT | LAND RESOURCES | PARLIAMENTARY & PUBLIC LAW | PLANNING & ENVIRONMENT | PRIVATE CLIENT | PUBLIC & REGULATORY | RESIDENTIAL PROPERTY | RESIDENTIAL PROPERTY DEVELOPMENT | RETAIL | SPORT & LEISURE

Stakeholder pensions

What are stakeholder pensions?

Stakeholder pensions are low cost, flexible pensions aimed particularly at people who do not have access to an occupational pension scheme and for whom a personal pension may not be suitable. They were introduced in 2001 as part of the government's commitment to encourage more people to save for their retirement. They offer a number of benefits to employees. For example:

- management charges are capped at 1.5% of the member's pension fund, reducing to 1% after ten years;
- members can change the level of their contributions, stop paying in, or transfer to a different scheme, without charge; and
- members can contribute as little as £20 per month.

Employer contributions to a stakeholder pension are optional. The employer's duty (unless he is exempt as described below) is simply to provide employees with access to a stakeholder scheme.

Stakeholder pensions are DC ('defined contribution') arrangements. This means that the scheme invests contributions in line with its statement of investment principles; the eventual size of the employee's pension fund depends on the amount paid in and the investment returns. As with other types of pension, tax relief on contributions means that, broadly speaking, employees paying basic rate tax of 22% will have £22 added to their fund by the Government for every £78 paid in.

Which employers must provide access to a stakeholder scheme?

As an employer, you do not have provide access to a stakeholder scheme if you have fewer than five employees.

You may also be exempt from the requirement to provide access if:

- you already offer an occupational scheme which staff can join within a year of starting work with you; or
- you offer to contribute at least 3% of salary into a personal pension scheme on behalf of all employees, and this scheme allows the employees to transfer out or stop making contributions without charge.

If none of these conditions applies to you, you must provide access to a stakeholder pension scheme. You must do this for all employees who:

- have worked for you continuously for three months or more; and

- have continuously earned more than the National Insurance lower earnings limit for the last three months.

What does 'providing access' mean?

Providing access to a stakeholder pension scheme does not mean setting up a scheme, appointing trustees or investing funds. It simply means putting employees in touch with an appropriate pension provider and offering them the option of contributing through your payroll. This process is described more fully in the following sections.

Even if you are exempt – for example, if you have fewer than five employees – you may wish to provide your employees with access to a stakeholder scheme. If the number of people you employ varies, it is a good idea to have a scheme in place even if you currently have fewer than five employees.

Once you cease to be exempt, you must provide access to a stakeholder scheme within three months. A fine of up to £50,000 may be imposed for failure to provide access: however, where employers have inadvertently failed to comply with the requirement, they are unlikely to be fined as long as they put the matter right promptly.

The employer's responsibilities

The provision of access to a stakeholder pension scheme can be broken down into a number of stages:

1. Choosing and designating a scheme.

2. Telling your employees about the scheme.

3. Offering payroll deduction.

4. Setting up payment information.

5. Making payments.

These stages are described in detail below.

Choosing and designating a scheme

'Designation' is the term used to describe the formal selection of one or more schemes which are available for your employees to join. Many major insurers, banks, finance companies and other organisations offer stakeholder pensions. To choose a suitable scheme, you could:

- look at the list of registered stakeholder schemes on the Pensions Regulator's website, www.thepensionsregulator.gov.uk;
- talk to an Independent Financial Adviser;
- ask employees for their views; or
- contact a range of providers.

If you talk to pension providers, these are some of the questions you could ask in order to come to a decision about the most suitable scheme:

- What support will you give me to administer payroll deductions?
- Is your charge less than 1.5%? What advice for members will you provide within this charge?
- Are there any restrictions on who can join the scheme?
- Must a certain number of members join in order for the scheme to be designated, or are individual members accepted?

Once you have chosen a scheme, you must check that it is on the Pensions Regulator's register of stakeholder schemes. Although the decision about which scheme to designate is yours, you must also consult your employees (for example, through a minuted meeting, or a letter asking for their views) before formal designation of a scheme.

The next step is to contact the scheme provider to tell them that you wish to designate their scheme. They will ask for some basic details so that they can contact your employees, and will send further information about the scheme.

Employees who are not happy with the choice of designated scheme are free to choose their own stakeholder scheme: however, in this case you are not obliged to offer them the choice of making contributions via payroll deductions. It may also be the case that no employees are currently interested in contributing to a pension. This does not exempt you from the requirement to designate a scheme.

Once a scheme is designated, it is your responsibility to check periodically (for example once a year) that the scheme is still on the Pensions Regulator's register of stakeholder schemes. You are not, as an employer, responsible for the scheme's future investment performance, and you will not be liable if the scheme does not perform as well as other stakeholder schemes.

Telling your employees about the scheme
Following formal designation, you must tell your employees and any representative

organisations about the scheme. As a minimum, you should give the scheme's name, address and a contact phone number: you may also want to circulate the scheme's marketing literature, and perhaps let someone from the provider visit the workplace to talk to staff.

You must also tell employees that they have the choice of paying into the scheme through the firm's payroll if they wish. You should explain that, if employees opt for payroll deductions:

- they can only change the level of contributions once every six months (unless you agree otherwise); and
- there is no charge for stopping or changing contributions.

You must also make it clear to employees that they can seek independent financial advice. As employer, you are not expected to give financial advice or to promote the scheme, only to make employees aware of scheme and to provide factual information. You could also provide them with the relevant leaflets from the Financial Services Authority (available at www.fsa.gov.uk).

Offering payroll deduction

You must offer employees the option of contributing to the designated scheme through payroll deduction. Your scheme provider may be able to help with this.

Contributions are voluntary. Individual employees decide how often and how much they wish to contribute (there may be a minimum contribution of £20, though some providers allow smaller amounts). Deducted contributions may be a fixed sum or a percentage of pay (either basic or gross taxable pay), as agreed with the employee.

Contributions must be deducted after statutory deductions such as tax and NI have been made. The pension provider will then claim tax relief and add it to contributions.

As mentioned above, you must explain to employees that they can only change the level of payroll-deducted contributions once every six months, unless you agree otherwise. While there is no charge for changing or stopping contributions, some employees may prefer to pay direct to the provider if they are unsure about the level and frequency of their contributions.

Setting up payment information

When you have established which employees wish to use payroll deduction, and how much they intend to contribute – and how much, if anything, you will be contributing on each employee's behalf – you must create a record of the payments due (the 'payment information' record). The payment information record is key to the correct operation of your designated stakeholder scheme. You must keep an accurate, up-to-date record of payments due, and ensure that the scheme provider has this by the time contributions are forwarded. This enables the provider to monitor that the correct payments have been made at the correct time.

There is no pre-defined format for payment information records. Your provider will normally be able to help with this, and in any case you should confirm your recording arrangements with the provider. Typically the record will be a table or spreadsheet showing, for each employee who has chosen payroll deduction:

- the employee's name and National Insurance number;
- the amount or percentage rate of the deduction (if necessary, including a description of what the percentage is based on, eg basic salary plus bonuses);
- the date of deduction from the employee's salary;
- the due date for payment to the provider;
- the amount or percentage rate of any contributions you choose to make on the employee's behalf, and the due date for payment.

Making payments

It is the employer's responsibility to ensure that the correct amount is deducted from pay and forwarded to the provider by the due date.

In all cases, the provider must receive employees' contributions by the 19th of the month following the month of deduction. This is the latest due date for contributions. For example, any deductions made in February (regardless of frequency) must be forwarded to the provider by 19th March. You may agree a premium pay date with the provider that is earlier than this. Employer contributions, if made, can have a different due date from employee contributions, but in practice it is usually easier to forward all contributions together.

The employer and provider should agree on a suitable payment method, for example cheque, direct credit or direct debit. Providers may refuse to accept payment in cash or by credit card.

The employer must ensure that payment information is sent in advance of, or at the same time as, the payment itself. The payment must match the supplied record, so it is essential to update the record if, for example, an employee stops contributions, and to ensure the provider has the updated record by the due date for payment.

Best practice is to make sure the payment information record is easy to maintain, and to send an updated record to the provider each month as a matter of routine.

As well as maintaining the payment information, the employer should keep a record of general correspondence and emails (whether to employees or to the provider) relating to the scheme.

The role of the Pensions Regulator

The Pensions Regulator is the UK regulator of work-based pension schemes. It maintains and publishes the register of stakeholder schemes, and regulates compliance with the legal requirements. It checks, for example, that stakeholder schemes continue to meet conditions such as the cap on charges.

Compliance

The regulator also checks that employers comply with their obligations. For example, it may investigate and take action if:

- non-exempt employers fail to provide their employees with access to a stakeholder scheme;
- deducted contributions are not forwarded by the due date (scheme providers have a legal duty to report this to the regulator);
- payment information is not recorded properly, or is not kept up to date; or
- payments made to the provider do not match the supplied payment information.

As a last resort, the regulator can impose fines, particularly where there is repeated failure to comply with the requirements: however, where possible, it will always try to work with employers and providers to put things right if a problem is identified.

Further help and information

The regulator is also a valuable source of help and information for employers. Its website (www.thepensionsregulator.gov.uk) provides a range of material including:

- a decision tree to confirm whether or not you are exempt from the stakeholder requirements;
- a range of guidance and quick reference leaflets;
- examples of the letters and posters about stakeholder pensions that you can use in your workplace; and
- the register of stakeholder schemes, including each scheme's contact details.

Acknowledgements

I would like to thank the Institute of Directors for their support with this publication. Thanks are also due to the many members of the Institute who have used the Directors' Advisory Service and who have, without knowing it, given me a valuable insight into the many and varied types of personnel problems faced by many small businesses that do not enjoy the benefit of a full-time personnel manager.

My thanks also go to the publishers Kogan Page for their usual efficiency and support.

ALL CHANGE

Employment and Health & Safety law are probably the fastest-changing areas of our current legal system – and employers need to be well prepared if they're to successfully tackle the challenges of this increasingly complex legal arena.

It's a well known fact that the law never stands still, and nowhere is this truer than in the areas of Employment and Health & Safety law where increasingly, year-on-year growth in new legislation is causing major challenges for employers. Often employers are unaware of the latest changes in the law, or don't appreciate the implications of new legislative processes; fortunately though, there are an increasing number of well-organised, well-informed specialist organisations in the market who deal exclusively with these two complex areas of legislation.

Employers frequently feel stifled in their ability to run their businesses successfully whilst working within these legislative frameworks. Theoretically then, the role of these specialist support companies is to help employers face up to their responsibilities with calmness and confidence, whilst giving them the added reassurance of knowing that they're being supported by professional and competent specialists.

Finding a specialist support service provider

If you're looking for a company to help you with your own Employment law and Health & Safety challenges, the least you should expect is that they'll put into effect policies and procedures that accurately reflect your company's particular needs. To this end, as a prospective customer, before you even entertain the idea of spending your hard earned cash, you should be asking yourself;

- What is your current level of exposure? *(Do you have any on-going tribunals or grievances?)*

- Are you a growing/static company? *(If you grow, will any potential supplier look to increase their charges on a regular basis?)*

- Is indemnity important to you? *(As this is often where a significant proportion of the charges will sit serious consideration should be given to whether it is necessary)*

- Do you want a generic or bespoke system? *(As a small company, you may only need to offer statutory policies to your employees – bespoke policies may be a service you simply don't require)*

– Do you already have policies and systems in place? If so, are these current? *(Why re-invent the wheel?)*

– What is the current level of Employment Law/Health & Safety knowledge within your organisation? *(Are you looking for ground-up support or are you just looking for a 2nd opinion?)*

– Do you want 24/7 support? *(It is frequently offered but rarely used so why pay extra for it? – do you really want to hold a grievance meeting at midnight?)*

In addressing these questions prior to meeting any potential suppliers, you will hone your requirements down to a more precise fit for your organisation and as such you should buy what you need, not necessarily what is for sale. Many prospective suppliers will offer you a 'one size fits all' solution, irrespective of your current position or requirements, typically because their indemnity model is inflexible. Be aware – inflexibility at the point of sale will frequently translate into inflexibility during service provision once the contract is in place. This may constrain rather than support your business as you move forwards.

Whose side are they on?
"Many employers feel that current Employment law favours the employee," comments Dean Gardner, Managing Director of NorthgateArinso Employer Services, a specialist provider of Employment Law and Health & Safety advice and support.

With this in mind, it is vital to find a service provider you can trust; the key to this trust is finding a partner that doesn't play both sides i.e. supports both the employer and the employee. Check out a supplier's website. Do they have a section for employers and employees? How can you expect to receive sound guidance and confidential advice if your prospective supplier may also be representing your staff?

"As a matter of policy, we only attend Employment Tribunals on behalf of employers and never represent employees," says Dean, "our advocates conduct meetings, respond to requests, follow tribunal procedures and negotiate on our clients' behalf, leaving employers free to do what they do best - run their businesses!"

Health & Safety law – far reaching consequences

Another challenge for employers is Health and Safety law. Potentially, this is an area of the law that can have the most far-reaching ramifications for both individuals and companies. However with all the other matters that company owners have to deal with, Health & Safety law is often pushed down the list of priorities when people are busy – which is not a wise approach.

The principles and practices for the successful management of Health and Safety are no different to those for managing the core activities of a business: setting policies, organising, planning and implementing, and measuring and reviewing performance. These principles are universal but the actions needed to implement them will vary according to the size of the organisation and the hazards presented by its activities.

Juries hearing cases brought under the Corporate Manslaughter and Corporate Homicide Act 2007, which became law in April, will be asked to consider a defendants safety culture as well as its compliance with Health and Safety law. Whilst a generic service may help an employer to tick the boxes regarding legislation, an organisation that wants to demonstrate that it has a positive safety culture, based on the principles of successful management principles, will require a bespoke service.

Be well prepared and well represented

So for employers dealing with the consequences of Employment and Health & Safety law, the secret is to be well prepared, well briefed and well represented. Investment in the services of a specialist firm will reap handsome rewards in terms of dealing successfully with legal obligations and legal challenges – plus it's a proven way for employers to save precious time and money trying to deal with complex laws that seem to change virtually every day. **"Health & Safety and Employment law are a fearsome trap for the unprepared which is why outsourcing is a successful business option" says Dean, "At NorthgateArinso Employer Services, we can provide the expertise, experience and reassurance that employers require if they are to deal with the law *and* run their businesses effectively at the same time."**

Introduction

AIM OF THIS BOOK

A key stage in the growth of any business comes when employees are appointed for the first time. With employees, however, comes a range of complications. Many of these arise from the complex legal framework that now governs UK employment law. Others arise from the sheer complexity of trying to manage and motivate people from diverse backgrounds with widely different attitudes and aspirations.

This book attempts to identify those aspects of employing staff that any employer must know to be able to manage this complexity successfully. These can be divided broadly into legal essentials (what employers are legally required to do) and non-legal essentials (those actions that, although not legal requirements, are fundamental for effective people management and are consequently critical to the success of any business).

The Employer's Handbook is not intended to be a comprehensive guide to UK employment law, but rather to point you in the direction of the actions you may need to take to deal with a variety of employment issues. A large number of letters, policy documents and flow diagrams have been included to assist you to deal with many of the topics covered. In many circumstances, however, you may need to refer to other publications, and in some cases obtain legal advice, before taking certain actions, particularly as employment law is a frequently changing area.

STYLE AND CONVENTIONS

The main aim has been to make this a user-friendly handbook with the emphasis on what you need to do as an employer or a manager to avoid people problems, rather than describing employment rights in detail. A certain amount of such description is unavoidable, as you need to know what you might be letting yourself in for when taking specific actions. However, you will not find separate chapters covering topics such as employment rights and discrimination (but see Table 0.1), as these have been covered when describing the actions you need to take at different stages of the employment relationship. Wherever possible, legalistic language and case references have been avoided.

He and she

One of the problems any author has is that of dealing with gender. The use of 'he' exclusively throughout the book would offend some people, as no doubt, would the similar use of the word 'she'. The use of the phrase 'he or she' throughout the text can lead to complex and clumsy sentences. Equally, the use of the plural 'they' can often be inappropriate or ungrammatical in a particular context. Consequently the convention adopted in this book has been to use 'he' or 'she' in alternate chapters, except where the subject relates specifically to one gender, such as maternity rights.

Employees and workers

There has been a tendency in recent legislation to refer to 'workers' rather than 'employees'. This is the case, for example, with the Working Time Regulations. The intention, where this applies, is that the legislation should apply not just to direct employees but also to those in a slightly different employment relationship, such as agency workers. Therefore, where the legislation specifically refers to 'workers', rather than 'employees' this has been reflected in the text.

EMPLOYMENT RIGHTS

Although the rights of employees at different stages of the employment relationship have been covered under each chapter heading, for convenience the main employment rights are set out in Table 0.1. These do not apply to all employees at all times and you should refer to the specific chapters relating to them for more information.

Table 0.1 *Summary of main employment rights*

Employment right	Required period of employment
Written statement of employment particulars	One month
Itemized pay statement	None
Equal pay	None
Not to be discriminated against on grounds of sex, sexual orientation, race, religion or belief, age, or disability	None
Medical suspension pay	One month
Not to be discriminated against because of trade union membership or non-membership	None
Not to be unreasonably excluded or expelled from a trade union	None
Time off work with pay for trade union duties	None
Time off work without pay for trade union activities	None
Time off work without pay for public duties	None
Time off work with pay to look for work or training if under notice of redundancy	Two years
Time off work with pay for antenatal care	None
Parental leave without pay	One year
Time off work to care for dependants	None
Time off work with pay for safety representatives	None

Table 0.1 *(Continued)*

Employment right	Required period of employment
Time off work with pay for employee representatives	None
Statutory sick pay (SSP)	None
Statutory maternity pay (SMP)	26 weeks
Ordinary maternity leave (26 weeks)	None
Additional maternity leave	None
Written statement of reasons for dismissal	One year
Not to be unfairly dismissed	One year
Not to be dismissed or disadvantaged in any way because of pregnancy or parental or maternity leave	None
Paternity leave	26 weeks (by 15th week before EWC)
Statutory paternity pay (SPP)	26 weeks
Adoption leave (Ordinary and Additional)	None
Statutory adoption pay (SAP)	26 weeks
Not to be dismissed or disadvantaged in any way for asserting certain legal rights	None
Not to be dismissed or disadvantaged in any way for whistle-blowing	None
Not to be dismissed or disadvantaged in any way for taking action on health and safety matters	None
Redundancy pay	Two years

Table 0.1 *(Continued)*

Employment right	Required period of employment
To be consulted about proposed redundancies	None
Guarantee payments	One month
To apply to Secretary of State for redundancy pay on insolvency of employer	Two years
To apply to Secretary of State for arrears of pay, holiday pay, notice, etc, on insolvency of employer	None
Minimum period of notice	None
National Minimum Wage	None
Not to have to work more than 48 hours per week, except by choice, and to receive 4.8 weeks annual holiday	None
To make a request to work flexibly	26 weeks

COMPANY SIZE

When considering the employment issues that affect you, a relevant factor is the number of people you employ. This is because certain rules only apply to companies of a certain size. Table 0.2 shows the stage at which different aspects of employment law begin to apply. Employment rights in general, which are set out in Table 0.1, apply to all employees with the required length of service.

Table 0.2 *Stages at which additional employment rules apply*

Number of employees	Additional employment rules
Five or more	Safety policy Safety committee, if requested Consultation on health and safety Stakeholder pensions
21 or more	Recognition of a trade union mandatory where a majority votes in favour

FURTHER INFORMATION

The following can provide useful guidance on general employment issues:

Armstrong, M (2006) *A Handbook of Human Resource Management Practice,* 10th edition, Kogan Page, London

Butterworth's Employment Law Handbook (2007) 15th edition, Butterworth, London

Chandler, P (2003) *Waud's Employment Law* (2003) 15th edition, Kogan Page, London

Department for Business, Enterprise and Regulatory Reform (BERR): www.berr.gov.uk

Essential Facts – Employment (2007) Gee Publishing Ltd, London

IRS Employment Review (published fortnightly) Industrial Relations Services, London

Personnel Manager's Factbook (2007) Gee Publishing Ltd, London

Stranks, J (2007) *Health and Safety at Work*, 8th edition, Kogan Page, London

1

Recruiting staff

This chapter describes the recruitment and selection process and the legal implications of that process. A summary of the process is set out in Figure 1.1, although you may need to modify this to reflect your particular requirements.

DECIDING WHETHER TO RECRUIT

Before recruiting any new or additional staff you should consider whether there really is a need to do so. This is especially important if the increase brings staff numbers up to a point at which additional employment regulations start to take effect.

Options that might avoid the need for an increase in permanent staff include:

- using contractors for certain activities;
- introducing more flexible working arrangements such as job-sharing, shift working or part-time working;
- redesigning jobs or changing the company's organization and/or structure;
- introducing or increasing overtime;
- improving productivity;
- using temporary staff;
- redeveloping and retraining existing staff.

Totaljobs.com *leads the way in recruitment sector with monthly ABCe audits*

Totaljobs.com is the UK's first online recruitment website to commit to monthly traffic and response audits. The audits are conducted to industry agreed standards, by industry-owned auditor Audit Bureau of Circulation electronic (ABCe). Included in the audit certificates will be totaljobs.com monthly Online Job Application figures.

Totaljobs.com has been auditing website traffic data with ABCe since April 2002 and the decision to move to monthly audits, as of January 2008, is part of the company's aim to reinforce its stance on complete transparency. In February 2008, ABCe verified that totaljobs.com attracted 1,746,234 Unique Users, and generated 3,140,011 visits and 909,694 online job applications to recruiters' vacancies.

Totaljobs.com is pleased to be joining a growing number of leading websites that deliver monthly certification through ABCe, including; guardian.co.uk, dailymail.co.uk, timesonline.co.uk, telegraph.co.uk, sky.com and sun.co.uk

Sophie Relf, Head of Marketing for totaljobs.com, said: "We are delighted to share our figures with the industry. Looking at the volume of jobs that we have, the number of companies that we work with; and the high volumes of response that we generate from jobseekers, we are confident that by publishing monthly audits recruiters and hiring managers alike will be able to share our success."

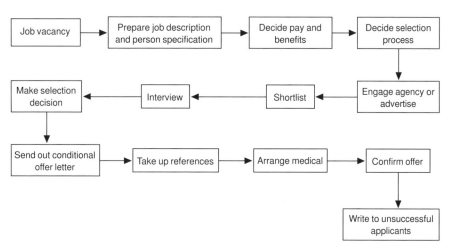

Figure 1.1 _The recruitment process_

PREPARING A JOB DESCRIPTION

Uses of a job description

Although there is no legal requirement for a full job description, it makes sense to prepare one, as this will:

- clarify the responsibilities of the jobholder;
- aid the recruitment process;
- provide a basis for assessing training needs;
- help in appraising performance;
- help in assessing future staffing needs or in changing responsibilities;
- be an essential requirement for any job evaluation process;
- be useful information in the event of any disciplinary action relating to job performance.

Content of a job description

There is no one formula for what should go into a job description but it should generally include the following:

- job title;
- name of jobholder;

- main purpose of the job, which should describe succinctly, in one or two sentences, the key role of the job in the company;
- reporting line – the title of the job to which this one reports;
- subordinates – the jobs reporting to this one;
- main tasks or accountabilities – some jobs will be routine in nature, in which case the main tasks should be listed (see the job description extract for secretary below), whereas others will be relatively complex with the emphasis more on the achievement of objectives, in which case the main accountabilities should be described in terms of end results (see the job description extract for finance director below);
- relevant statistics, such as budgets managed, sales targets, and caseloads;
- main contacts and the reason for these;
- signature of jobholder and immediate line manager;
- date.

Job description for secretary

Job purpose:

To provide a full secretarial support service to a director.

Main activities:

- Type letters, reports and other documents, as required.
- Draft routine correspondence.
- Screen telephone calls, take messages and respond to routine enquiries.
- Maintain a diary of appointments.
- Arrange meetings, travel and accommodation as required.
- Act as receptionist for visitors.
- Open and deal with post.
- Take minutes of meetings.
- Order stationery and office supplies.
- Maintain the office filing system and records.

Job description for finance director

Main purpose of job:

Contribute to the attainment of the company's business objectives by providing strategic and financial guidance and by ensuring that the company's financial commitments are met.

Main accountabilities:

- Direct and control finance staff to ensure that they are appropriately motivated and developed and so that they carry out their responsibilities to the required standard.
- Contribute to the achievement of the company's business objectives by providing advice and guidance on financial strategy.
- Provide financial advice and guidance to the company's managers and staff to enable them to achieve their objectives.
- Oversee the preparation of the company's financial accounts to ensure that these are presented accurately and on time.
- Develop and implement an internal audit programme to ensure that the company complies with financial procedures and regulations.
- Develop and maintain all necessary systems, policies and procedures to ensure effective and efficient financial management within the company.
- Monitor external contracts and services provided by suppliers to ensure that these are operating effectively and provide the best value to the company.
- Carry out all necessary actions to ensure that the company meets its financial and legal obligations.

PREPARING A PERSON SPECIFICATION

A person specification is complementary to a job description. Whereas a job description describes the content of the job, a person specification describes the desired characteristics of the person required to do that job. Like a job description it is not a legal requirement, but is very useful for recruitment and in determining training needs (see sample person specification below).

Sample person specification

Job:	Secretary/PA	
Reporting to:	Managing director	
	Essential	*Desirable*
Qualifications:	Educated to GCE 'A' Level GCSE English Secretarial training	Degree GCSE Maths

Experience:	Two years' office experience	Three years' office experience including at least two years in a similar role
Skills/competencies:	Keyboard skills including word processing and DTP Familiarity with 'Word', 'Excel' and 'PowerPoint' Tact and discretion Good team worker Good written and verbal communication skills Highly organized Conscientious with a desire to do the job to a high standard Able to exercise initiative	Web publishing skills including HTML Report writing skills
Physical requirements	Good health and smart appearance	
Circumstances	Living within commuting distance of London Able to work overtime on occasions	

Two long-standing approaches used in the preparation of person specifications are Alec Rodger's seven-point plan and Munro-Fraser's five-fold grading system. Both of these suggest headings under which the attributes of an ideal candidate can be classified.

The seven-point plan

The seven points are as follows:

- *Physical make-up* – health, appearance, bearing and speech.
- *Attainments* – education, qualifications, experience.
- *General intelligence* – intellectual capacity.
- *Special aptitudes* – mechanical, manual dexterity, facility in use of words or figures.

- *Interests* – intellectual, practical, constructional, physically active, social, artistic.
- *Disposition* – acceptability, influence over others, steadiness, dependability, self-reliance.
- *Circumstances* – any special demands of the job, such as ability to work unsociable hours, or travel abroad.

(Rodger, A (1952) *The Seven Point Plan*, NIIP, London)

The five-fold grading system

This involves the following five considerations:

- *Impact on others* – physical make-up, appearance, speech and manner.
- *Acquired qualifications* – education, vocational training, work experience.
- *Innate abilities* – quickness of comprehension and aptitude for learning.
- *Motivation* – individual goals, consistency and determination in following them up, success rate.
- *Adjustment* – emotional stability, ability to stand up to stress and ability to get on with people.

(Munro-Fraser, J (1954) *Handbook of Employment Interviewing*, Macdonald & Evans, London)

It should be borne in mind that only factors relevant to the job should be taken into account, including any which may not be necessary for effective job performance, eg requiring a high level of physical fitness for a sedentary job, could leave you open to claims of discrimination in selection.

You should describe the characteristics required for a particular job, determined by reference to the job description, against the various headings used. It is a common practice to enter two levels – the ideal and the minimum acceptable requirements to do the job. Job applicants can then be compared against these headings, although making the necessary assessments can be a complex and unreliable process.

HOW TO RECRUIT

The first step when filling a vacancy is to consider whether there is anyone internally who might be suitable, perhaps after a period of retraining. Where you take the decision to recruit externally the main ways of filling the job are by:

- word of mouth;
- advertising;
- using recruitment agencies and selection consultants;
- using executive search firms ('headhunters');
- recruitment fairs.

Word of mouth

Recruiting staff by encouraging existing employees to tell their friends and relatives about vacancies is very common and some companies even offer financial incentives to staff who persuade someone else to join. Probably the main advantage of using this approach is that you may know more about the employee's background and there is likely to be a certain amount of peer pressure to do a good job. The main danger is that recruiting from a limited pool in this way could be discriminatory if all the recruits come from one section of the community and this does not reflect the mix in your catchment area.

Advertising

The aim of an advertisement is to encourage applications from suitable candidates for the job and also to promote the image of the company. The wording and layout should attract a sufficient number of candidates of the right quality but it should also discourage applications from those who would be unsuited to the job.

The basic content of the advertisement should be:

- the job title;
- the location;
- salary and main benefits;
- a brief description of the key responsibilities or duties;
- the qualifications, skills and experience required;
- the advantages of the job;
- how and to whom application should be made.

Information about salary is sometimes omitted from advertisements, for various reasons, but experience shows that this generally reduces the number of applications. You can usually obtain assistance with the design and wording of job advertisements from newspapers and professional journals, although it is clearly in their interests to sell as much advertising space as possible. An alternative approach would be to place the whole matter in the hands of an advertising or recruitment agency.

If you are preparing a job advertisement yourself you need to ensure that it is not discriminatory by implying that the job is open only to persons of a particular race or sex, or that marital status, sexual orientation, religion or belief, age, or disability will exclude applicants, unless there are compelling reasons for any such exclusion. Some disabilities will prevent a person from effectively carrying out certain types of work. This also means that words with a sexual connotation, such as 'salesman', should be avoided. You also cannot insist that an applicant must, or must not, join a trade union.

Avoiding age discrimination

The Employment Equality (Age) Regulations 2006 came into effect on 1 October 2006. These mean that, with some rare exceptions, you cannot now discriminate on grounds of age when recruiting an employee (or during employment generally). When advertising you should:

- not specify a particular age or age range or use terminology that implies that you are looking for someone of a certain age, eg 'dynamic young graduate', 'mature person', etc;
- avoid asking for a specific number of years of experience but instead describe the type of experience required;
- make clear that where certain qualifications are required an equivalent level will be acceptable; older candidates, for example, may not have taken GCSE examinations;
- use advertising media that can include a wide field of candidates rather than advertising only in publications that might appeal to a specific age range;
- review advertising and publicity information about the organization to ensure that there are no hidden messages about the age of applicants you are seeking to recruit.

Most organizations include an equality statement in their advertisements and an example is provided below (reproduced with the kind permission of the NCVO).

Equal opportunities – statement of policy

.... [insert company name] is an equal opportunities employer and will apply objective criteria to assess potential suitability for jobs.

We aim to ensure that no job applicant or employee receives less favourable treatment on the ground of race, colour, nationality, religion, ethnic or national origins, age, gender, marital status, sexual orientation or disability.

Selection criteria and procedures are reviewed to ensure that individuals are selected, promoted and treated on the basis of their relevant merits and abilities.

All employees will be given equality of opportunity and, where appropriate and possible, special training to enable them to progress both within and outside the organization.

.... [insert company name] is committed to a continuing programme of action to make this policy effective and bring it to the attention of all employees.

Recruitment agencies and selection consultants

One of the main advantages of using a recruitment agency or a selection consultant is that they can bring considerable expertise to the selection process and can frequently give advice on the kinds of reward and benefits package that is likely to attract suitable candidates. They can take many aspects of the recruitment process out of your hands including, for example, advertising vacancies, interviewing and shortlisting candidates and providing assistance with the final selection. They can also allow you to remain anonymous until the final stages, if desired.

The greatest drawback is probably cost, fees usually being based on a percentage of salary and ranging from about 15 per cent to 25 per cent. The service will usually be provided on a no-result-no-fee basis and it may also be possible to recoup the fee if the candidate leaves within a certain period.

Executive search consultants (headhunters)

This approach is more appropriate for the most senior vacancies where the company has very specific requirements. In this case the consultants will conduct a market search, often targeting people in senior positions in other companies or referring to their own database of candidates. This is a very useful way of approaching individuals who are known to be suitable but without revealing the name of the company.

The main drawbacks are that it can be costly and will automatically exclude those outside the headhunter's network who may nevertheless be very able but with a low profile. One other possible drawback is that there is an assumption that those who are currently occupying comparable positions would be suitable candidates, but this takes no account of how well they might be performing in those positions.

Recruitment fairs

Recruitment fairs provide an opportunity for the employer to give information about the organization and job vacancies in an informal setting. Candidates are able to see what opportunities are available without having to attend a formal interview. The fairs have the added advantage that they might attract applicants who possibly would not otherwise respond to job advertisements.

These fairs are generally professionally organized, with employers having stands to display information about their organizations. In the past these have proved particularly popular for recruiting graduates. To avoid infringing age discrimination legislation you must be careful to use other selection methods as well and also not to debar older candidates, who may still be graduates, even if not recent ones.

APPLICATION FORM OR
CURRICULUM VITAE (CV)?

One of the decisions you will have to make when recruiting staff is whether to ask candidates simply to submit a CV or whether to require them to complete an application form. The more appropriate approach will depend primarily on the seniority of the job and the number of vacancies to be filled. Where you are filling a senior job it is more common to ask for a CV and experience shows that asking for application forms in such cases can reduce the number of applicants. However, where you expect to receive a large number of applications, forms can be very useful in screening applicants, primarily because you are asking everyone for the same information in a structured way, which makes comparison easier.

Some of the relative advantages and disadvantages of application forms and CVs are set out in Table 1.1. An example of an application form that complies with the latest age discrimination legislation can be found at www.efa.org.uk/policy/steps_recruitment.asp.

Table 1.1 *Advantages and disadvantages of CVs and application forms*

CVs

Advantages	*Disadvantages*
Speed – most applicants will have a prepared CV.	Many CVs are professionally prepared and may not accurately reflect the applicant's true presentation skills.
The standard of presentation can give information about the applicant.	The applicant can conceal or leave out vital information.
Some applicants may be deterred by having to complete an application form.	Varied content and presentation can make comparison of different applicants complex.
It is simpler to ask for a CV than to design and issue an application form.	They may not give the information you actually require.

Application forms

Advantages	*Disadvantages*
They can be designed to provide the information you require.	One form may not be suitable for all jobs.
Because the information is structured it is easier to compare applicants.	Forms put some people off.
Gaps in information can easily be seen.	They are not as fast and convenient as CVs.
The form can be used as a template for the interview.	Poorly designed forms may not obtain all the information you require and often do not provide sufficient space for certain answers.
Information from a form can easily be transferred to a personnel database.	There is a cost involved in producing and dispatching forms.
The standard of completion gives an indication of a candidate's ability to follow instructions.	They do not give applicants the opportunity to highlight the aspects of their career they consider the most relevant.

INTERVIEWING

General rules

Probably the most common way of selecting a person for a job is through the face-to-face interview. The most important points to bear in mind when you conduct an interview are:

- Ensure that the interview is free from interruptions and outside noise and that the location is suitable for the purpose.
- Ensure that enough time is set aside for each interview.
- Ensure that all parties involved have been told the date, time and venue for the interview.
- Read all CVs and/or application forms in advance.
- Prepare questions in advance (see example questions below).
- Avoid any questions that might appear to be discriminatory on grounds of sex, race, religion or belief, age, or disability, such as 'Do you intend to start a family in the near future?' or 'Are you likely to want to take long holidays in your own country?' or 'Will your disability mean that you have to have time off for hospital visits?' or 'Do you think you would be able to work in a team of younger people?' These all suggest that factors other than ability to do the job are likely to be taken into account.
- Ensure that you ask a large number of open questions, questions which encourage discussion, rather than closed questions, which elicit a 'yes' or 'no' answer. For example, it is better to ask 'What do you like about your present job?' rather than 'Do you like your present job?'
- If disabled persons are attending the interview ensure that appropriate facilities are provided.
- If more than one person is involved in conducting the interview ensure that it is clear who will ask which questions.
- Keep notes of decisions reached and the reasons for them, as these will be important in the event of any candidate querying the selection decision. Remember, though, that candidates can have access to such notes through the Data Protection Acts.

Using the following checklist will help you ensure that you have covered all relevant points when you are about to conduct a selection interview.

Preparation for interview – checklist

Consider the following factors when preparing for an interview:

- Do you have all relevant information about the candidates, including:
  - application forms/CVs;
  - all other correspondence with the candidates;
  - medical report forms if obtained;
  - references if obtained;
  - results of any tests carried out;
  - personal files of any internal candidates;
  - other relevant information?
- Have you identified important issues to be discussed at the interview?
- Do you have the job description?
- Do you have the person specification?
- Have the candidates been told the date, time and venue of the interview?
- Have you taken account of their travelling or work constraints?
- Have reception and security staff been told who to expect and at what times?
- Have the other members of any interview panel been told of the time and place of the interviews?
- Have the other panel members all been given the above information about the job to be filled and the candidates?
- Have the panel members been fully briefed about their roles in the interview?
- Have arrangements been made to pay any travelling expenses?
- Do you have all necessary information about the salary and terms and conditions relating to the job in question?
- Have you decided on the information you require and prepared a list of relevant questions (see below)?
- Have you considered the questions that candidates are likely to ask and your responses to these?
- Has a suitable interview room been prepared?
- Have you arranged to divert telephone calls and avoid interruptions?
- Have waiting and cloakroom facilities been provided for the candidates?
- Have candidate assessment forms been prepared and made available to the panel members (see example below)?
- Has the decision-making process been agreed?

- Has the process for notifying candidates of the result of the interview been agreed?
- Have the candidates been told about the stages in the interview process?

Interview structure

When carrying out an interview you should have a structure in mind. This should comprise an opening, a middle and an end, and you need to take specific actions at each stage.

When opening the interview:

- try to stick to the timetable; interviews too frequently overrun;
- start by welcoming the candidate and try to establish rapport, perhaps by chatting about something inconsequential;
- introduce yourself and any other interviewers;
- state the purpose of the interview and describe how it is to be conducted.

In the middle stage:

- try to ask questions that are open-ended and encourage discussion – basically questions that begin with 'who?' 'what?' 'where?' 'when?' 'why?' and 'how?' or phrases such as 'tell us what you think about . . .';
- ensure that you avoid questions that could be construed as discriminatory;
- avoid just going back over the application form or CV, repeating the information that is already there, but do clarify anything that is not clear;
- do not hesitate to probe if the need arises; it is better to get any doubts out into the open than to wonder about them afterwards;
- listen carefully to the replies, remembering that the candidate should do most of the talking, and try to read between the lines;
- ask the interviewee to supply examples of the kinds of things he has done to get a clear idea of current and past experience;
- keep notes of what is said, and if a number of candidates are being interviewed it is a good idea, in the absence of a photograph, to write a short pen-portrait of each of them; it is surprisingly easy to become confused after interviewing, say, six people in one day.

At the end of the interview:

- invite the candidate to ask any questions about the job or the company;
- tell the candidate what will happen next and when he can expect to hear the outcome;
- ask the candidate if he has any expenses and explain how these can be claimed.

After the interview:

- discuss and record your conclusions;
- notify the candidates of the outcome as soon as possible; you may wish to delay telling any reserve candidate until the first choice has accepted but this delay should not be too long;
- negotiate the salary and terms of employment with the successful candidate and prepare a contract of employment.

Note: It is important to retain a note of your reasons for appointing a particular candidate in case you receive any complaints of discrimination from those who were unsuccessful.

Example interview questions

Some examples of the kinds of questions that can usefully be asked at interviews are set out below. However, you should remember that these are only examples and will need to be modified to meet your own precise requirements and in relation to the information provided by the candidate:

- Tell me about yourself and your career to date.
- What interests you about this job?
- What do you know about this company?
- What contribution can you make to this company?
- Why did you leave your last job?
- What do you consider to be your main strengths?
- What areas do you think you need to improve?
- Describe your current responsibilities.
- What have been your major achievements in your career to date?
- Looking back over your career, what would you have done differently?
- What have been the biggest problems in your current (or previous) job?

- What experience do you have of managing staff?
- Can you give examples of the types of people problems you have had to deal with?
- What experience do you have of managing budgets?
- Where do you see yourself in, say, five years time?
- What other jobs have you applied for?
- How much sickness have you had over the past two years?
- What salary and benefits are you looking for?
- If offered this job, when could you start?
- Why should we appoint you in preference to any other candidate?
- Can you give an example of a time when you have had to:
  - make an important decision;
  - deal with a sensitive issue at work;
  - introduce a new system or process;
  - work as part of a team to achieve an important objective?

Candidate assessment form

Name ....

Job applied for ....

Interviewer(s) ....

Date ....

Rate the candidate as follows on the criteria below:

1 = Exceeds minimum requirements
2 = Meets minimum requirements
3 = Does not meet minimum requirements

				Comments
Qualifications	1	2	3	
Relevant experience	1	2	3	
Skills/Competencies	1	2	3	
Team fit	1	2	3	
Personality	1	2	3	
Analytical ability	1	2	3	

Organizational skills	1	2	3
Presentation skills	1	2	3
Decision making	1	2	3
Management skills	1	2	3
Business acumen	1	2	3
Drive/enthusiasm	1	2	3
Health record	1	2	3

Overall conclusion ....

OTHER SELECTION METHODS

A detailed discussion of other selection methods is beyond the scope of this book. However, some other techniques that might be appropriate in certain circumstances are described below.

Psychometric tests

Psychometric tests provide an analytical and quantifiable way of measuring personality traits and abilities, intelligence and aptitudes that are likely to be relevant to the job.

Such tests should satisfy six criteria. Any test should be:

- a sensitive measuring instrument that discriminates between subjects;
- standardized, so that an individual score can be related to others;
- reliable, in that it always measures the same thing;
- valid, in that the test measures what it is designed to measure;
- acceptable to the candidate;
- non-discriminatory.

There are a number of different types of psychometric test that, for selection purposes, may be classified as intelligence tests, aptitude and attainment tests, and personality tests.

Intelligence tests

Intelligence tests are the oldest kind of psychometric test, having been designed in 1905. However, they are rarely, if ever, used for selection purposes these days. The main problem with intelligence tests is that they are attempting to measure something that is very complex and about which there is much disagreement. It is possible that intelligence tests only measure an ability to do intelligence tests. In any case, they have limited application in the selection context and their use in the wrong circumstances could provoke resentment if candidates feel that they have already proved their intellectual capacity through their qualifications and experience.

Aptitude and attainment tests

These are designed to test particular aptitudes or abilities and can therefore be made very relevant to the job in question. Aptitude tests measure an individual's potential to develop, whereas attainment tests measure skills that have already been acquired. Aptitude tests can examine such things as verbal and numerical reasoning skills, spatial ability, manual dexterity, and so forth. Some of the most common attainment tests are typing tests, which are widely used and accepted. The most important aspect in designing all such tests is to ensure that they are properly validated.

Personality tests

Personality is an even vaguer concept than intelligence and this is probably the biggest problem with personality tests. What exactly are they measuring? There are a number of different theories about personality and a number of different definitions, with some people taking the view that it cannot be defined and measured.

Personality tests can take a number of different forms, testing, for example, individual traits or characteristics, interests, or values. Others may concentrate on specific workplace behaviour.

Some of the more common tests include the 16PF, Myers Briggs Type Indicator (MBTI), the FIRO-B and Saville and Holdsworth's OPQ. There has been much debate about the validity of personality tests and studies have given variable results, but they are generally found to be more valid than the standard interview, especially when used in combination with other techniques.

Using tests

Whatever tests are used, they should:

- ideally, be used as part of and integrated with the selection procedure and supported by other approaches;
- be rigorously designed and validated;
- be administered by, or supported by advice from, someone trained to the standards of the British Psychological Society.

Assessment centres

An assessment centre is not a single building or place, as the name might imply, but a range of tests and exercises, such as in-tray exercises, group discussions, or presentations, given to a group of candidates, who are evaluated by a number of assessors. They can last for several hours or several days. Because of their duration, the complexity of designing them, and the associated costs, they are unlikely to be appropriate for small companies. However, they have generally been shown to be good predictors of job performance.

Outdoor selection

Outdoor selection involves using a series of outdoor activities as part of the selection process. Participants are put into challenging situations requiring them to demonstrate how they interact with others, for example by working with an appointed leader to solve a complex problem such as crossing a river by making the best use of their collective skills and materials provided, or by undertaking a physical challenge. This type of approach is most appropriate for large organizations with groups of applicants moving into new roles, and will not generally be suitable for small companies.

Work samples

A work sample is an approach that requires applicants to perform the kinds of tasks they will be required to carry out in the job. Although in the past this approach was confined to jobs requiring practical skills, such as craftsmen, it is now often used for office jobs. Examples of work samples for such jobs include getting an applicant to carry out a role play, such as conducting a disciplinary interview, if that is likely to be part of the job, or writing a report about some aspect of the company. A common technique is the in-tray exercise, which requires applicants to show how they would deal with a typical range of internal problems and correspondence.

Biodata

Biodata selection involves selection on the basis of biographical information including age, qualifications and jobs held. It is based on the assumption that past experience and attainments are likely to be a good predictor of job performance. Biodata questionnaires vary in the number and types of question asked but will typically seek information such as number of jobs, length of employment, hobbies and interests. Their main drawbacks are that they can be discriminatory because of the nature of the questions asked, they need to be individually designed for different organizations, and they can quickly become out of date.

AVOIDING DISCRIMINATION IN SELECTION

It is unlawful to discriminate in selection on grounds of sex, sexual orientation, race, religion or belief, age, disability, pregnancy, or trade union membership or non-membership.

The only exception to the rules on sex or race discrimination is where there is what is called a 'genuine occupational qualification' (GOQ) (see below), for example in dramatic performances where the role calls for a specific race or sex, where a social worker is required to deal with a particular ethnic group, or where the work is of such an intimate nature that members of the public might object to a member of the opposite sex carrying it out.

Discrimination may be direct or indirect. Direct discrimination arises when one applicant is treated less favourably than another for reasons relating to sex, sexual orientation, race, religion or belief, age, or disability. An example would be restricting certain jobs to members of one sex or a particular race.

Indirect discrimination arises when the selection criteria are such that a smaller proportion of one sex or race can comply with them and they are not justified by the requirements of the job. An example would be requiring applicants to take tests not relevant to the job and which would have the effect of putting certain groups of people at a disadvantage – for example, physical lifting tests, which would discriminate against women or those with certain types of disability.

Genuine occupational qualifications (GOQs)

Sex discrimination

A person's sex is likely to be a GOQ for a job:

- where the essential nature of the job calls for a man (or woman) for reasons of physiology (excluding physical strength or stamina); or
- where considerations of decency or privacy require the job to be held by a man (or woman); or
- the jobholder has to live in premises provided by the employer but which cannot reasonably provide facilities for both sexes; or
- where the job is in a single-sex establishment for persons requiring special care, supervision or attention; or
- where the holder of the job provides individuals with personal services promoting their welfare or education, or similar personal services, and those services can most effectively be provided by a man (or a woman); or
- where the job involves work outside the United Kingdom in a country whose laws or customs are such that the job can only be done, or can only be done effectively, by a man (or by a woman).

Race discrimination

Being of a particular racial group is a GOQ for a job:

- where the job involves participation in a drama performance or other entertainment in which a person of the racial group in question is required for reasons of authenticity; or
- where the job involves participation as an artist's or photographic model in the production of a work of art, picture or film, for which a person of the racial group in question is required for reasons of authenticity; or
- where the job involves working in a restaurant or similar place and a person of the racial group in question is required for reasons of authenticity; or
- where the jobholder provides persons of the racial group in question with personal services promoting their welfare and only a person of the same racial group can provide those services.

Age

Age can be a GOQ provided it is a genuine requirement of the job and it is appropriate to apply this criterion in the circumstances, However, it is likely to be unlawful if the person appointed does not meet that requirement.

Avoiding discrimination against disabled people

The Disability Discrimination Act 1995 applies to all companies, regardless of size. This means that it is unlawful to refuse to offer employment just because someone has a disability that would not prevent that person from doing the job.

When considering applications from disabled persons you should:

- consider what adjustments you can reasonably make to the job or the workplace to enable the disabled person to meet the requirements of the job – failure to make a 'reasonable adjustment' amounts to unlawful disability discrimination;
- emphasize the essential elements of a job in the person specification and job description so that any disabled person who can meet these require-ments can be considered seriously;
- modify the recruitment process where necessary, for example by adapting tests;
- adapt physical arrangements if practical, for example by providing wheel-chair ramps;
- consider allowing a disabled candidate to be accompanied, if appropriate;
- train managers and staff in their responsibilities in relation to the law.

Avoiding age discrimination

The Department for Work and Pensions suggests that you should:

1. Remove the date of birth section from any application form and instead put this information on a separate monitoring form that interviewers will not see.
2. Also remove any other age-related questions. You can still ask applicants to describe their experience and jobs held.
3. Ensure that any special recruitment programmes for graduates or managers are open to all ages.
4. If you use a recruitment agency, check that they do not exclude people because of their age.
5. Focus on skills held and avoid preconceptions such as wondering whether an older person will be able to work with the latest technology or at a particular speed.

6. Train interviewing staff in all aspects of avoiding discrimination, including age discrimination.
7. Use people of different ages on an interview panel (where possible) to avoid any accusations that judgements were based on age.
8. Ask job-related questions.
9. Use selection criteria to assess candidates.
10. Monitor the ages of the candidates who applied, those who were short-listed and that of the person appointed.

Much of this advice amounts to no more than good selection practice, so should not present a problem for most employers.

MAKING A JOB OFFER

Once you have made the selection decision your next action should be to write to the successful and unsuccessful candidates. You can make an unconditional job offer but it is more usual to make any offer subject to the candidate meeting certain criteria, such as providing satisfactory references or passing a medical examination. At this stage it is better to defer writing to other shortlisted but unsuccessful candidates because your first choice may decline the offer.

The job offer should contain, as a minimum:

- the title of the job being offered;
- any conditions attaching to the offer;
- the location of the job;
- details of salary or wage, payment intervals and the annual review date;
- any significant benefits;
- the starting date;
- the hours of work;
- holiday entitlement;
- to whom the new employee should report;
- what the employee should do next.

Examples of offer letters are shown below.

You may also wish to consider making any appointment subject to a probationary period. If you do so this should be clearly stated in the offer letter, as should any special conditions attaching to this period.

It is important to remember that what goes into the offer letter forms part of the contract of employment.

Example offer letter 1

Dear .....

Following your recent interview at these offices I am pleased to be able to offer you the job of .... [insert job title] with this company.

This is subject to:

(a) the receipt of satisfactory references;

(b) a medical report from the company's medical adviser;

(c) [insert any other conditions attaching to the appointment, such as the completion of a satisfactory probationary period].

If in the opinion of the company your references and/or medical report are not satisfactory, the company will withdraw this offer, or if your employment has already commenced, terminate your employment without notice.

The full details of this offer are as follows:

Job title You will be employed as a .... [insert job title], although you will be expected from time to time to carry out other duties appropriate to a job at this level. You will report to .... [insert job title].

Place of work Your place of work is .... [insert location], although you may be required to work at any of the company's premises on a permanent or temporary basis.

Salary and benefits Your starting salary will be £ .... [insert amount] per annum [insert any other agreed period] and this will be paid on the last day of each month by bank credit transfer [insert any other method agreed]. Your salary will be reviewed annually on 1 January [insert any other review date].

In addition to your basic salary you will also be entitled to the following benefits .... [set out details of any bonus, company car, medical insurance or other fringe benefits].

Hours of work Your normal hours of work will be from .... [insert start time] to .... [insert finish time], Monday to Friday [or other working days] with a paid one-hour break for lunch each day [or other appropriate wording]. The nature of your role means that you may be required to work overtime without additional payment.

[Any requirement to work more than 48 hours on average and any need for the employee to sign an opt-out under the Working Time Regulations should be mentioned.]

Holidays You will be entitled to .... [insert number] days' holiday per annum in addition to all public holidays. The company's holiday year runs from .... [insert date] to .... [insert date] and holidays cannot be carried over from one year to the next. During your first year of employment you will accrue holiday at the rate of .... [insert accrual rate] for each completed month of employment.

Sick pay Your entitlement to sick pay and the procedure for reporting absences are set out in the Staff Handbook.

Pension The company operates a pension scheme which you will be entitled to join on appointment and details will be sent to you separately.

Notice period The company will give you .... weeks/months' notice [insert notice period] of the termination of your employment (on grounds other than gross misconduct), or any longer period required by statute. You are required to give the company .... weeks/months' notice [insert notice period] if you decide to terminate your employment.

Acceptance Further information about the detailed terms and conditions applying to your employment can be found in the Staff Handbook.

I would be grateful if you would confirm your acceptance of this offer on the terms and conditions set out above by signing and returning the attached copy of this letter to me. I would also be grateful if you could contact me to confirm your likely start date.

I look forward to you joining us and hope that this is the start of a long and happy association with this company. If you require any further information or would like clarification of any aspect of this offer please let me know.

Yours sincerely,

Example offer letter 2 (for larger companies)

Dear .....

Further to your recent interview I am pleased to offer you a job at this company based at .... with a start date of ....

This letter of appointment, together with the terms and conditions outlined in the enclosed Staff Handbook, which should be read in conjunction with this offer letter, constitutes the basis of your continuous employment with the company.

Job title and grade

Your initial job title and grade will be .... Further details are given in the section on grades in the handbook. As a term of your employment, you may be required to undertake, from time to time, such other duties as may be commensurate with your position in the company.

Pay

With effect from .... your remuneration will be at a rate of £......... per annum and comprises a basic pensionable salary of £......... per annum plus a non-pensionable regional allowance of £......... per annum. Your non-pensionable car allowance will be at a rate of £......... per annum. Payment, which is subject in all cases to statutory deductions of income tax and National Insurance contributions, will be made into your bank account in 12 monthly instalments on or around the .... of each month. You will receive a monthly pay statement detailing gross pay and deductions and any subsequent changes to your salary will be highlighted on that statement.

Salary arrangements

The company operates a performance-related pay policy and individual managers are rewarded according to their objectively assessed performance. Each year the amount of money available for distribution is expressed as a percentage of the basic salary bill for managers.

An individual manager's performance is reviewed against his or her annual objectives at the end of each year and a performance rating determined. The performance rating influences the pay award but comparisons with peers or peer groups within the company and market information of similar jobs outside the company will also be taken into account. Any awards are normally made in April. Full details of the company's performance-related pay policy will be available at your place of work.

Healthcare plan

You will be eligible for private health cover during your employment in accordance with the rules of the company scheme. The scheme operates on terms and conditions that are in force from time to time. The company reserves the right at any time to vary the scale or level of benefits in force.

Details and registration documents will be sent to you from head office. Full cover under the scheme will commence from the date of acceptance of your signed application for scheme membership.

Car scheme

You are eligible to participate in the company's car scheme subject to the rules of the scheme, which may change from time to time. For full details of the scheme please contact [insert appropriate person]. Alternatively, you may elect to take a cash option.

Hours of work

The normal working week is 35 hours and this is normally for seven hours per day (excluding a one-hour unpaid lunch break) Monday to Friday inclusive. Your initial start and finish times will be 9.00 am to 5.00 pm Monday to Friday inclusive unless you have been advised otherwise.

Leave

Annual leave

The holiday year runs from .... to .... For further details including the entitlement for one completed year of service and above, refer to the handbook.

You are required to take a minimum of two working weeks of your annual leave as consecutive weeks. Further information on arrangements for taking annual leave will be available at your place of work.

Public and bank holidays

In addition to annual leave you are entitled to paid leave on public and bank holidays. Different arrangements may apply to shift workers and details are available at the relevant work location.

Absence from work

No salary will be paid for periods of unauthorized absence. Subject to you following the absence rules laid down by the company, normal pay will be continued during periods of authorized absence due to sickness, subject to any service criteria that may exist from time to time. Any statutory sick pay entitlement will be included within this pay. Further details are given in the section on sickness in the Staff Handbook.

Place of work and mobility

Your initial location will be ....; however, you may be required from time to time to work at or from any company location. Full details are set out in the Staff Handbook.

Pension

Details of the company pension scheme are available from the company secretary.

Data protection

It is important that the our confidential personal records are maintained as accurately as possible and under the Data Protection Acts 1984 and 1998 the company and employees have a mutual responsibility in this regard. You must notify the company in writing of any change in your personal circumstances, such as your address, marital status, birth of children, attainment of professional qualifications, and so forth. For further details refer to the 'data protection' section in the Staff Handbook.

No smoking

A 'no smoking' policy operates in all company premises. Staff who smoke on these premises may be subject to formal disciplinary procedures, which may ultimately lead to dismissal.

Disciplinary rules

Contravention of any disciplinary rules, misconduct or a failure to achieve the required standards of performance is likely to result in action being taken under our disciplinary procedures, which could include dismissal. General disciplinary rules are set out in the Staff Handbook.

Grievance procedure

If you have a grievance related to your employment, you have a right to apply for redress. Details of the procedure are set out in the Staff Handbook.

Termination of your employment by the company

You are entitled to one calendar month's notice from the company to terminate your employment, or by such notice as may be required by statute, unless your employment is terminated on the grounds of gross misconduct. For further details please refer to the 'notice period' section in the Staff Handbook.

Termination of employment by you

You are required at any time to give the company at least one calendar month's notice in writing.

Acceptance

I should be grateful if you would kindly sign and return the attached copy of this letter to your line manager to confirm your acceptance of this offer.

Yours sincerely

I hereby accept the offer and the terms and conditions with the company as set out in this document, together with the other conditions contained in the Staff Handbook, which I have read in conjunction with this offer letter.

Signed:
Name:
Date:

TAKING UP REFERENCES

Although there is generally no legal obligation on an employer to give a reference (apart from certain jobs regulated by the Financial Services Authority), most are happy to do so. Any reference you are given must be fair, honest and accurate. However, there is nothing to stop an employer from providing a neutral reference – one that confirms that the employee was employed in a particular job with that company for a particular period, but makes no other comment about performance or attitude.

To ensure that you obtain all the required information about a prospective employee, the safest course of action is to provide a reference form, such as that set out below, or, better still, to obtain references by telephone. Previous employers may be willing to disclose information about a prospective candidate over the telephone that they would be reluctant to put in writing, and it may also be possible to judge attitudes by the tone of voice used. However, for a telephone reference to be of real value, you need to ensure that you ask the right questions. Using the application reference form will help ensure this. In addition, you may want to confirm impressions gained at the interview or clarify any doubts you may have.

Most employers ask for two references: one from the last employer, and one from another person who knows the candidate. In practice, it is only the reference from the candidate's last employer that is of real value because the other will generally be from a personal friend.

You should always get the candidate's permission to take up any references. A common practice is to take up references from previous employers at the offer stage, and to make the job offer subject to a satisfactory reference from the current employer. This allows the candidate time to give notice before the company is approached.

An example letter asking for a reference is set out below.

Application for reference

Name of prospective employee:
Company name:
Company address:
Name of person requesting reference:
Job title:
Telephone number:

Information required:

Date employee began employment with your company:
Job title:
Main responsibilities:

Number of days sickness in last year of employment:
Has the employee been subject to any disciplinary proceedings? YES/NO*
If YES, please give details.

In your opinion was the employee:
Honest? YES/NO*
Reliable? YES/NO*
Punctual? YES/NO*
A satisfactory performer? YES/NO*
Would you re-employ him/her? YES/NO*
Do you know of any reason why we should not employ him/her? If so, please specify.

Please give any further information that you feel might be relevant.

Would you be prepared to discuss this further over the telephone? YES/NO*

Signature:

Name:

Date:

Position:

Telephone number:
* Delete as appropriate

Letter applying for reference

Dear .....

Re: [applicant's name]

The above-named person has applied for a job as a .... with this company and has given your name as a referee.

We would be grateful if you would give us your opinion of his suitability for the job described by completing the enclosed form. We will also appreciate any other information you can give us that you feel might help us in making our decision, and which has not been covered adequately on the form.

Any information given will be treated as confidential. If a subject access enquiry is received from the applicant, under the terms of the Data Protection Act, we would be obliged to disclose the content of the reference, but the source of the information will be kept confidential.

Thank you for your cooperation.

Yours sincerely,

MEDICAL REPORTS

You can make an appointment subject to a satisfactory medical report from the company's medical adviser or the candidate's own doctor. It is preferable to employ a company medical adviser because that person will have the company's interests at heart and the employee will have no right of access to the report. Where the report is prepared by the person's own doctor he has the right to see it and to amend it or to withhold information (Access to Medical Reports Act 1988).

CHECKING QUALIFICATIONS

There is ample evidence that a significant minority of applicants lie about, or exaggerate, their qualifications in job applications. You should make a point of checking qualifications by reference to professional yearbooks, by asking the applicants to bring any certificates along for verification, or by direct reference to the examining body.

REJECTING CANDIDATES

When rejecting job applicants the general rule is that you should try to notify them speedily but avoid entering into detailed explanations of the reasons for their lack of success. However, it is good practice to offer a verbal explanation if this is likely to help the candidate in any subsequent application. An example of a rejection letter is set out below.

Example rejection letter

Dear ......

Job of:

Thank you for [attending the interview for the above job at these offices on .....]/[applying for the above job].*

I regret that, after careful consideration, we will not be [taking your application any further]/[making you an offer]* as there were a number of other candidates whose qualifications and experience more closely matched our requirements.

I would like to thank you for your interest in the company and to take this opportunity to wish you every success in your job search.

Yours sincerely,

*Delete as appropriate

You should also retain the notes relating to any selection or shortlisting decision, so that in the event of any complaint about your decision you can produce evidence in support of it. There have been a number of cases where members of ethnic minorities have been able to show that just by putting a different name on an application this can affect whether a person is invited for interview.

WITHDRAWING A JOB OFFER

You might sometimes have to withdraw a job offer that has already been made. Where this is not because of any fault of the candidate, such as failure to provide a satisfactory reference where that was a condition of the appointment, you should give the candidate pay in lieu of the notice period set out in the contract.

EMPLOYMENT OF OFFENDERS

Under the Rehabilitation of Offenders Act 1974 an offender does not need to give the employer details of any past offence for which he or she is now considered to be rehabilitated. Equally the employer must not take into account any such offences. These periods of rehabilitation vary depending on the nature of the offence and some, such as a sentence of custody for life, are excluded completely. The practical effect of the Act is that not only does the applicant not have to mention any 'spent' conviction, but could effectively lie about having committed an offence if asked directly whether he or she had any convictions. The relevant offences and time periods for rehabilitation are set out in the Act.

Exceptions

There are some jobs for which people are required to declare their convictions regardless of whether they might otherwise be spent under the provisions of the Act. These include:

- appointment to any post providing accommodation, care, leisure and recreational facilities, schooling, social services, supervision or training to people aged under 18 (including teachers, school caretakers, youth and social workers, and child minders);
- employment providing social services to elderly people, mentally or physically disabled people, alcohol or drug misusers or the chronically sick;
- appointment to any office or employment involving the administration of justice, including police officers, probation officers, traffic wardens, etc;
- admission to certain professions that have legal protection, including lawyers, doctors, dentists, nurses, chemists, accountants, etc;
- appointment to certain jobs regulated by the Financial Services Authority;
- appointment to jobs where national security may be at risk (eg certain posts in the civil service and defence contractors).

A full list of these exceptions is contained in the Rehabilitation of Offenders Act 1974 (Exceptions) Order 1975.

Where appointments are to be made to jobs that are excepted from the Act you should make it clear to the applicant that checks about any previous convictions will be made and that the appointment is conditional on these.

Criminal records checks

The Police Act 1997 established the Criminal Records Bureau (CRB) to provide easier access to criminal records checks for employment and voluntary appointments. The CRB will provide disclosure of records to employers who register with them to enable them to carry out pre-employment checks to establish whether a particular candidate is suitable for a specific job.

There are three types of check:

- Standard;
- Enhanced; and
- Protection of Vulnerable Adults (POVAFirst check).

The Standard check contains details of any unspent convictions as well as any cautions, reprimands, etc, or states that there are no such convictions. It also indicates whether an individual is banned from working with children or vulnerable adults.

The Enhanced check contains the same information as the Standard check but is reserved for use in connection with certain jobs such as those involved in the regular care, training or supervision of people under age 18 or vulnerable adults.

The POVAFirst check is a scheme run by the Department of Health and applies to:

- registered service providers of care homes;
- domiciliary care agencies;
- adult placement schemes;
- agencies who supply care workers to the above.

It comprises mainly a list of people who are unsuitable to work with vulnerable adults. Service providers are required to check the list and must not offer jobs in care positions to anyone on it. They should also refer people to the list if they have abused or harmed vulnerable adults in their care or placed them at risk of harm.

Further information is available from www.disclosure.gov.uk.

RESTRICTIONS ON EMPLOYING CHILDREN

There are certain restrictions on the employment of children. These are:

- no children may be employed under the age of 14, except on 'light work', information about which should be available from the local council;
- children aged 15 may only work for up to eight hours on a non-schoolday;
- children under 15 may only work for up to five hours on a non-schoolday;
- children must not work for more than two hours on schooldays and Sundays;
- they must not work for more than 35 hours in any week in the school holidays if over 15, or for more than 25 hours if under 15;
- they must not work for more than four hours in any day without a rest break of one hour;
- they must not be employed for more than 12 hours in any week in which they are required to attend school;
- there must be at least two consecutive weeks in the school holidays without employment.

EMPLOYMENT OF OVERSEAS NATIONALS

All European Economic Area (EEA) nationals have the right to work in the United Kingdom. Other nationalities will generally need a work permit, although there are a number of exceptions to this general rule. Further information can be obtained from www.homeoffice.gov.uk or www.workpermits.gov.uk.

The EEA includes the following countries:

Austria	Greece	Netherlands
Belgium	Hungary	Norway
Bulgaria	Iceland	Poland
Cyprus	Ireland	Portugal
Czech Republic	Italy	Romania
Denmark	Latvia	Slovakia
Estonia	Liechtenstein	Slovenia
Finland	Lithuania	Spain
France	Luxembourg	Sweden
Germany	Malta	

However, you should note that if the new employee is a national from one of the new members of the EU, ie Czech Republic, Estonia, Hungary, Latvia, Lithuania, Poland, Slovakia or Slovenia, you must follow a three-stage procedure:

1. Check documents to ensure that the employee is a national from one of these countries.
2. As soon as the employee begins working notify him of the need to register with the Home Office. You have to check that such registration has taken place within one month of the employee starting work.
3. If the registration process is successful the Home Office will send the employee a registration certificate and you will be provided with a copy, which must be retained. If you do not register with the Home Office within the period of one month but continue to employ the person, you may be guilty of committing a criminal offence and could face a maximum penalty of £5,000.

On 1 January 2007 Bulgaria and Romania joined the EU, but citizens from those countries are subject to certain restrictions. These are:

*   Skilled Romanian and Bulgarian workers with the right qualifications and experience will continue to be allowed to come to the United Kingdom on work permits to take up specific jobs where no suitable UK applicants can be found.
*   Workers with particularly high levels of skills and experience will continue to be admitted under the Highly Skilled Migrants Programme.
*   Low-skilled migration will be restricted to those sectors of the economy where the United Kingdom already has low-skilled schemes and will be subject to a strict quota.
*   There will be time limits on certain workers and no access to benefits and public housing.

Employers and employees not abiding by the new rules could face fines.

Given the relative complexity of this area and the frequent rule changes, you are strongly advised to check government websites before employing overseas nationals.

More information is available from www.workingintheuk.gov.uk and www.homeoffice.gov.uk.

ASYLUM AND IMMIGRATION ACT 2006

The Immigration, Asylum and Nationality Act 2006, which is being introduced in stages up to 2008, repeals and replaces the Asylum and Immigration Act 1996, though the essential requirements of that Act remain in place. You need to refer to relevant websites for the latest developments as the various stages of the Act commence. Under the Act it is a criminal offence to employ persons aged 16 or over without authorization by the immigration authorities. This means that you must check to ensure that any potential employee has a National Insurance number or, failing that, can provide evidence of his entitlement to work in the United Kingdom.

There are now two types of document that can be checked to meet the Act's requirements. These are one original document from List 1 or two from List 2.

List 1 documents are:

- a UK passport;
- an EEA passport or national identity card;
- a UK residence permit issued by the Home Office;
- an application registration card issued by the Home Office to an asylum seeker stating that the holder is permitted to take up employment.

List 2 documents are:

- an official document bearing a national insurance number plus:
  - a birth certificate, or
  - a letter from the Home Office, or
  - an immigration status document;
- a work permit plus:
  - a passport, or
  - a letter from the Home Office.

The documents must confirm the jobholder's right to remain in the United Kingdom and take up the employment in question.

The Home Office has issued a code of practice for employers describing how to meet obligations under the Act without being guilty of race discrimination.

FURTHER INFORMATION

Access to Medical Reports Act 1988

Asylum and Immigration Act 1996

Data Protection Act 1998

Disability Discrimination Act 1995

Edenborough R (2002) *Effective Interviewing – A handbook*, 2nd edition, Kogan Page, London

Employment Act 1989

Home Office (2006) A points based system: making migration work for Britain. Cm 6741

http://www.homeoffice.gov.uk

http://www.ind.homeoffice.gov.uk

Immigration, Asylum and Nationality Act 2006

Race Relations Act 1976

Rehabilitation of Offenders Act 1974

Sex Discrimination Acts 1975 and 1986

The Children (Protection at Work) Regulations 1998 and 2000

The Executive Grapevine, Executive Grapevine International Ltd

2

Writing employment contracts

DECIDING WHETHER SOMEONE IS AN EMPLOYEE

A key decision you have to make at the outset of any employment relationship is whether, in fact, the person being employed is actually an employee and therefore subject to a whole range of employment protection measures, or whether that person is self-employed with any contract being a contract for services, rather than a contract of employment.

A person is likely to be self-employed if some or all of the following conditions are met:

- she is in business on her own account and carries all the financial risk;
- she also works for other companies;
- no guarantee of work is given by the company;
- she provides her own tools and equipment;
- she is not under the control of the company's management;
- she can decline work.

There is an increasing tendency in legislation to refer to 'workers' rather than employees, such as in the Working Time Regulations, but although this definition would include persons such as those providing domestic services or working for an agency, it would not apply to the genuinely self-employed person.

THE CONTRACT OF EMPLOYMENT

The contract of employment between you and the employee is not one single document but comprises the contents of any offer letter, any verbal promises made by you to the employee that are intended to be part of the contract, and any other written terms and conditions applying to this type of job in the company, such as those that might be contained in any staff handbook. There may also be customary practices in the company that would also form part of the contract. For example, if you customarily pay a Christmas bonus to all staff this would be likely to be equally applicable to any new employee, unless there were conditions attached to the payment, such as a minimum length of employment.

There are also aspects of the employment contract that are not written anywhere, but are implied. For example, it is to be expected that any employee will follow any reasonable instructions given by an authorized manager and, equally, that you as the employer will provide all the necessary facilities to enable an employee to be able to do her job effectively.

Where the company has collective agreements, ie agreements negotiated between the employer and any unions or employees' representatives, these will also be part of the employee's contract although they may not actually be contained in a staff handbook.

STATEMENT OF EMPLOYMENT PARTICULARS

What is written into a contract is a matter for agreement between the employee and you and is not specified by law. However, it is a legal requirement that you issue any employee with a written statement of employment particulars within two months of commencing employment. The content of this statement is specified by statute (Employment Rights Act 1996) and must include the following information:

- the parties to the agreement – the name of the employer and the employee;
- the date employment began (in this job);
- the date continuous employment began, including service with any predecessor organization;
- the rate of pay, the method of calculating it and the intervals at which it will be paid;
- terms and conditions relating to hours of work;

- holiday entitlement and holiday pay;
- the title of the job or a brief description;
- the place of work and any mobility requirements.

You must also give the employee other information as part of the written statement, but this does not have to be set out in a single document and may be given in instalments, provided it is given within the two months' time limit.

This additional information includes:

- where the employment is temporary, the date it is to end;
- any terms and conditions relating to sickness or injury, including sick pay provisions;
- terms and conditions relating to pensions;
- whether a contracting-out certificate for pensions is in force;
- the length of notice required from both parties;
- details of any collective agreements that might affect the employee;
- information about the conditions attaching to any requirement to work outside the United Kingdom;
- the procedure for dealing with grievances (or where it can be found);
- the disciplinary procedure and any disciplinary rules (or where they can be found).

If there are no details to be entered under one of the above headings, that fact should be clearly stated at the appropriate point in the statement.

As indicated above, the statement of employment particulars is only part of the contract of employment, but it is strong evidence of the intentions of both parties. Two copies of the statement should be sent to the employee for signature, with one being retained for your records.

An example of a statement of employment particulars for a management job is set out below. A statement for clerical and other jobs should contain the same headings but the details might need to be modified. You should note that there is no legal requirement for the contract to be signed, and it still applies if the employee declines to sign it. However, a signature does indicate that the employee has read the contract and is hopefully aware of the content.

Example statement of employment particulars for a manager

This statement is a legal requirement of the Employment Rights Act 1996 and forms part of your contract of employment.

It sets out the main particulars of the terms and conditions of employment between:

[Name of company]

and

[Name of employee]

Date on which employment commenced:

Continuous employment: Your period of continuous employment began on [the same date] *OR* on .... [taking into account any employment with previous employers which counts towards continuous service].

Job title:

You should note that the company might require you to undertake other duties and responsibilities appropriate to a job at this level. You must carry out your work diligently and faithfully and comply with any general or specific instructions given to you by the company.

Reporting to:

Confidentiality

You must not at any time during your employment, or after it has ended, make or permit any unauthorized disclosure of any information that is confidential to the company or any customer of the company. Confidential information includes information relating to the transactions, finances, business or affairs of the company or customers of the company.

Place of work

Your main place of work is ...., although you may be required to work at other company locations on a temporary basis.

Work outside the United Kingdom

If you are required to work outside the United Kingdom for a period of time of more than one month you will receive separate particulars of the relevant terms and conditions applicable to that work and to your return.

Normal hours of work

Your normal working hours are 35 hours per week, plus a one-hour lunch break each day. However, you will be expected to work the hours necessary to reach your targets. [As this might occasionally require you to work more than the maximum of 48 hours per week specified in the Working Time Regulations you will be required to sign an agreement opting out of this provision in the Regulations. You can terminate this agreement at any time by giving the company three months' notice.]

Overtime is not paid.

Pay

Your salary is £ .... per annum.

Your salary is payable by equal monthly instalments in arrears on the last working day of each calendar month. Payment wil be made by cheque or by credit transfer to your bank account. Your salary will be reviewed annually on [insert date].

Expenses

The company will reimburse all travelling and other out-of-pocket expenses properly incurred by you in the performance of your duties, subject to the production of invoices, vouchers or other reasonable evidence of expenditure.

Deductions from your pay

The company shall be entitled to recover any debt owed by you to the company or any other sums lawfully due from you to the company by deduction from your remuneration, including holiday pay and pay in lieu of notice, or any other payment on termination of employment.

You are not entitled to any remuneration or other payment from the company during any period of unauthorized absence from work.

Holiday entitlement

You are entitled to [insert number] working days' holiday per annum with full salary in addition to public holidays. During your first year of employment your holiday entitlement will be in proportion to the number of complete months worked based on the accrual rate described below. All holidays must be approved in advance by the company. [Unused holiday cannot be carried over from one holiday year to the next].

On the termination of your employment for any reason (except misconduct) you will be entitled to holiday pay for each day that may remain after deducting from your accrued holiday entitlement the amount of holiday already taken in the holiday year in which your employment ceases. Accrued holiday entitlement is calculated by taking, for each completed calendar month of employment during the holiday year in which your employment ceases, one twelfth of your annual holiday entitlement for that holiday year to the nearest whole day. The daily rate of holiday pay will be your annual salary at the date of termination of your employment divided by [260] [insert any other agreed figure].

If you have taken holidays in excess of your accrued holiday entitlement the company may deduct from your final salary or any other payment due to you on the termination of your employment the amount overpaid to you for the excess holiday, calculated on the same basis as for holiday pay.

Absence from work

If you are unable to come to work for any reason, you must notify your manager as early as possible on the first day of absence, or arrange for someone to do so on your behalf. You should provide evidence of any incapacity and the reason for it. If you do not comply with this requirement the company may take disciplinary action against you and you may forfeit your right to sick pay.

Sickness absence

If you are absent because of sickness you must complete a company self-certification form for the first seven days and give this to your manager on your return. For illnesses of more than seven days, a doctor's certificate must also be produced on the eighth day and weekly thereafter.

If you realize that your sickness will last for more than the working week, you should contact the company and ask us to send a certificate to you at home, which you should complete and return by post.

Your certificates should show all the actual days of sickness even if they are not days you would normally work, such as weekends and public holidays.

Company sick pay

Company sick pay will be at the discretion of management but will not be unreasonably withheld. To qualify, you must have had six months' service with the company and have complied with the requirements on notification of absence and the provision of medical certificates. The entitlement increases with length of service as follows:

- six months to two years – one month's full pay, one month's half pay;
- two years to five years – two months' full pay, two months' half pay;
- over five years – three months' full pay, three months' half pay.

Company sick pay includes any entitlement to statutory sick pay (SSP) but the total of company pay and SSP will not be greater than your normal basic salary. If you are not entitled to company sick pay, you may still be entitled to SSP, which will be paid in accordance with the regulations for the time being in force. The rules relating to the payment of sick pay and SSP are set out in the Staff Handbook.

The company can at any time require you to submit to an independent medical examination, by a medical practitioner nominated by the company, which we will pay for.

Pensions

You are entitled to become and remain a member of the [insert name] pension scheme, subject to and in accordance with the rules of the scheme in force for the time being, and an explanatory booklet is available from ....

[A contracting out certificate is] *OR* [There is no contracting out certificate] in force in respect of your employment.

Termination of employment

You are required to give not less than [insert period of weeks or months] notice to terminate your employment.

You are entitled to receive not less than [insert period of weeks or months] notice if the company terminates your employment, for any reason other than gross misconduct, or any longer period required by statute.

The company reserves the right to give you pay in lieu of notice.

On the termination of your employment for any reason you must return all documents, equipment or other property belonging to the company or relating to the company's business which are in your possession or control and you must not make or retain any copy, extract or duplicate of any such document.

OR [where the period of employment is for a fixed term]

You are employed on a fixed term contract which will expire on .... [insert date].

Disciplinary rules and disciplinary procedure

The disciplinary rules and procedure which apply to you are attached as an appendix to this contract.

Grievance procedure

If you are dissatisfied with a disciplinary decision or if you have any grievance relating to your employment you should apply in the first instance to [insert name of supervisor or line manager], either orally or in writing. If the matter is not resolved you should follow the following procedure .... [set out grievance and disciplinary appeals procedures or refer to other documents such as Staff Handbook].

Collective agreements

Your terms and conditions of employment are affected by the following collective agreements between the company and .... [insert name of union/employer's association/staff association, etc].

[list relevant agreements]

OR

No collective agreements directly affect the terms and conditions of your employment.

Personal information

You must notify the company of your current address and any changes, your bank account to which salary payments are made, details of the person(s) to contact in an emergency, and other information which is needed by the company to maintain accurate records and to ensure compliance with its statutory obligations.

You agree to give the company permission to collect, retain and process relevant personal information about you. The company will keep such information confidential and will make every effort to ensure that it is accurate and kept up to date.

Signed: .... for the Company

Date: ....

Signed: .... Employee

Date: ....

NB Insert in the square brackets words appropriate to your particular requirements.

SPECIFIC CONTRACTUAL CLAUSES

In addition to the employment particulars contained in the written statement, employment contracts will usually contain a number of other clauses or variations on standard clauses. Some of the more common ones are described below.

Probationary period

Employers sometimes wish to apply a probationary period before offering an employee permanent employment. An example of this type of clause is as follows:

> The first six months of your employment with the company are probationary. During this period, the company may terminate your employment by giving you one week's notice. At the end of the probationary period, your employment with the company will be reviewed.

Non-competition clause

A non-competition clause or restrictive covenant is put into a contract to prevent the employee from competing with the company, or revealing trade secrets, once that person has left. Any such clause must be worded to give the company only the protection that may be considered reasonable to protect its business interests, and should therefore be limited in time and scope. If the clause is too widely drawn it may not be enforceable. An example is:

> For the protection of the company, its business, its employees, and its customers, you agree that: you shall not, during the 12-month period starting with the date of termination of your employment, either on your own account or with or on behalf of any other person, solicit or entice away or try to solicit or entice away from the company, any individual who is an employee of the company; you shall not, during the six-month period after the date of termination of your employment, either on your own account or with or on behalf of any other person, solicit or entice away or attempt to solicit or entice away, any company customer; and you shall not, during the six-month period after the date of termination of your employment, either on your own account or on behalf of any other person, have dealings, directly or indirectly, with any company customer. However, you are not prohibited by any of these restrictions from seeking or doing business with a company customer who is not in direct or indirect competition with the company.
>
> You agree that these restrictions are reasonable and necessary for the protection of the company and that if any of these are found by any court to go beyond what is reasonable to protect the company's interests, that the remainder of the contract will still apply as modified.

Benefits

You may wish to refer in the written statement to some of the main benefits applicable to the job. These might include for example:

- a discretionary bonus (be careful to ensure that you do not word this in such away as to create a contractual entitlement, unless you intend to do so);
- a company car;
- medical insurance;
- season ticket loan;
- life assurance.

The full range of benefits that might apply to any job is covered in Chapter 4.

Termination of employment

The period of notice you give to the employee or require from her will depend on the type of job. For monthly paid staff, one month on either side is typical. For more senior jobs or those where the employee has to continue providing a service to a client or customer, longer periods might be required. There is also a statutory right to notice, which is one week for anyone with more than one week's but less than two years' service, rising by one week for every year of service thereafter up to a maximum of 12 weeks after 12 years.

It is a good idea to insert into the contract a clause that gives you the right to give the employee pay instead of requiring that her notice be worked out. Adding such a clause removes the danger of you being in breach of contract in these circumstances. See also the section below relating to garden leave.

An example of a termination of employment clause is:

> Your employment may be terminated by either party on the giving of one month's written notice and the company reserves the right to pay salary in lieu of notice during the notice period.
>
> When you have completed five years' employment with the company you are entitled to one week's notice for every year of employment up to a maximum of 12 weeks after 12 years.
>
> Notwithstanding the other provisions of this contract, the company shall be entitled to terminate your employment without notice or payment in lieu of notice for dishonesty or gross or persistent misconduct, whether in connection with your employment or not.
>
> On termination of your employment for whatever reason you shall return to the company all books, documents, papers, computer data, materials, credit cards, and other property relating to the business or belonging to the company, which may then be in your possession or under your power or control.

Garden leave

When an employee leaves the company, either through resignation or dismissal, that person has the right to continue attending the place of work during the notice period. However, this is not always desirable because she might continue to have access to commercially sensitive information. To prevent attendance during the notice period you should insert a provision into the employment contract giving you the right to require the employee not to report for work. You can attach conditions to this 'garden leave', such as not permitting the employee to work for another company, but these should be clearly spelt out in the contract.

An example of a garden leave clause is as follows:

> The company shall have the right during the period of notice, or any part of that period, to place you on leave, paying the basic salary and benefits to which you are entitled. During this period you are not to visit company premises, other than at our request.

Exclusive employment

You may wish to ensure that an employee devotes all her energies to her job and is not distracted by external activities. For example, someone who works late evenings and early mornings in a nightclub may not be on top form during the day. Also, you could fall foul of the Working Time Regulations (see below and Chapter 8) if an employee works more than 48 hours a week in total because she has another job. It may therefore be advisable to insert a clause in the contract similar to this:

> Employees are not permitted to take second jobs, for example in the evening, without written company agreement. Any person in breach of this requirement will be subject to disciplinary action and may be dismissed.

Confidentiality

It is an implied term of the contract of employment that an employee should remain loyal to the employer and act in good faith, which clearly includes not giving confidential information to competitors, but you may wish, nevertheless, to protect such information with a confidentiality clause, such as the following:

> Except for information already in the public domain, you will not disclose any confidential information concerning the business or affairs of the company, or any associated company, or our customers or suppliers, to any other person or organization. This also applies after you have left the company.

Any information relating to the company, our customers or suppliers remains the property of the company, and when you leave any such information must be handed back to the company.

Working Time Regulations opt-out

Where a member of staff may be required regularly to work more than 48 hours per week you should ask that person to sign an opt-out similar to that in the following extract.

Agreement to opt-out of the 48-hour working week

Company ....

Name of employee ....

I understand that under the provisions of the Working Time Regulations I am not required to work more than 48 hours per week on average.

I agree that I may work more than an average of 48 hours a week. If I change my mind, I will give you [insert period of notice – up to three months] notice in writing to end this agreement.

Signed ....

Dated ....

Other clauses

In addition to the clauses set out above there are a number of other employment terms and conditions that are usually contained within a staff handbook, as set out in Chapter 9, but that could, if desired, be incorporated into the written statement. The main problem is that this can tend to make the statement a long, complex and possibly off-putting document. On the other hand, it does mean that all the key terms and conditions can be found in one place.

TYPES OF CONTRACT

Open-ended and fixed-term contracts

Most employment contracts are for an indefinite period of time and only end when the employee leaves. However, it is also common to have a fixed-term contract when the employment is for a specified period of time, such as one year, and automatically ends when that period has elapsed. To avoid any doubt such a contract should specify a definite end date. You should bear in mind that non-renewal of a fixed-term contract is a dismissal and is subject to the normal rules applying to any dismissal. If the principal reason for the dismissal is that the contract has expired and no further work is available then the dismissal is likely to be fair (see Chapter 14). You should note that with effect from 10 July 2006 anyone employed for four years on successive fixed-term contracts automatically becomes a permanent employee.

Joint contracts

In a joint contract it is a condition of the job that two people are employed jointly to carry out the work. An example of a joint contract would be where a husband and wife are employed to run a hostel. In this type of contract, ending the employment of one party to the contract will result in the automatic ending of the employment of the other person.

Directors' service contracts

A director's service contract is very similar to any other employment contract and should contain everything required in the statement of particulars of employment. However, such contracts usually contain a number of other provisions that may only be appropriate for company directors. These typically include:

- longer notice periods, six months or a year being common;
- a non-competition clause, requiring the director not to enter into competition with the employer, nor to solicit the employer's customers or staff, for a period following termination of employment;
- a garden leave provision;
- confidentiality clauses;
- special bonus provisions;
- wide-ranging mobility provisions;
- a requirement not to carry on any other employment or professional activities outside this employment;
- a requirement to relinquish all directorships on leaving;
- special compensation arrangements on losing office.

Although these provisions are more commonly found in directors' service contracts some could also appear in ordinary employment contracts.

Bear in mind that where the contract contains generous bonus provisions these should be subject to stringent conditions, so that you do not end up rewarding failure. This problem has been highlighted in recent years when a number of senior executives have been given generous settlements on leaving companies despite those companies suffering a serious decline in profitability and share values.

An example of a director's service contract is set out as an appendix to this chapter.

Casual employees

Casual employees are those who are employed only for a certain number of hours and who receive payment only for those hours and who do not otherwise benefit from the terms and conditions of employment applying to permanent staff (although you should assume that statutory employment rights will apply). When you employ casual staff the basis of the employment, including its duration and the terms and conditions applying, should be made clear in the offer letter.

An example of wording in a contract for a casual worker is set out below:

You will provide services to the company on a casual basis and as required by the company. However, we cannot guarantee to provide you with work and there is no obligation on your part to accept any work offered.

You will be paid at the rate of £........... for all hours actually worked. You will not be entitled to any other company benefits.

You are not an employee of the company and consequently you will be responsible for accounting to the Inland Revenue for all taxes payable and any National Insurance or other statutory reductions [alternatively, the company may be obliged to deduct tax and National Insurance, but it should be made clear that, if so, this is 'for administrative convenience only'].

AMENDING CONTRACTS

A contract of employment is an agreement between you and the employee and can only be changed by agreement. Although certain common changes such as an increase in pay will be mutually agreed between both parties, any unilateral change by you will be likely to be a breach of contract. You should always therefore try to obtain the employee's agreement to any contract changes.

Problems most commonly arise when an employer, for business reasons, tries to make changes to the existing contract, which are not accepted by the employee. If the employee cannot be persuaded to accept the new terms the only options are either not to change the contract, or to terminate the existing contract and offer to re-employ on a new one. The danger is that any such action could amount to an unfair dismissal, unless justified by strong business reasons. Imposing the changes without consultation could give rise to claims for breach of contract, and constructive dismissal if the employee resigns.

FURTHER INFORMATION

Chandler, P (2003) *Waud's Employment Law*, 14th edition, Kogan Page, London
Employment Rights Act 1996
Essential Facts – Employment (2007) Gee Publishing Ltd, London
Personnel Manager's Factbook (2001) Gee Publishing Ltd, London
Working Time Regulations 1998

APPENDIX: SPECIMEN SERVICE AGREEMENT

The following service agreement is an example of what such a contract will typically look like. It comprises various sections from a number of such contracts with further amendments by the author. You should not use it as it stands because the precise wording to go into any service agreement will depend on what is agreed between the parties and you will need to seek advice to ensure that the agreement covers all salient points and that it is legally sound.

Service Agreement

This agreement is made the ...... day of .... 2008 between

(1) ....
[company name and address] ('the Company'); and

(2) ....
[employee name and address] ('the director')

1. Definitions and interpretations

1.1 In this agreement:

'Company' includes any successors to the ownership of the Company;

'Associated Company' means any company or other organization over which the Company (either alone or with any connected person) has direct or indirect control;

'Board' means the board of directors of the Company from time to time;

'Chairman' means the Chairman of the Board from time to time;

'Effective Date' means the date that the agreement is signed by the parties.

1.2 Any reference to a statute or statutory provision includes a reference to any amendment or re-enactment of it.

1.3 Any reference to one gender includes a reference to all other genders.

1.4 Any reference to the singular includes a reference to the plural and vice versa.

1.5 References to any clause, sub-clause, paragraph or schedule is to a clause, sub-clause, paragraph or schedule of or to this agreement.

2. Job title and duties

2.1 You are employed as .... [job title]

Further information about your duties and responsibilities are set out in your job description, as amended from time to time.

2.2 You are to exercise the powers and functions and carry out the actions required of your position, and to undertake such other duties consistent with your position which may be reasonably assigned to you from time to time by or with the authority of the Board, and as directed by the Board.

2.3 You shall report to [job title of line manager] or to such other person as the Board may direct.

2.4 The Company reserves the right to transfer you to any subsidiary or associated company on the same terms and conditions set out in this agreement. In any such circumstance your employment will be treated as continuous.

2.5 You agree to serve the Company and any associated company faithfully and well and to use your best endeavours to promote and protect the interests of the Company and any associated company.

2.6 You agree to give the Board any information or assistance it may require relating to the business of the Company, and any associated company about which you have knowledge, and to keep the Board regularly and promptly informed of the development and progress of the Company's and any associated company's business.

3.   Date of commencement

Your period of employment with the Company commenced on .... [date].

Your period of continuous employment commenced on .... [date].

OR

You have no period of previous service that would count as continuous employment for the purposes of the Employment Rights Act 1996.

4.   Hours of work

4.1 You shall devote the whole of your time, attention and abilities to the performance of your duties during the Company's normal business hours of 9.00 am to 5.30 pm Monday to Friday inclusive [amend as appropriate], and at such other times as may reasonably be necessary for the effective discharge of your duties (unless prevented by illness or other incapacity and except as may from time to time be permitted or required by the Board) and you accept that by signing this agreement you have agreed that regulation 4 (1) of the Working Time Regulations 1998 shall not apply.

5.   Place of work

5.1 Your normal place of work will be at the Company's offices at [location]. However, you agree to work at such other place within the United Kingdom as the Company may reasonably require. If you are required to relocate the Company will give you as much notice as possible and will reimburse such removal and other incidental expenses as the Company considers fair and reasonable in the circumstances.

5.2 You may be required from time to time to work abroad. If the Company requires you to work outside the United Kingdom for a period of more than one month it will provide you with written details of any terms and conditions which may apply to that work and to your return to the United Kingdom.

6. Remuneration and benefits

6.1 Your basic salary is £...... [salary] per annum, or such other sum as the Company may subsequently determine, and will accrue from day to day. The salary is payable by equal monthly instalments in arrears on the last working day of each month and includes any sums receivable as director's fees.

6.2 The salary will be reviewed annually by the Company with any change taking effect from 1 January of that year. Annual salary increases are awarded on merit and depending on your performance.

6.3 You may at the discretion of the Company be entitled to receive a bonus from time to time. Any such bonus will be related to performance, based on targets to be agreed between the parties to this agreement. Details of any agreed bonus or incentive scheme and the terms and conditions applying to it will be set out in a separate document. You shall have no right to receive any bonus if you are no longer employed by the Company or are working out a period of notice.

6.4 You shall in addition receive the following benefits:

- Membership of the Company's medical insurance scheme for you and your family, including dependant children, provided that you and your family, including dependant children, meet the normal underwriting requirements of that scheme and are accepted at normal rates of premium.
- Membership of the Company's Life Assurance Scheme for a sum insured equal to four times your annual remuneration (ie basic salary plus bonuses averaged over the previous three years) provided you meet the normal underwriting requirements of the scheme and are accepted at normal rates of premium.
- Membership of the Company's permanent health insurance scheme provided you meet the normal underwriting requirements of the scheme and are accepted at normal rates of premium.
- Further information about these schemes is set out in the Staff Handbook.

7.   Expenses

7.1   The Company will reimburse all reasonable hotel, travelling, entertainment and other expenses necessarily and properly incurred by you in the course of carrying out your duties and responsibilities for the Company, subject to the Company's approval of completed expenses claim forms, production of valid receipts or other documentary evidence and compliance with the Company's regulations relating to expenses. Further information about the Company's expenses policy is set out in the Staff Handbook.

7.2   Any credit card issued to you by the Company must be used only for expenses necessarily and properly incurred by you in the course of your employment and in accordance with the Company's regulations.

8.   Car or car allowance

8.1   The Company will provide you with a fully expensed Company car, equivalent in value to a .... [car make and model] and including a car telephone for business and personal use during your employment. The Company will pay all costs relating to the car as set out in the Company car policy, a copy of which is contained in the Staff Handbook. You undertake to take good care of the car and to ensure that it is maintained in a legal and roadworthy condition.

8.2   Alternatively you may receive a car allowance of £......... [amount] per month. This is on condition that any car you drive shall be a private car and the Company shall have no responsibility for any aspect of owning or running the car except that the Company shall reimburse you the cost of insuring the car and the cost of all petrol (whether for personal or business use).

8.3   It is a condition of your employment that you maintain a valid UK driving licence at all times.

9.   Pension

9.1   The Company shall pay a contribution of [x per cent] of your basic salary into the Company's pension scheme subject to any Inland Revenue requirements and overriding legislation.

9.2   A contracting-out certificate is [is not] in force in respect of your employment.

10.   Holidays

10.1   You shall be entitled to [insert number] days holiday each calendar year in addition to all public holidays normally applying in England and Wales. The holiday year runs from 1 January to 31 December. Holidays may not be carried forward from one year to the next without the express permission of the Board. No payment shall be made during your employment in lieu of holidays not taken.

10.2   On commencement of employment you shall accrue holiday on a pro rata basis for each complete month of service in that holiday year. On termination of your employment you shall be entitled to receive a payment representing holiday accrued, but as yet untaken, on a pro rata basis for the number of completed calendar months you have worked during the current holiday year. Any such payment will be calculated at a rate of [accrual rate, for example $^{1}/_{260}$th] of your annual basic salary per day of holiday. [Alternatively, the Company may, at its discretion, require you to take any unused holiday entitlement during your notice period.]

10.3   If at the date of the termination of your employment you have taken holidays in excess of your accrued entitlement this excess will be deducted from any sums due to you from the Company. This will be calculated at a rate of [accrual rate, for example $^{1}/_{260}$th] of your annual basic salary per day of holiday.

10.4   The Company will try to accommodate all reasonable requests relating to the time and duration of holidays but reserves the right to arrange holidays in its interest. Your entitlement to holidays and to holiday pay is subject the rules of the Company from time to time in force relating to holiday entitlement and holiday pay.

11.   Sickness or injury

11.1   If, in the opinion of the Board, you are unable to perform your duties properly for a period, or periods, not exceeding a total of 13 weeks (including both normal working days and non-working days) in any period of 12 months because of illness (including mental illness), accident or any other cause beyond your control, you shall be entitled to receive your full basic salary (inclusive of any Statutory Sick Pay to which you may be entitled) for the duration of that period. Thereafter any payment shall be subject to, and in accordance with, the terms of the Company's permanent health insurance scheme.

11.2 If you are unable to work because of illness or an accident you must notify your line manager as early as possible by telephone on the first morning of absence or as soon as reasonably practical thereafter, indicating the reason for your absence and its likely duration. If you are absent for more than three consecutive working days you must complete a self-certification sickness form on your return and give it to your line manager. If you are absent for more than five working days you must provide an appropriate medical certificate from your doctor in the manner required by the rules of the Company. Thereafter you should send in further medical certificates at weekly intervals during the whole period of absence.

11.3 Failure to comply with Company's rules relating to the reporting of sickness or injury, as amended from time to time, could result in you losing the right to be paid during any such absence.

11.4 Statutory Sick Pay ('SSP') shall be paid by the Company in accordance with the legislation in force at the time of absence. Any payment of remuneration under sub-clause 11.1 for a day of absence will discharge the Company's obligation to pay SSP for that day.

11.5 The Company reserves the right to require you to be medically examined at its expense by a medical practitioner nominated by it and for a report of that examination to be made available to the Board.

11.6 If, in the opinion of the Board, you are or have been unable to perform your duties properly for a period or periods exceeding 13 weeks in total, or if the Board has good reason to believe that you are unlikely to be able to perform your duties properly for a continuous period of 13 weeks or more, the Company shall be entitled at any time to give you at least six months' notice of the termination of your employment less the total of any periods for which you have been paid salary under sub-clause 11.1 during the 12 months prior to the giving of such notice. However, the Company may not terminate your employment if you are receiving, or are entitled to receive, benefits under the terms of the Company's permanent health insurance scheme unless the Company first provides you with benefits no less favourable than the net benefits payable to you by the insurer under that scheme.

12.   Outside interests

12.1 During your employment you must not, without the prior written consent of the Board:

(a) be directly or indirectly engaged or concerned in any capacity with any business, trade or occupation where this may conflict with the interests of the Company or adversely affect the effective discharge of your duties. However, this does not prevent you holding, for investment purposes only, not more than five per cent of the issued shares or securities of any companies which are listed or dealt in on any recognized stock exchange. For this purpose 'occupation' shall include any public, private or charitable work which the Board considers may hinder or interfere with the performance of your duties; or

(b) introduce to any other person, company or undertaking, except an associated company, or carry out on your own behalf, any business that the Company is able to carry out.

13. Confidential information and trade secrets

13.1 You shall keep secret and shall not at any time either during your employment, or after its termination, for whatever reason, use, communicate or reveal to any person for your own purposes or those of any other person, company or undertaking, any secret or confidential information about the business, finances or organization of the Company or any associated company, or its or their suppliers or customers obtained in the course of your employment.

13.2 You shall also use your best endeavours to prevent the publication, disclosure or use of any such information.

13.3 Examples of the types of information that will be regarded as secret and confidential, will include, but not be limited to, the following examples, whether relating to the Company, an associated company or to any client, customer or supplier of the Company or any associated company:

- relevant hardware, software or source codes;
- details of research and development activities;
- marketing and sales policies and information, price lists, pricing structures, credit management policies and procedures, payment policies and procedures;
- business plans;
- suppliers and their production and delivery capabilities;

- customers and details of their particular requirements;

- financial information and plans;

- product lines and the development of new products;

- production or design secrets;

- technical design, specifications or formulae of products;

- information about officers and employees;

- any information marked 'confidential' or which you have been told is confidential or which you might reasonably expect to be regarded as confidential; or

- any information given in confidence by clients, customers, suppliers or any other person.

13.4 The restrictions in this clause do not apply to:

(a) any disclosure authorized by the Board or required by any court or tribunal or other authorized regulatory authority; or

(b) any information that has come into the public domain, except a breach of this clause or of any equivalent provision.

14. Intellectual property

14.1 You agree that any invention made by you in the course of your employment or originated by you using equipment or facilities owned by the Company shall belong to the Company.

14.2 You agree to assign to the Company with full title guarantee all present and future intellectual property rights in any invention made by you during the course of your employment with the Company and agree to disclose promptly to the Company all documents and other materials relevant to any such intellectual property.

14.3 You agree to waive any moral rights that you have or may have against the Company or any of its employees, officers or agents in any intellectual property originated by you in the course of your employment by the Company.

14.4 You agree to take such actions and execute such deeds and other documents that the Company consider may be necessary to substantiate, protect and maintain the intellectual property rights of the Company, without compensation additional to that provided for in your contract of employment. This clause will continue to apply following the termination of your employment for whatever reason.

14.5 You agree that decisions relating to the substantiation, protection and maintenance of any intellectual property originated by you shall be at the sole discretion of the Company and you shall have no claim against the Company in the event of any decision not to proceed with any such substantiation, protection or maintenance.

14.6 You appoint the Company to be your attorney and to take such actions and execute such deeds and other documents as may be necessary in your name and on your behalf and to give the Company or its nominees the full benefits of rights conferred under this agreement.

15. Grievance procedure

15.1 If you have a grievance relating to any aspect of your employment you should raise the matter in the first instance with the Chief Executive [or other appropriate person]. If the matter remains unresolved, it may be raised in writing with the Chairman of the Board. The grievance will then be considered at the next appropriate meeting of the Board, which will give you a written response as soon as practicable following the meeting. The decision of the Board shall be final.

16. Disciplinary procedure

16.1 Except in the case of gross misconduct and subject to the provisions of sub-clause 17.4, the policy of the Company is not to dismiss an employee for a first breach of the contract of employment that is capable of being remedied until that employee has been warned that dismissal could result from that breach. However, you accept that for an appointment at your level it may not always be appropriate to give any such warning prior to dismissal.

16.2 A copy of the disciplinary rules and procedure of the Company are set out in the Staff Handbook. These do not form part of your contract of employment.

17. Termination of employment

17.1 Your employment may be terminated by either you or the Company giving to the other six months' [or other agreed period] notice in writing.

17.2 Your employment shall in any event terminate without notice on your sixty-fifth [or other agreed retirement age] birthday. However, you have the right to ask to work beyond this retirement age and the Company has a duty to consider any such request.

17.3 If written notice of termination of employment is given either by you or by the Company, the Company may in its sole and absolute discretion terminate your employment immediately by paying you salary in lieu of any required period of notice together with any accrued holiday pay up to the date notice is given. You will not be entitled to any additional compensation in respect of any holiday that would otherwise have accrued during the notice period.

17.4 The Company reserves the right to terminate your employment summarily by oral or written notice and without any payment in lieu of notice if it has reasonable grounds for believing that you are guilty of gross misconduct, gross negligence or any other serious breaches of Company rules or your contract of employment, including any of the following events:

(a) Commission of any criminal offence, dishonesty or serious misconduct, whether during the performance of your duties or otherwise, and which in the opinion of the Board renders you unfit to continue as a director of the Company or which would be likely to prejudice adversely the reputation or interests of the Company or any associated company;

(b) In the event of any bankruptcy order being made against you or by you becoming prohibited by law from being a director or taking part in the management of the Company whether under the Company Directors Disqualification Act 1986 or otherwise;

(c) If any information relating to your suitability for employment by the Company and provided in the course of applying for employment is subsequently found to be false or misleading; or

(d) If you fail or cease to meet the requirements of any regulatory body whose consent is required to enable you to carry out effectively your duties and responsibilities under your contract of employment.

17.5 If written notice of termination of employment is given either by you or by the Company, the Company reserves the right either to require you during the notice period to perform such duties as the Board may determine, or to require you not to undertake any duties and to exclude you from any premises of the Company or any associated company. In either case the Company will continue to pay your normal salary and provide all other benefits during the notice period.

17.6 On the termination of your employment, for whatever reason, you shall immediately:

(a) return to the Company all documents, books, materials, records, correspondence, notes, reports, papers, data, software, manuals and information, in whatever form held (including summaries and extracts of these), relating to the Company or any associated company, and any other property of the Company or any associated company including, but not limited to, any car, computers, software, keys, credit cards which are in your possession, custody, care or control. You will be required to confirm in writing that you have complied fully with the terms of this sub-clause;

(b) delete any information or records, however stored, relating to the business of the Company or any associated company, which you possess or control outside the Company premises. You will be required to confirm in writing that you have complied fully with the terms of this sub-clause;

(c) resign any office or appointment you hold in the Company or in any associated company without any claim for compensation or damages for loss of office and you hereby appoint the Company as your agent to execute any necessary letters of resignation on your behalf; and

(d) transfer to the Company all shares and share certificates you hold in any company as nominee or trustee for the Company, and appoint the Company to execute any such transfers on your behalf.

18. Suspension

18.1 If the Board has reasonable grounds to suspect that any one of the events specified in clause 17.4 has occurred the Board may suspend you on full salary together with associated benefits while the matter is investigated. You have the right during any such suspension to terminate your employment immediately by notice in writing to the Company, but without any claim for compensation.

19.   Restrictions

You agree to be bound by the following restrictions:

(a) You shall not for a period of six months after the termination of your employment, either personally or through an agent, either on your own account or for any other person, directly or indirectly canvass or solicit orders from any customer to supply goods, services and supplies that are provided by the Company or an associated company or which are substantially similar to those provided by the Company or an associated company.

(b) You shall not for a period of six months after the termination of your employment, either personally or through an agent, and either on your own account or for any other person, directly or indirectly canvass or solicit orders from any person, firm or company who within the period of 12 months prior to the termination of your employment was a client or customer of the Company or an associated company and with whom you have had dealings.

(c) You shall not during your employment or for a period of 12 months after the termination of your employment, either personally or through an agent, and either on your own account or for any other person, directly or indirectly solicit or endeavour to entice away from the Company any director, employee or consultant of the Company.

20.   Data protection

20.1 You agree that personal data relating to you and to your employment with the Company required for the effective administration of the Company may be collected, held (in hard copy and computer readable form) and processed by the Company.

20.2 You agree that the Company may process sensitive personal data relating to you, including medical details and details of gender, race and ethnic origin. Personal data relating to gender, race and ethnic origin will be processed by the Company only for the purpose of monitoring the Company's equal opportunity policy and for ensuring that equal opportunities in employment are promoted and maintained. You agree that the

Company may disclose or transfer such sensitive personal data to other persons if it is required or permitted by law to do so or, in the case of personal data relating to gender, race, ethnic origin, religious belief, age, sexual orientation or disability, for the purpose of monitoring the Company's equal opportunity policy. Where the disclosure or transfer is to a person resident outside the European Economic Area, the Company shall take reasonable steps to ensure that your rights and freedoms in relation to the processing of the relevant personal data are adequately protected.

21.   Notices

Any notice under this agreement shall be in writing and may be delivered personally or sent by first class post (airmail if overseas) or by facsimile machine.

The address of the Company for service of notices shall be its registered office and any such notice should be marked for the attention of the Chairman of the Board. Any notice to you from the Company will be to the address stated in this agreement or to any other permanent address that you notify to the Company. You are required to notify the Company of any changes to your address and telephone number.

22.   Collective agreements

22.1   This agreement sets out the entire agreement and understanding between the parties in connection with your employment save only for any terms implied by law. There are no collective agreements that directly affect the terms and conditions of your employment.

23.   Variation

23.1   Any term or provision of this agreement may only be amended by written agreement between you and the Company.

24.   Miscellaneous

24.1   You consent to the deduction from any sum otherwise payable to you during or on the termination of your employment the value of any claim the Company has against you, including but not limited to, the following:

(a) overpayment of wages or salary;

    (b) overpayment of any expenses incurred by you in the course of your employment;

    (c) any loans made to you by the Company;

    (d) any advances on wages or salary that the Company may have made to you.

25.   Severability

25.1 The various terms and provisions of this agreement are severable and if any term or provision in this agreement is held to be illegal, invalid or unenforceable, in whole or in part, under any rule of law or enactment, such term or provision or part shall to that extent be deemed not to form part of this agreement, but the enforceability of the remainder of this agreement shall not be affected.

26.   Previous agreements

26.1 The agreement cancels and is in substitution for all previous letters of engagement, agreements and arrangements (whether verbal or in writing) between you and the Company, all of which shall be deemed to have been terminated by mutual consent.

27.   Law and jurisdiction

27.1 This agreement shall be governed by and construed in accordance with English law and each party to this agreement submits to the non-exclusive jurisdiction of the English courts.

EXECUTED by

.... Director

SIGNED by ....
in the presence of:

....

Name:

Address:

Occupation:

DATED ....

3

Paying staff

DECIDING HOW MUCH TO PAY

You are free to decide how much to pay for a particular job provided this is above the National Minimum Wage (see below). In deciding the appropriate pay level you should take into account:

- what the company can afford;
- the market rate for jobs of this type in the area;
- the size of the job in comparison with other jobs in the company;
- the overall value of the remuneration package including benefits.

Finding out the market rate

As you will normally have to compete with other employers for staff it is clearly important to ensure that you are paying at a comparable level for jobs of similar size.

There are a number of sources of information about the going rate for particular types of job. These are:

- job advertisements in local newspapers and professional journals;
- pay surveys and publications;
- employment agencies;

- consultants;
- market research;
- professional bodies and employer organizations.

Job advertisements are a readily available source of information about pay levels. The main danger with this type of information is that the jobs in question may not be directly comparable to those in your own company and they also tend to state the maximum, rather than the typical, earnings for that type of job. This is particularly the case when terms such as 'total package' or 'OTE' (on-target earnings) are used.

There is also a substantial variation in pay levels depending on the size of the organization, the industry sector and its location. Wherever possible, you should try to compare like with like. There are numerous pay surveys on the market and these can provide a reliable source of data, provided they cover the jobs you are seeking to fill. The main points to bear in mind when using surveys are:

- they can be expensive to buy and are not usually available from local libraries;
- the size of the survey sample is critical – generally the larger the sample the more reliable the data;
- survey data is often collected on the basis of job title, which gives very little information about the real size and range of accountabilities of any particular job, making comparisons difficult;
- survey data quickly becomes out of date and will need to be adjusted to take account of inflation;
- the composition of the survey can vary from year to year, which can lead to some inconsistencies in the data.

Other sources of pay information include a range of personnel and pay publications that are available in some libraries, including, for example, the Industrial Relations Services Pay Bulletin, Incomes Data Services Reports and so forth, and professional bodies such as the Chartered Institute of Personnel and Development (CIPD) and the Institute of Directors (IoD). The surveys by Croner Reward in association with the IoD are particularly useful for determining pay for senior staff. Finally, companies' annual reports are another useful source of information about board-level pay.

It is possible to conduct your own market research by contacting similar companies, or companies with similar jobs. The main problem is that this can be time-consuming and there may be reluctance on the part of many companies to give what they might regard as commercially sensitive information to a potential competitor.

If you are using recruitment consultants to fill a vacancy they will generally have a good idea of the pay level that will be sufficient to attract a good candidate. However, it should be borne in mind that it is in their interests for the recommended pay level to be higher rather than lower, as this will make it easier for them to find a suitable candidate and will increase their fee, which is normally based on a percentage of the salary offered.

Finally, there are a number of reward consultants who will advise on pay levels. However, in view of the fees involved this is usually only a sensible option for senior jobs or where there is a need to review the pay of several jobs.

Internal relativities

In deciding the pay level for a particular job it is not only the external market that has to be taken into account but also the relative pay levels in the company. It is important for motivation and morale to ensure that individuals feel they are being paid fairly in relation to their colleagues. In a small company all that needs to be taken into account is the relative size of jobs based on their content, and the experience and performance of the persons doing the jobs.

In a large company it may be necessary to have a job evaluation scheme. Such a scheme might be essential to ensure that jobs of equal value receive equal pay, which is a legal requirement and, arguably, is more important since the introduction of the Equal Pay Questionnaire in April 2003. Job evaluation is described in more detail in the next section of this chapter.

JOB EVALUATION

What is job evaluation?

Job evaluation is the process of systematically assessing the relative importance of jobs in a company so that they can be placed in a rank order. Usually each job is compared with all other jobs in the same company using an analytical framework that enables the user to make logical judgements about job size.

Job evaluation does not determine pay rates; it only helps the company decide how jobs should be grouped. The determination of the appropriate pay and benefits packages for different jobs comes at the end of the job evaluation exercise.

Benefits of job evaluation

There are a number of benefits of job evaluation. The most important of these are:

- most people want to feel that they are being rewarded fairly in relation to others in the company and job evaluation can help to ensure that rewards are allocated fairly between jobs;
- job evaluation provides an objective way of assessing job size;
- judgements are made by managers about how much jobs should be paid anyway, so it is better to do this systematically rather than on 'gut-feel';
- depending on the method used, it can enable comparisons to be made between completely different types of jobs;
- without a systematic method of job evaluation it might be difficult to provide a strong defence to any equal value claims (see below);
- job evaluation can assist in salary planning and pay negotiations;
- job evaluation can be a valuable tool in the analysis of a company and can help to identify any gaps or overlaps in responsibility.

A systematic method of job evaluation may not be necessary for all companies. If your company is comprised of only a few employees the rank order of jobs will generally be obvious. Similarly in some environments the pay rates are determined solely by the market and trying to assess job size would be superfluous.

Disadvantages of job evaluation

There are of course some disadvantages to job evaluation. These include the following:

- no system of job evaluation can be completely objective and there will always be some who feel that the approach adopted does not adequately reflect their own jobs;
- some systems can be time-consuming and costly to install and maintain;
- external consultancy will usually be required to introduce job evaluation;
- many managers and employees prefer the vagueness surrounding non-analytical ways of determining job size as this gives more scope for negotiation and manipulation;
- some systems may be difficult for employees to understand, thereby leading to suspicion and mistrust;

- the process of introducing job evaluation can bring to light organizational anomalies that many may have wished to keep hidden.

Equal pay and job evaluation

It has been a requirement of UK law since the Equal Pay Act 1970, effective from 1975, that men and women are paid on the same terms where:

(a) the woman is employed on like work with a man in the same employment; or

(b) the woman is employed on work rated as equivalent with that of a man in the same employment; or

(c) the work is of equal value.

This is reinforced by the Treaty of Rome, which states that equal pay should be given for equal work without discrimination on grounds of sex, and by the Equal Pay (Amendment) Regulations 1983, which state that 'equal pay for work of equal value' must be observed by employers. In addition, the Equal Pay Directive states that where a job classification system is used for determining pay, it must be based on the same criteria for both men and women and so drawn up as to exclude any discrimination on grounds of sex.

You should note that while it has been generally assumed in this section that an equal pay claim will be brought by a woman, such a claim can also be brought by a man and this is becoming increasingly common.

The three grounds on which a woman may make a claim for equal pay are where:

1. she is doing work that is the same or broadly similar to that of a man, ie 'like work';
2. the job has been rated the same under a proper job evaluation study; or
3. the work is of equal value to a man's in terms of effort, skill, decision making and the other demands it makes that have not been assessed under a job evaluation study.

Under point 1, above, a tribunal will decide whether the work is broadly similar or whether there are any material differences that would justify different rates of pay. Under point 2, above, where a woman's job has been rated as equal to a man's under a job evaluation scheme a tribunal will award equal pay. If it has been rated as lower the woman would not normally be able to bring a claim under this heading unless she could prove that the job evaluation scheme itself was discriminatory.

A woman can make a claim for equal pay for work of equal value where she can prove that her work is equal to that of a man in terms of the demands it makes of her in terms of effort, skill, decision making or other significant factors. Where no job evaluation scheme exists or any such scheme is biased, and the tribunal considers that the comparison made is reasonable, it can appoint an expert to undertake a job evaluation exercise.

For job evaluation schemes to be seen as valid and non-discriminatory they should conform to the following criteria:

- they must be analytical;
- the comparison should be of the whole job;
- factors and weightings must be objective and non-discriminatory;
- the evaluation scheme and the basis for allocating pay rates to jobs should be capable of being explained by the employer;
- the scheme must be based on the same criteria for men and women;
- one overall scheme for all jobs is the safest option;
- a job evaluation scheme may not be discriminatory just because one of its criteria is more common to men, but it should take into account other criteria which may be more common to women;
- the time at which the work is done will not, per se, normally be viewed as justifying a difference in evaluation;
- the job evaluation process must be free of bias, with women being involved in the evaluation of jobs;
- job information must be obtained in a way that is non-discriminatory;
- market issues can sometimes justify a material difference in pay between certain jobs, but care should be taken to ensure that the comparisons are not themselves biased.

Types of job evaluation scheme

Job evaluation schemes divide broadly into analytical and non-analytical schemes. Non-analytical schemes are ranking, paired comparison and classification. These are considered further below.

Ranking

Ranking compares each job with every other job and places them in order of importance to the organization. Evaluators compare whole jobs rather than the separate components of jobs, but may make these comparisons on the basis of one or more key factors, such as the decisions made or the accountabilities of each post.

The advantages of ranking are simplicity and speed and it may be perfectly adequate for a small organization. However, it has a number of disadvantages:

- its lack of sophistication means that it may be difficult to defend the results as there will be no way of demonstrating any analysis;
- there can be no guarantee that bias has not been built into the system;
- the lack of objective criteria is likely to mean that judgements made about jobs are inconsistent;
- it is difficult to compare very different jobs for which different aptitudes might be required;
- while a rank order can be obtained, the magnitude of the difference between jobs cannot be measured;
- it does not easily enable jobs to be grouped for grading or pay purposes;
- the rationale behind the decisions cannot easily be communicated and the approach is therefore likely to lack credibility with staff.

Paired comparisons

The paired comparisons method of job evaluation is similar to ranking in that complete jobs are compared with all other jobs. However, in this case scores are allocated in terms of whether a particular job is as important, more important or less important than another. In this way, by giving points to each job in turn on the basis of these comparisons, a rank order may be produced.

This approach again has the advantages of simplicity and speed, and correlation of results can be made even faster by the use of a computer. Again it may be perfectly adequate for a small organization. Although it is a slightly more sophisticated way of comparing jobs, it suffers from all of the disadvantages of ranking, plus the fact that as the number of jobs increases so do the number of comparisons that have to be made, and the calculations involved.

Job classification

Job classification involves the identification of a number of classes or grades of employee, each of which will have certain characteristics and into which all jobs with these characteristics can be placed. Frequently organizations have a grading structure into which jobs are placed on a felt-fair basis but without any detailed analysis of the size of those jobs. Such systems are very common in the public sector and in large highly structured organizations.

Job classification again has the advantages of speed and simplicity, but with the added advantage that there are clear grade or job family definitions that enable jobs to be more accurately allocated to the appropriate grade or class. The main disadvantages of classification are that:

- it compares job descriptions with grade criteria, rather than jobs with jobs, which is a less reliable way of getting a rank order;
- it can be difficult to grade more complex jobs;
- the grade definitions may be difficult to formulate and may not always be helpful when allocating jobs to grades;
- there is no easy way of justifying why a job has been allocated a particular grade;
- it is not usually accepted as being a valid approach in equal value cases;
- there is no guarantee that bias has not been built into the process;
- this approach can be subject to grade drift whereby, over time, the grades of various jobs will tend to creep up, usually depending on the advocacy skills of the manager seeking any increase;
- it can result in the introduction of too many grades and job categories, which in turn can have implications for the organization structure, and will complicate pay policy.

Points rating

Points rating or points factor rating consists of the identification of a number of factors considered to be relevant to all the jobs under consideration, with points allocated to the different levels of these factors. Jobs are then compared against each of these factors, and points allocated accordingly, and then the separate factors are totalled to give an overall score.

Once all the jobs have been evaluated the organization will have a rank order of scores which can then be further divided into grades against which pay levels can be set. There are numerous examples of such schemes and a number of factors that commonly occur, such as knowledge and experience, decisions made, complexity, etc. Such schemes may be bought 'off-the-shelf', or can be designed specifically for the organization in question. The main advantages of using an off-the-shelf scheme are that it saves a lot of the time required to design a bespoke scheme and it will have been tried and tested in other organizations. The main drawbacks are that the factors may not be entirely appropriate to the jobs in the organization, or may not reflect its culture, and such schemes often need to be maintained by external consultants. Tailor-made schemes are considered further below.

Points schemes have the following advantages:

- as evaluators have to consider each job in terms of a number of factors they are able to be more objective in their judgements;
- because all jobs are being considered against the same criteria there is likely to be greater consistency in the judgements made;
- evaluators are able to demonstrate analytical reasons for making particular judgements about jobs;
- the allocation of points makes the process of developing a grade structure or pay bands easier;
- the size of the difference between jobs can be measured;
- the system is more likely to be perceived as fair than one in which the criteria are not known;
- the approach is more likely to be accepted in equal value cases;
- such schemes are relatively easy to computerize.

The main disadvantages are:

- their analytical nature can give a spurious impression of scientific accuracy when in fact they are still dependent on evaluators' judgements;
- they can be expensive and time-consuming to install and maintain;
- they are based on an assumption that all the factors used are equally relevant to all jobs, which may not be the case.

Factor comparison

Factor comparison differs from points rating in that jobs are compared with each other on a number of different factors rather than as whole jobs. This produces a number of different hierarchies of jobs as some will be high on some factors but low on others. Comparisons are made of the lists of factor rankings, with judgements about how much of each job is attributable to the various factors, eg what percentage of the job's total size might relate to a factor covering responsibility.

While this approach is analytical and objective, it is relatively little used nowadays because it is time-consuming, complex and costly to install.

Other methods

Over the years a variety of approaches to job evaluation have been developed. A number of these have concentrated on a single factor rather than a range of factors and would therefore be less likely to be accepted from an equal value viewpoint.

Tailored schemes

Tailored schemes are those designed specifically for a particular organization. They have the advantages that they can be designed to reflect precisely the needs of the organization in question, that they will use the terminology recognized within it, and that by involving staff in their design they will give the scheme greater credibility and a sense of ownership on the part of employees. While there is likely to be more development time involved, this can be kept to a minimum if support is provided by an experienced job evaluation specialist who will know from past experience what factors and weightings are likely to best reflect job size in a particular environment.

The job evaluation process

A very important aspect of introducing job evaluation is the process that supports it. Even where a very robust, well-established scheme is introduced it can still fail, not because of any inherent faults in the scheme, but because the process has not been properly managed. While the detail of any process will vary depending on the type of job evaluation method used, there are a number of issues you need to consider when introducing any approach.

Scheme objectives

It is important first of all to be clear about the objectives of any job evaluation scheme and to take account of the organization's business goals, its culture, and previous history. You need to be clear about what you expect the scheme to deliver and about those matters you consider central to business success. The organization's culture will affect the way in which the process is carried out.

The range of jobs

The numbers and types of jobs within the organization will affect both the kind of evaluation methodology required and the process. Manual and craft jobs will have different outputs and skills from managerial and professional jobs and both groups may need to be evaluated using different factors. Where only a few jobs are involved one of the simpler and less analytical methods might be appropriate.

Selecting the method

Once you are clear about the objectives of the job evaluation exercise and you know what types and numbers of jobs are involved, the next stage is to decide the job evaluation method to be used. While the cost of the method and its necessary consultancy support will be a factor in the decision, it is as well to bear in mind that the real costs are likely to be in implementation, and that the consultancy fees are relatively insignificant as a proportion of the total.

There are a number of proprietary schemes on the market, of which the Hay Guide Chart and Profile Method is the most widely used. Other major schemes include those operated by KPMG, Towers Perrin, Wyatt and a range of other consultancies. While it is beyond the scope of this book to cover these in any detail, it is as well to note that all these off-the-shelf schemes have the advantage of being tried and tested and so the various factors and scores can be applied with a degree of confidence. Their main drawback is that they often try to cover a very wide range of jobs and organizations with the same selection of factors. Clearly, however, there are differences between the components of jobs on the shop floor and those in the boardroom. For this reason some of the companies mentioned have different schemes for manual and non-manual jobs, and sometimes for different industry sectors.

Some other schemes are tailor-made and design factors and weightings that are specific to a particular organization. This kind of approach can ensure that the factors chosen are those that are the most relevant to that organization and the fact that it has been involved in the selection and design of them should help to ensure greater credibility. The main difficulty is in getting factor definitions agreed and correctly weighted, although there are statistical techniques for achieving the latter. One other drawback is that the use of different factors, levels and scores in different organizations makes comparison between them more difficult and complicates the pay comparison process.

An extract from the BCHR job evaluation scheme is shown after the end of this section (Figure 3.1).

Costs

There is usually a cost involved in introducing job evaluation. This stems not just from the cost of buying or designing a suitable scheme, with any necessary consultancy support, and the staff time involved in evaluating jobs and maintaining the system, but also from the implementation of any salary increases.

Typically, when you introduce job evaluation you will find that some jobs are underpaid and some are overpaid in relation to others. Since it is very difficult to reduce pay, and it would be demotivating and probably a breach of the employment contract to do so, those who are overpaid will usually continue to receive their existing level of pay on a personally protected basis – a process sometimes described as red-circling. On the other hand, those who are underpaid will usually expect to have their salaries brought up to the appropriate level. It is incumbent on you to do this, as the whole point of the exercise is normally to ensure that pay relativities are right, and any failure to make these adjustments is again likely to be demotivating.

Communication

It is very important to ensure that the job evaluation exercise is effectively communicated to the employees. Precisely what is communicated and in how much detail is something that has to be carefully considered. As a minimum, the employees should be:

- told that a job evaluation exercise is to take place;
- informed of the aims and objectives of the exercise;
- notified of the process and the timescale involved;
- informed of the scheme principles;
- notified about the results of the exercise, although the amount of detail they are given will vary from organization to organization.

Wherever possible you should get the cooperation of any trade unions and they should be involved in the process. In this way they are more likely to buy into the process. If they remain outside it, then they can oppose the results at a later date.

Job evaluation panels

Although jobs can be evaluated by an individual, it is more common in organizations of any size to have a job evaluation panel. This reduces the danger of individual bias, as everyone has prejudices about the worth of particular jobs and these will be diluted by a group process, gives access to a wider range of knowledge about the organization and its jobs, and is generally perceived to be fairer.

Panel or committee members should be persons who have sound judgement and credibility within the organization. You should also try and ensure that as wide a range of job types as possible can be covered by the group's combined knowledge. Similarly, the panel should be representative of the organization's employees. For example, if there are no women evaluators the process may be discriminatory, even if the scheme itself is free of any such bias. However, you should keep the panel as small as possible, otherwise it becomes unwieldy and might involve too much time and resources.

Decisions should be by consensus. If there is no agreement this is likely to mean that the evaluators do not understand the job and require more information or clarification.

HOW PAY IS MADE UP

There are a number of different elements that can make up an employee's total pay. Some of the more common ones are:

- base pay – which is the contractually agreed rate of pay set out in the contract of employment, before any additions, and usually expressed as an annual, monthly, weekly or hourly rate;
- overtime – which is the rate of pay for any work over and above the basic hours; the conditions for payment should be clearly described in the contract of employment;
- bonus – this is any amount additional to the base pay that is paid subject to certain conditions, such as the achievement of performance targets;
- shift pay – an amount paid to compensate staff for regularly working hours outside the normal working day;
- regional allowances – to compensate for the higher cost of living in certain locations;
- other allowances;
- standby and call-out payments.

PAY STRUCTURES

In small companies the simplest way to pay people is to pay an individual weekly wage or annual salary, which is reviewed annually, generally known as a spot rate. In larger organizations with several jobs of similar size, it is more common to pay jobs within a pay range or grade with the position within that

Interpersonal skills Knowledge and experience	1 Basic – Basic social skills only	2 Limited – Requires an ability to present the right image to external clients and to interface well with other departments	3 Advisory – Requires some influencing skills and an ability to communicate clearly and provide advice	4 Persuasive – Requires significant motivational, persuasive or influencing skills	5 Critical – Role requires expert counselling skills and an ability to reconcile differences and shape attitudes in conditions of emotional stress
A Basic – Secondary education only required	35	45	55	70	95
B Clerical – Knowledge of elementary systems and procedures and relevant skills	45	55	70	95	120
C Administrative/ technical – Knowledge of more advanced systems and procedures plus relevant skills	55	70	95	120	160
D Advanced technical/basic professional – Requires a body of specialist technical knowledge and an understanding of principles related to that knowledge	70	95	120	160	210
E Professional – Requires a high level of specialist expertise involving professional judgement and the breadth of knowledge necessary to manage others	95	120	160	210	270

Figure 3.1 *Knowledge and skills (extract from BCHR job evaluation scheme)*

F Senior professional/ managerial – Requires substantial managerial and/or professional knowledge gained through broad and deep experience	120	160	210	270	350
G Directing – Requires sufficient knowledge and experience to be able to direct and control a major function or to contribute substantially to the formulation of strategic objectives	160	210	270	350	455
H Strategic – Requires the knowledge and experience necessary to direct the organization	210	270	350	455	590

Figure 3.1   _Knowledge and skills (extract from BCHR job evaluation scheme)_
(Continued)

range being generally dependent on the individual's performance and experience. There are many variations on this theme.

The most appropriate approach for you will depend on the number and types of jobs within your company. As companies increase in size, spot rates become more difficult to manage. Pay ranges, on the other hand, give the flexibility to reflect differences in performance. The various types of pay structure with their advantages and disadvantages are described below.

Pay ranges

The most common approach to pay, at least in the private sector, is to apply pay ranges. These may either be applied to individuals or to groups of jobs and typically comprise maximum and minimum salary points, constructed about a mid-point, based on the job size and/or market rate for a particular category of jobs, but usually without incremental steps.

There are no hard-and-fast rules about how wide such ranges should be, but 80 to 120 per cent or 90 to 110 per cent of the mid-point are very common. Similarly, the basis for determining the mid-point, or the maximum and minimum, will vary from company to company. Managers may be given the discretion to appoint anywhere within the range for a particular type of job or certain points may be identified, for example at 90 per cent, 95 per cent, 100 per cent, 105 per cent of the range and so forth. Application of these percentages may be related to performance, and where this approach is used a performance matrix such as that set out in Figure 3.2 can be used to assess the size of any bonus. The figures in the boxes refer to the percentage increases in salary. Typically pay ranges overlap, but this is not obligatory. Where ranges are applied there may often also be one-off cash bonuses for the attainment of agreed targets.

The matrix shows the percentage of base salary payable as bonus, related to the position in the salary range, for different levels of performance

Performance rating	Position in range		
	Below 90%	**90%–110%**	**Above 110%**
Well above target	15%	12.5%	10%
Above target	12.5%	10%	7.5%
On target	10.0%	7.5%	5%

Figure 3.2   *Performance matrix*

Advantages

The advantages of pay ranges are that:

- they are more flexible than incrementally based grades;
- managers are usually given relatively wide discretion in deciding salaries and are under no obligation to give an increase if this is not justified by market data or performance, and provided there is no contractual obligation to do so;

- they give the company wide scope to reward individual development and academic attainments or qualifications;
- they can give the company more control over its reward policy;
- they can be based on either job size or market rates, or a combination of the two, and may be applied differently for different job categories;
- they tend to break down the historical attitudes that can arise with grades.

Disadvantages

The disadvantages of pay ranges are that:

- although they are generally less structured than grades with fixed increments, they can be applied just as rigidly, thus generating none of the advantages described;
- because of their flexibility they require more managing;
- they are likely to result in greater variations in individual pay for similar jobs and could therefore lead to dissatisfaction in some staff.

Competency bands

Pay ranges can be adapted to suit the particular needs of the company. For example, they can be related to competencies by the use of competency bands. Staff would move to different levels within the pay scales on the attainment of certain levels of competence, although the ranges would need to be sufficiently wide to accommodate these.

Job families

Pay ranges can also be applied to job families. In this approach the various job families are identified – for example, administrative and clerical, finance, information technology and so forth – and pay ranges relevant to those groups are applied. This enables the company to reflect the differing pay markets in which these job categories operate and can provide clear career paths. It does, however, make the establishment of one overall reward policy more difficult.

Spot salaries

Spot or spot rate salaries are those where specific individual salaries, rather than a salary range or grade, are paid to staff. In this case the rate paid usually depends on what the individual employee can negotiate with the employer. Obviously this kind of arrangement gives the employer a substantial degree of freedom in agreeing the reward package. Spot rates are most appropriate in small companies with a variety of jobs, for jobs at the most senior level, or where the job is such that only a few people with rare capabilities are able to fill it. Where substantial numbers of staff are employed, spot rates can become difficult to apply and manage and could raise equal value issues.

Broad banding

Features

Broad banding entails the introduction of fewer but much broader pay ranges. The typical features of a broad-banded structure are:

- four to six pay ranges covering all employees;
- each pay range containing jobs of perceptibly different size;
- a very wide salary range with significant overlap between ranges;
- the position in the range is determined by a variety of factors, including job size, market pay, performance and the acquisition of new skills and competencies.

Implications

The main implications of a broad-banded pay structure are as follows:

- there is less movement between pay bands but more movement within them; moving from one pay band to another would be a significant promotion;
- staff would have to be prepared to move between jobs without necessarily moving to a higher pay range;
- the actual pay of any employee would be determined by a number of factors including job size, market rate, performance and the acquisition of knowledge, skills or competencies.

A job evaluation process may be necessary to determine the appropriate pay band for jobs and to establish boundaries. This could be installed relatively quickly, but would be likely to be less participative than is usually the case and would be likely to be less effective for defending equal value claims.

Pay discussion will centre more on the individual's pay than the rates for a particular pay band.

Team leaders could be placed in the same band as their team members.

BONUSES

The design of bonus schemes can be complex, as any such scheme has to be carefully tailored to the needs of the company and to the type of job involved. For example, the type of scheme that might be appropriate for a salesperson would be completely different from one for a plumber or a secretary. When you are thinking of introducing a bonus scheme, therefore, you need to consider the following issues:

- The reason for the scheme – is it because you want the employees to share in the company's success or is it to reward the achievement of specific targets?
- If the scheme is to reward performance, do you have a process for setting targets and for assessing whether those targets have been met?
- How much is any bonus going to be?
- Are you going to have different schemes for different jobs?
- Are bonuses going to be paid on an individual or a group basis?
- How will you reward office and managerial staff who may not be able to earn bonuses through meeting productivity targets?
- How will any bonus relate to the rest of the remuneration package?
- How often will any bonus be paid?

THE NATIONAL MINIMUM WAGE

The law relating to the National Minimum Wage is laid down in the National Minimum Wage Act 1998, the National Minimum Wage Regulations 1999 and in the National Minimum Wage Act (Amendment) Regulations 1999.

The National Minimum Wage applies to any worker who is not genuinely self-employed. From October 2007 the rate is £5.52 per hour for all workers aged 22 or over. There are lower rates for workers below this age and for certain trainees who may be aged 22 or more.

The hourly rate is calculated by working out a worker's total pay over the relevant pay reference period and dividing by the number of hours worked. The pay reference period is normally a month for monthly paid staff, but for any workers paid over a shorter period, such as a week, it will be that shorter period. The calculation should be based on gross pay (before deduction of tax and National Insurance) and after deduction of certain payments above the base pay, such as overtime, shift payments, expenses, statutory sick pay, and maternity pay.

93

Piece workers, or output workers, including home workers, must be paid a 'fair' piece rate linked to the National Minimum Wage. For this purpose, output work means work that is paid on the basis of the number of pieces made or processed by the worker, or according to some other measure such as the number of tasks or transactions carried out by the worker.

These workers must either be paid at least the minimum wage for all hours worked or, alternatively, be paid the fair piece rate for each piece produced or task performed, determined by reference to the rate of performance of an average worker (called the 'rated output system'). To apply this you must have conducted a test to determine the average speed at which the job can be completed. This test has to be carried out using all workers, or a representative sample, and in similar conditions to those of the piece rate workers.

You must then issue the piece rate worker, in advance, with a notice which:

- states that such a test has been conducted (or that the speed has been estimated);
- states what the average hourly output is;
- states that the worker will be treated as having worked for the time that it would have taken him (or her) to complete the job at the average speed;
- states the rate to be paid for the work in question; and
- gives one of the National Minimum Wage helpline numbers.

You are required to pay 120 per cent of the minimum wage for the time established by the testing procedure to ensure that workers who may be below the average speed also receive the National Minimum Wage.

It is essential that you keep adequate records if you use the rated output system.

Further information about the National Minimum Wage can be obtained from the BERR website: www.berr.gov.uk.

GUARANTEE PAYMENTS

Guarantee payments were introduced to safeguard employees in the event of short-time working. They must be made to any employee who might normally expect to work, for any day when no work is provided because of a lessening of demand for your product or service. These payments are made for a maximum of five working days in any three months and are subject to a limit specified by the government (£20.40 per day from 1 February 2008).

EQUAL PAY

In April 2003 an Equal Pay Questionnaire was introduced. Through that questionnaire, any employee who feels that he or she is not receiving pay equal to a member of the opposite sex can ask the employer to provide information about the pay of that person. While giving information about the pay of another employee could potentially infringe data protection legislation if that person does not wish the information to be disclosed, this danger can usually be averted by describing the grade or pay range applying to the comparator employee rather than giving the actual salary.

DIRECTORS' REMUNERATION REPORT REGULATIONS 2002

These Regulations give shareholders more opportunity to express concerns over directors' remuneration. They provide that:

- quoted companies must publish a detailed report on directors' pay as part of their annual reporting cycle. Disclosure requirements both about facts and policies have increased. The report must be approved by the Board of Directors;
- a graph of the company's total shareholder return over five years, against a comparator group, must be published in the remuneration committee report;
- the names of any consultants to the remuneration committee must be disclosed, as must be whether they were appointed independently, along with the cost of any other services provided to the company;
- companies must hold a shareholder vote on the directors' remuneration report at each annual general meeting.

DEDUCTIONS FROM PAY

Restrictions on deductions

You are not allowed to make deductions from pay unless:

- there is a statutory authority to do so, as with income tax and National Insurance;

- there is a clause in the employee's contract agreeing to a specific deduction; or
- the employee has agreed in writing to the deduction.

Overpayments

Where overpayments of wages or expenses have been made these can be deducted from earnings without the need to get prior permission from the employee.

Attachments of earnings orders

Where an employee defaults on debt repayments the courts have the power to require the employer to make deductions from that employee's pay.

Check-off agreements

A check-off agreement is an arrangement whereby trade union subscriptions are automatically deducted from pay. It is a legal requirement for you to ensure that such deductions are lawful, which can only be done by ensuring that the employee gives his consent in writing to the deduction.

Generally, check-off arrangements can be viewed as a convenient way of ensuring that trade union subscriptions are paid, for maintaining good industrial relations and as a means of enabling the company to monitor the level of union membership. You can, if desired, charge the union an administrative fee for carrying out this arrangement.

TAX AND NATIONAL INSURANCE

PAYE

Any employee has to pay tax (PAYE – Pay As You Earn) to HM Revenue & Customs under Schedule E and it is your responsibility to deduct the tax and account for it to them. Each employee is given a tax code by HM Revenue & Customs and it is the responsibility of the employee to ensure that the code given is the correct one and the responsibility of the employer to ensure that the correct amount is deducted.

You have to deduct the correct amount, keep records of the pay and deductions and pay the correct amount to HM Revenue & Customs each month. At the end of the tax year a return has to be sent to HM Revenue & Customs showing all the payments and deductions made throughout the year.

The tax code is notified to the employer by a P45 certificate issued by the previous employer or by direct notification from the tax office. In the absence of any such notification an emergency code has to be applied.

National Insurance

As an employer it is your responsibility to pay National Insurance contributions to HM Revenue & Customs for all employees whose earnings are above the Lower Earnings Limit. These are described as Class 1 NIC contributions and comprise a contribution from the employee and one from you as the employer. It is normal to collect the employee's contribution by making a regular deduction from salary.

All NI payments must be made by the 19th day of the month following the month of deduction and can be incorporated into the monthly PAYE return.

Contributions should be calculated by reference to the employer's pack, which is sent automatically to you before the start of each tax year.

National Insurance is payable on all earnings and on a range of benefits, but not on expenses. It is not usually payable on redundancy payments.

Contributions do not have to be paid for employees aged under 16 years, and for those over retirement age only the employer's contribution is payable.

What does or does not count for National Insurance purposes is a relatively complex area, although the payment process itself should be fairly routine once it has been set up. To help employers there is a range of information available contained in publications that are available from the National Insurance Contributions Office. This can be accessed online through their website at www.hmrc.gov.uk. Alternatively there is a national employers' helpline on 0845 7143143.

ITEMIZED PAY STATEMENT

You must issue any employee with an itemized pay statement at the time of payment with details of:

- gross earnings;
- the amount of any fixed deduction and the reason for the deduction;
- the amount of any variable deduction and the reason;
- the net pay.

FURTHER INFORMATION

Armstrong, M (1996) *Employee Reward*, Institute of Personnel and Development, London

Armstrong, M and Baron, A (1995) *The Job Evaluation Handbook*, Institute of Personnel and Development, London

Armstrong, M and Murlis, H (2007) *Reward Management*, 5th edition, Kogan Page, London

Essential Facts – Employment (2007) Gee Publishing Ltd, London

HM Revenue & Customs, www.hmrc.gov.uk

Incomes Data Services Ltd, 77 Bastwick Street, London EC1V 3TT; Tel: 020 7250 3434

IRS Employment Review, Industrial Relations Services, London, published fortnightly

Personnel Manager's Factbook (2007) Gee Publishing Ltd, London

4

Employee benefits

There is no legal requirement for you to give benefits, above the minimum statutory entitlements, but most employers do so because of the need to be competitive in the jobs market and also to encourage a high level of staff satisfaction. Benefits can include:

- pension;
- car;
- share options;
- medical insurance;
- death-in-service benefits;
- holidays (above the statutory minimum);
- sick pay (above the statutory minimum);
- relocation expenses;
- enhanced maternity leave;
- sabbatical leave;
- payment of professional subscriptions;
- season ticket loans;
- subsidized meals or luncheon vouchers;
- sports and social facilities;
- childcare facilities.

Maintaining employee heath and combating the costs on *"pulling a sickie"*

Employee health has never been a hotter topic for British businesses, with sick days costing the economy £13.4bn in 2006, according to the CBI. Health Secretary Alan Johnson has also indicated his determination to stamp out 'sick-note culture' with the introduction of well-notes to demonstrate what activities employees are actually able to do. Add to this the continued interest surrounding public health issues such as obesity and fitness, and it is clear that employers are increasingly responsible for aspects of the health of their workforce. Good workplace health also manifests itself in increased productivity and reduced costs due to absence and staff turnover, making the wellbeing of employees an issue that needs to be tackled from the top.

Health cash plans, such as those offered by HSF health plan, bridge the gap between relatively expensive private medical insurance (PMI) and public health services. Unlike PMI, however, cash plans are the ideal way to manage everyday health such as GP visits and dental or optical care. For a relatively small monthly premium, contributors are reimbursed with a percentage (up to 100%) of the cost of routine appointments or treatment.

Making a GP appointment is often cited as one of the most inconvenient health chores. HSF health plan offers a 24-hour, doctor-run telephone helpline that helps callers assess their needs and decide on best course of subsequent treatment. This gives workers the flexibility to manage their health at times to suit them and their working life. With HSF health plan, spouses and dependent children are covered at no extra cost - ideal for working parents with the responsibility of managing the whole family's health.

Chronic non-serious illness, such as back pain, can mean a valued member of staff is off work long-term, which has a potentially huge impact on business. Many sufferers of these types of conditions feel unable to return even to light duties without the support and advice of health professionals such as physiotherapists, yet waiting lists can make this treatment impossible to access. HSF health plan includes provision for appointments with practitioners such as physiotherapists, osteopaths and podiatrists, as well as for specialist investigations such allergy testing, x-rays and health screening as again enabling employees to proactively manage their health in a way and time that suits them.

Employees often feel under pressure to be 'present' and can be reluctant to schedule routine health appointments, such as dental care. Unfortunately, this strategy can backfire if it results in longer-term absence. With HSF health plan, dental care is included, enabling employees to schedule regular checks and treatment – making absence planned and fully accountable. With the financial peace of mind having a cash plan brings, employees can seek treatment at an earlier stage before their condition worsens, necessitating time away from work.

Stress is thought to be one of the biggest causes of workplace absence, blamed for 13.8million days of absence each year. To put that into context, last year British businesses lost £9.6billion due to employees suffering a high level of stress. HSF health plan offers a Stress Advice Line as part of every scheme, helping employees recognise and reduce workplace stress.

Companies can either entirely fund a health plan on behalf of employees as a workplace benefit, provide part funding or simply encourage voluntary participation. HSF offers a beneficial rate to corporate contributors, whether self or employer funded. Providing a health cash plan does more for workplace health than simply provide access – this kind of employee benefit sends a clear message to the workforce that positive health is at the very heart of the company. By funding contributions, at least in part, employers are encouraging their workforce to invest and become interested in their health. Along with other health-living initiatives this can have a marked effect on absenteeism.

Originally founded as the Hospital Saturday Fund, HSF health plan was established in 1873 to allow workers to save for their healthcare. How called HSF health plan, it's a not-for-profit organisation, which makes regular donations to hospitals, hospices and medically-associated charities, as well as to individuals whose health problems have caused financial stress and hardship. For more information log on to **www.hsf.eu.com**

IT'S A WIN-WIN

In the ongoing drive to retain staff and build their loyalty, many companies are looking at ways to offer additional benefits to their employees. Many of those added value elements are costly at a time when margins are squeezed, but offering a **Childcare Voucher Scheme** is a win-win for employers and employees alike. A childcare voucher sacrifice scheme gives you the opportunity to offer your employees a Tax and National Insurance benefit while making savings in Employer's National Insurance for your organisation.

What are Childcare Vouchers? They are Tax and NI exempt salary deductions which can be paid to carers direct through a childcare voucher provider. Up to a maximum amount of £55 a week or £243 a month is subtracted by the employer from the employee's salary prior to the calculation of Tax and NI. The money is paid to a childcare voucher company who then pays the carers at the request of the parent.

Childcare vouchers can be used for a wide variety of care ranging from day nurseries, registered childminders and nannies to after-school and holiday clubs for older children.

How much can be saved? An individual taking the maximum amount in vouchers will save between £857 and £1195 per annum (other allowances may be affected). Your company could save up to £373 per person depending on the rate of Employers NI that you pay. This will far more than cover the administration fee charged by the Voucher Company, leaving you with an overall saving and a great employee benefit!

So why use Corporate Childcare Solutions Group? We are a small company with a strong philosophy of personal service. We offer employers, employees and carers full on-line access, so they can check their voucher balance, set up payments or amend details 24/7. We also tailor our communications to your business so each company has its own documentation. Furthermore we do not operate a call centre; a named account manager who knows your business is at the end of the line ready to assist. We are a small company offering exceptional service at a great price.

The main issues that you have to consider as an employer are the common practice in your market sector, and especially in those companies you might compete against for staff, and whether benefits are applied equally and fairly to all staff. You will also need to consider the tax implications of various benefits packages.

You might also wish to consider whether you want to offer a flexible benefits package, whereby employees can pick and mix from a range of options. More information on flexible benefits is set out later in this chapter.

In July 2005, research was carried out for www.employeebenefits.co.uk on 199 companies giving voluntary benefits, defined as products and services made available through an employer but paid for by staff out of their own income. The most common benefits are shown in Figure 4.1.

STAKEHOLDER PENSIONS

Stakeholder pensions are low-cost pensions designed for people who are not currently in a pension scheme.

If you have five or more employees you must arrange access to a stakeholder pension scheme for all your employees who earn more than the National Insurance Lower Earnings Limit. This does not mean that you have to set up a scheme, merely that you need to contact a commercial provider and pass the details to your employees. Failure to do so could result in you being fined.

Exemptions

You do not have to provide a stakeholder pension scheme if:

- you employ fewer than five people;
- you offer an occupational pension scheme that all your staff can join within a year of starting;
- you offer all employees a personal pension scheme to which you contribute an amount equal to at least 3 per cent of the employee's basic pay and which has no penalties for members who cease contributing or who transfer their pension.

Introducing a scheme

To introduce a stakeholder pension scheme you need to take the following actions:

Voluntary benefit	%
Additional voluntary contributions to a defined benefit or money purchase pension scheme	66%
Group personal pension	63%
Healthcare/hospital cash plan	59%
Private medical insurance	58%
Gym membership	57%
Childcare vouchers	54%
Stakeholder pension	52%
Life assurance	49%
Season ticket loan	49%
Leisure/entertainment services	47%
Employer's own products or services	46%
Legal advice/helpline	40%
Retail products, eg electrical goods	40%
Travel insurance	39%
Optical care vouchers	39%
Debt counselling/helpline	37%
Health screening	36%
Dental insurance	36%
HMRC-approved save as you earn (SAYE) sharesave plan	35%
Personal accident insurance	35%
Financial advice/education	35%
Income protection/permanent health insurance	34%
Critical illness insurance	30%
Retail/leisure vouchers	30%
Non-vocational training	27%
Mobile phones	27%
Motor insurance	26%
House insurance	25%
HMRC-approved share incentive plan	21%
Pet insurance	19%
Fuel for private use	14%
Discounted cars to staff through an all employee car ownership plan	11%
Mortgage subsidy	4%
Luncheon vouchers	3%

Source: www.employeebenefits.co.uk, July 2005

Figure 4.1 *The most common voluntary benefits as reported by 199 surveyed companies*

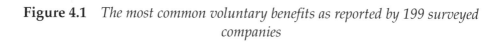

- choose a registered stakeholder pension scheme or schemes;
- discuss the scheme or schemes with those employees who qualify for access;
- formally choose the agreed scheme;
- give your employees the name and address of the pension scheme provider;
- arrange to deduct contributions from the pay of those employees who have chosen to contribute to the scheme through you;
- give your employees information about the payroll deduction arrangements;
- make any agreed payroll deductions;
- send any employee and employer contributions to the pension scheme provider within the stated time limits;
- record payments made to the pension scheme provider.

Further information about stakeholder pensions is available on www.dss.gov. uk.

SHARES AND SHARE OPTIONS

You can use employee share schemes to attract and retain staff who are considered critical to the future success of the company, and also as a useful means of linking rewards to company performance. However, they should always be viewed as part of the company's overall reward strategy.

Share schemes may be 'approved' or 'non-approved'. Approved schemes are those that are approved by HM Revenue & Customs. The main advantage of approved schemes is that employees who receive shares or share options under them are not liable to income tax under schedule E.

The main advantage of non-approved schemes is that they are not subject to the same restrictions as approved schemes, such as the value of shares that may be issued and the terms on which they are offered.

CARS

Cars are usually allocated to employees either because they are needed for the effective performance of the job, or because the status of the job in the company is such that a car is an expected part of the package. It is now common for a car allowance to be paid instead of a car being provided. If a car is provided, probably the most straightforward option is to use a contract hire company.

You don't have off the shelf challenges, so we don't have off the shelf solutions.

Whilst there are often common themes, no two businesses share the exact same circumstances. Our Consultants will explore your objectives and recommend a benefits strategy to meet your needs.

Whether simple or complex, traditional or innovative, our solutions build on a core level of governance, essential given ever-increasing levels of legislation and regulation. We appreciate the importance of advice and will deliver clearly structured recommendations rather than provide you with lists of options. To achieve this there are key elements which underpin our services:

Expertise

Our services cover all aspects of employee benefits:

- defined benefit and defined contribution pension schemes
- risk benefits
- health and wellbeing services
- flexible benefits
- independent financial advice

From consultancy and design to implementation and administration, our client focussed approach draws on expertise from varying disciplines to deliver a tailored solution.

Partnership

In order to provide appropriate advice and a valued service it is vital that we understand your business and your employees. This is achieved by building long-term relationships founded on trust. Central to this is providing appropriate support to all relevant functions within your business – us working in partnership with you.

Communication is the most influential factor in maximising the impact and effectiveness of your employee benefits programme. There is a wide range of media options available for benefit communication and these can be used in combination to meet objectives and budget. From total reward statements which emphasise the scope and value of a benefits package, to one-to-one support educating employees about their retirement planning, effective communication is key to employee engagement.

HSBC Actuaries and Consultants Limited is an independent employee benefits consultancy, wholly owned by the HSBC Group.

For more information please contact Mark Pemberthy on 01727 775090 or mark.pemberthy@hsbc.com

HSBC Actuaries and Consultants Limited is authorised and regulated by the Financial Services Authority Registered in England: number 676122 Registered offices: 8 Canada Square, London, E14 5HQ www.hacl.hsbc.com info.hacl@hsbc.com

Attract, retain and motivate has been a long-standing validation for employee benefits. Whilst clichéd, these outcomes are still highly relevant in today's competitive environment and employee benefits continue to play an important part in achieving these. Mark Pemberthy, Senior Consultant as HSBC Actuaries and Consultants Limited takes a brief look at what employers can do and what the issues are.

It's all about you and your employees

Every company will have their own combination of objectives from their reward strategy, which may include:

- being an employer of choice
- projecting the culture of the employer
- improving employee's work-life balance
- enhancing return on investment by reducing employee turnover, managing absenteeism, or increasing productivity
- controlling costs
- providing employees with the tools to ensure they can afford to retire

Whichever sector your company operates in, there will be some advantage to be derived from providing employee benefits which are relevant and valued by employees and potential recruits alike.

Changing focus

Traditional benefits such as pensions, life cover and ill-health benefits are understandably still core to most employers' benefits packages. There continues to be development in these areas, fuelled by innovation and legislation – most notably in the pensions arena.

However the most significant growth in recent years has been in complementary and voluntary benefits, such as child-care vouchers. These products and services provide immediate value to an employee, in contrast to the more long term and contingent nature of pensions and life cover, which are more paternal but less tangible.

Benefits can be employer funded, employee funded, or integral to a Flexible Benefits programme. Some benefits can be enhanced by tax efficient funding methods which legitimately harness income tax and National Insurance contributions to reduce costs or boost value.

Size doesn't matter

Technology has enabled providers to develop scaleable services which enable SME's to take a customised approach to employee benefits, an option that has historically been impractical for all but the largest employers.

With benefit options ranging from health and wellbeing initiatives to carbon-offsetting, employers of all sizes can now offer a tailored combination of benefits to suit the demographics of employees and recruitment targets.

The value of Trust

Employees naturally trust employer sponsored services and as a result the workplace is a powerful environment for financial education. Given the growth of defined contribution pension schemes, employee education may ultimately prove vital in ensuring that employees are able to secure a comfortable retirement.

Communication is the vital ingredient in any successful employee benefit strategy. There are a host of communication media that can be used to ensure that employee benefits are understood, valued and ultimately deliver the identified objectives.

To discuss any of the areas covered by this article please contact Mark Pemberthy of HSBC Actuaries and Consultants Limited at **mark.pemberthy@hsbc.com**

Imagine...Childcare Vouchers

Imagine...Childcare Vouchers can be offered to the employees of any organisation wishing to provide this benefit. Put simply, they are just a different way of paying for childcare costs, whilst still allowing the parent to choose the kind of care they think best suits their child. The most popular way of providing childcare vouchers is through a salary sacrifice scheme (whereby an employee exchanges part of their salary for vouchers and saves tax and national insurance contributions) or flexible benefit, although some clients do prefer to offer childcare vouchers as a benefit in addition to salary.

Imagine...the benefits to your business

Key to the growing number of organisations implementing childcare voucher schemes is that they financially benefit the employer as well as the employee. Childcare vouchers are national insurance exempt for the employer – the NI savings will more than cover any service charge, creating savings which can be invested in other family-friendly initiatives.

Childcare vouchers can be made available to all employees with children up to the age of 15 years (or 16 for children with disabilities), and can be used to pay for any form of registered or approved childcare. All working parents within your organisation may therefore benefit from the scheme, not just those with pre-school children.

Childcare vouchers have been shown to positively enhance recruitment and retention within both public and private sector organisations, as well as actively demonstrating a commitment to family-friendly working – a great boost for the image of any organisation.

A key concern for any employer wishing to embark on a childcare voucher scheme is the amount of time and administration involved. We have developed a fully HMRC compliant scheme which is fully electronic, simple to implement and run, and requires minimal administration.

To find out more about Imagine Childcare Vouchers, please contact us:
Imagine Co-operative Childcare
Co-operative House
234 Botley Road
Oxford
Oxon OX2 0HP
Tel: **0800 458 7929**
Email: **vouchers@imagine.coop**
Web: **www.imagine.coop**

advertisement feature

Whether or not the car fleet is owned by the company, you still have to decide about:

- the choice of makes and models;
- any restrictions on these;
- the replacement policy, ie whether the vehicle will be replaced after a stated number of years or a specific mileage, or whichever of the two is reached first;
- the extent to which you will allow those entitled to a company car to trade up or down (within the approved list) and the related salary adjustment;
- offering a cash alternative to all drivers (see below).

Where an employee is entitled to a company car, you should state in the employment contract:

- the make and model of vehicle the employee is entitled to;
- whether it is available for private use and whether there are restrictions on its use;
- who is allowed to drive the car;
- when it will be replaced;
- who is responsible for the cost of fuel, maintenance, tax, insurance and repairs;
- whether the car user is required to make a contribution in return for private use of the car;
- whether there are circumstances (such as extended leave or during a driving ban) when the vehicle may be withdrawn;
- health and safety rules to be followed;
- the car user's responsibilities in respect of the vehicle.

Information about the taxation of company cars is available from www.hmrc. gov.uk.

FLEXIBLE BENEFITS

Flexible benefits schemes, also described as 'cafeteria benefits', are formal schemes which allow employees to change their individual pay and benefits package to suit their specific requirements. These can involve a choice within benefits, eg a choice of car models with employees being given the option of upgrading by paying an additional cash contribution, or downgrading with a cash refund, or a choice between benefits. Generally, references to flexible benefits schemes relate to those which provide a menu of benefits options.

Schemes generally allow employees either to retain their existing salary and choose from a range of benefits or to have a salary reduction in exchange for certain benefits.

The CIPD identifies advantages and disadvantages of flexible benefits schemes, which are listed below.

Advantages

- Employees choose benefits to meet their needs and value these benefits more highly.
- Employers and employees share the responsibility for providing benefits.
- During periods of change, flexible benefits help to harmonize rewards.
- Employers provide benefits at a known cost that is fixed regardless of the choices that employees make, so allowing them to cap future benefit costs.
- Employees have a true idea of the full worth of the benefits package they receive and employers do not provide benefits that are not valued.
- Employees are given a sense of control and involvement by having a choice.
- Dual career couples avoid having benefits duplicated by their respective employers.
- Employers are seen to be more responsive to the needs of an increasingly diverse, demanding and ageing workforce.
- A competitive benefits package is valuable in attracting and retaining key personnel.
- The awarding of benefits such as a company car becomes less divisive.
- Employers' demands for flexible working practices are more justifiable if employees enjoy flexible benefits.
- They may help to align the total reward strategy to the HR and business strategies.

Disadvantages

- Employers find them complex and expensive to set up and maintain (although new technology is reducing both the cost and administrative burden).
- The choices made may cause problems both to employers and employees.

Old benefit gathering new momentum

The call from employers for cash plans has gathered significant momentum in recent months, driven partly by increased competition to attract and retain staff and partly by the innovation from providers.

The staff retention issue now engages the employer beyond its top management. Staff with transferable skills and knowledge are becoming more difficult to retain in a competitive labour market and are often in positions that do not attract 'big' benefits such as Private Medical Insurance, high death in service cover, Critical Illness and the like. In this market cash plans are a highly valued low cost benefit that can help reward these key employees.

Innovation too is driving the market as suppliers such as BHSF build into their plans employee assistance plans, screening benefits and other back-to-work benefits to address absence management. Aiming at the holy grail of "Good for employee + Good for employer" the cash plan market has really raised its game.

Cash plans can even be a no cost option. The ability of BHSF and others to deliver the product as a voluntary benefit through benefit fairs, road shows and work-site marketing allows an employer to introduce the benefit and not impact tightening budgets.

Cost does remain an issue. Employer sponsored plans can be introduced on a voluntary basis from around £5 per month for employees and where a company contribution is available even less, but beware expensive imitations. There are plans on the market that offer little extra genuine value but cost employees 30%-70% more.

If this is an area that employers have not previously looked at the "Good for employee + Good for employer" proposition can seem too good to be true – but true it certainly is.

For more information contact **sales@bhsf.co.uk 0121 629 1165**.

The design of any scheme will vary between organizations but most schemes will typically include certain core benefits such as:

- holidays;
- life assurance;
- private medical insurance;
- critical illness insurance;
- personal accident insurance.

If you are considering a flexible benefits scheme it is best to get professional advice before doing so because of the complexities involved.

TAXATION OF BENEFITS

Most benefits are subject to tax, but the following are generally tax free (though NICs may be payable in some cases):

- contributions paid into an approved occupational or personal pension scheme for the employee;
- cheap or free canteen meals, if these are provided for all employees, even if separate facilities are provided for different groups of employees;
- luncheon vouchers up to 15p per working day;
- in-house sporting or recreational facilities;
- redundancy and outplacement counselling;
- a workplace nursery financed and managed by the employer;
- childcare vouchers;
- Christmas party or other annual social event up to £150 per person per annum;
- works buses, or subsidies to public bus services, to get employees to and from work;
- bicycles and cycling safety equipment provided for employees to get to and from work and workplace parking for bicycles and motorcycles;
- removal and relocation expenses up to £8,000;
- genuine personal gifts given for reasons unconnected with the job, for example, retirement gifts other than cash, or wedding gifts;
- gifts, other than cash, received from someone other than the employer, for example, seats at sporting or cultural events, providing that any gift or outing is not worth more than £100;
- equipment and facilities provided for the disabled to carry out their jobs.

Finding the right solution for your business isn't difficult

When you know where to look

Corporate pensions and benefits, covered from every angle

Every business in the AEGON family is recognised as a specialist in its own area. AEGON Scottish Equitable, for example, has 175 years' experience in the pensions, savings and protection markets. Whatever your business needs, from pension plans and risk benefits to trustee services and more, you'll find AEGON can put together the perfect solution. Visit **aegon.co.uk**

AEGON

Pensions | Investments | Protection

April 2008

Employee benefits – making the most of what you offer

In a competitive marketplace, your employees make a huge difference to your business success. Generally speaking, the more they're 'engaged' and aligned to your company's objectives and strategy, the better your business will do.

Rewards and benefits can drive engagement and make it easier to recruit and retain people, but providing benefits is an expense. How can you get the best value for your spend?

First, we'll take a look at some of the tools you can use to make the connection between benefits and engagement. Then we'll talk about measuring engagement and the Return on Investment (ROI) that you can get from your benefits spend.

Employee benefits and engagement

Pensions form the core of most employee benefits packages. There are many different types of pensions, but they share the valuable advantage of tax relief on contributions made by both employers and employees. It's important that employees understand the cost-effectiveness of saving in a pension and really appreciate the value of the contributions you make on their behalf. A yearly statement is the minimum needed for employee communications, but helping people understand where they have choices in their pension can drive their interest and understanding. Providers can help by producing easy-to-follow communications for employees – on paper or through a website – to support and guide them through.

Salary sacrifice is a key tool to reduce the net cost of benefits. If employees 'sacrifice' their salary to obtain benefits, there are potential tax savings for both employer and employee. A number of benefits work well through salary sacrifice – including pensions. From a recent employer survey*, around half of the respondents used the savings from salary sacrifice to fund benefits. The most common benefit offered on a salary sacrifice basis is childcare vouchers. For those who use it, it's a highly valued service and brings a feel-good factor because of both the savings made and the convenient service through the workplace. It has the potential to drive ongoing engagement for people who otherwise could choose to take time out from work.

Some of the proof of the benefit of employee benefits lies in the management of risk. **Life cover** is one of the simplest and cheapest products you can offer to employees and it's a basic core benefit within most employers' benefits packages. Other risk benefits, such as **critical illness** are less well-known, but are valuable in helping people make it through difficult times, such as a diagnosis with one of the life-threatening illnesses specifically included in the cover.

The treatment of other types of risks can be more complex. Employee assistance plans (EAPs) are services that offer help and advice to employees with many different kinds of problems – home- and work-related. These services can reduce employees' calls on other more expensive benefits such as **income protection**. This is particularly relevant for you where the ongoing cost of the income protection depends in part on the number of claims made. Having access to a confidential welfare counselling service mitigates the risk of absence and its cost. The EAP may be able to help people with things that would otherwise cause distraction or require the employee to take time out at work to deal with their problem. The key thing is to collect the relevant absence data and measure the impact of your benefits to obtain a clear ROI benefit.

If your benefits package acts as a retention tool for your current staff, the money you'll spend on recruitment and induction will reduce. Your HR team can focus on adding value to your business instead of spending time on attracting, evaluating, selecting and inducting new people to the business. The ROI on employee benefits could include the cost that the business has avoided by not needing to recruit to 'stand still'.

Measuring engagement

A new market has sprung up in the last few years for **web-based software** that makes the administration of benefits packages of all sizes simpler to manage. The tools make flexible benefits plans easier from the HR perspective and aid employees' awareness of the benefits available. One key benefit of using the software is its ability to provide up-to-date and accurate data on the uptake of benefits and the actual costs against the benefits budget. Combined with measurements of engagement – perhaps through staff surveys – it's feasible to look analytically at the benefits package and its value.

Employee benefits are well-established in today's business world. Like every other source of cost, proving the benefit of what you spend is vitally important. Building a focus on value and measurement is the key to getting benefit from your benefits. Employee engagement is the bigger prize and benefits can be a useful tool in engaging and retaining the people you want in your business.

*Employee benefits/Towers Perrin flexible benefits research 2008

FURTHER INFORMATION

www.adviceguide.org.uk
www.cipd.co.uk
www.hmrc.gov.uk
www.peoplemanagement.co.uk

5

Performance management

THE IMPORTANCE OF MANAGING PERFORMANCE

It is vital to the long-term success of your business that your employees carry out their jobs well. This is particularly important if you are in a competitive field where the only differentiator may be the respective performances of individuals and teams within the competing companies.

The effective management of your employees' performance should:

- contribute to business success by ensuring that individual efforts are linked to business objectives;
- improve the motivation and performance of staff by giving them positive feedback and by providing them with opportunities for training and development;
- give the company more information about individuals and their needs.

THE PERFORMANCE MANAGEMENT PROCESS

The main steps in the performance management process are:

- setting objectives;
- managing performance;

Aligning individual pay and performance with corporate goals

Gavin Lawrie of 2GC Active Management describes a new to set personal goals and incentives that are demonstrably aligned with corporate objectives.

According to the UK's Chartered Institute of Personnel and Development (CIPD), individual pay and performance management systems can deliver very positive results for organisations, but to do so they must be designed to drive correct behaviours at all levels of the organisation[1]. But designing such systems and getting them to work is not easy. Success requires organisations to ensure that there is consistency between individual and corporate goals, and that these are set and managed within a sympathetic control system. Two factors dominate advice on how to achieve this:

- First, organisations need to provide sufficient, relevant and meaningful information about corporate goals to enable teams and individuals to set objectives against which they can be measured: the content of the performance management system must be made relevant to each level.

- Second, the practice of performance management must "fit" with the organisation's strategy at each level of the organisation[2]. While performance also depends on other factors, if individual activities are in conflict with organisational goals these may lead to poor organisational performance.

For very good reasons, responsibility and accountability for designing, implementing and managing such systems typically falls to staff functions, even though staff functions often have limited knowledge of or influence over the activities required for the delivery of corporate strategic objectives. To do this job effectively, those charged with delivering the system need to find a way to capture the insight and support of those in the organisation who will use them.

Modern Balanced Scorecard – A new tool with a familiar name

The Harvard Business Review considers it to be one of the top 15 management tools introduced in the 20th Century. It is a fixture in the 'top 10' of Bain & Company's annual survey of management tools in use in US and Europe. The Balanced Scorecard, which started life in the early 1990s as a simple but popular performance management

---

[1] See "Understanding the People and Performance Link: Unlocking the Black Box" by John Purcell and others. CIPD 2003, London (ISBN: 0852929870).
[2] See "What is Wrong with Performance Appraisal? a Critique and a Suggestion" by Keith Grint in the Human Resource Management Journal, Vol. 3, No.3 (1993).

framework has evolved over the past 15 years into a powerful and flexible strategic performance management tool. This article looks at the extent to which the most modern version of the tool – the 3rd Generation Balanced Scorecard[3], can enhance the ability of HR and other staff functions to manage the delivery of relevant and actionable individual goals and incentives that are nonetheless explicitly linked to key strategic objectives.

Effective Balanced Scorecards help management teams track progress (either their own or the organisation's) in achieving strategic objectives. Where progress is insufficient, a well designed Balanced Scorecard triggers interventions from these managers to correct whatever shortfall has been noted. To be able to trigger these interventions therefore, the Balanced Scorecard must reflect the strategic priorities of the team that is going to use it. But since different management teams have different functions and responsibilities, this necessarily means each team will have to have its own unique design of Balanced Scorecard. In the past, this requirement for local relevance was too complex to incorporate into a Balanced Scorecard design project, and teams typically got Balanced Scorecards that had generic goals shared across many within the organisation. These sub-optimal designs were easier to build, but less useful to the teams that had to use them, and many failed to deliver value as a result.

The latest best practice design processes, as embodied in the 3rd Generation Balanced Scorecard approach, provide a solution to this design problem. By using insights drawn from years of practical experience and academic research in related fields, these modern methods make it possible to deliver sets of multiple Balanced Scorecards that are explicitly aligned behind corporate goals, but nonetheless specifically relevant to each management team.

No other management tool is more effective at translating high-level strategic goals into locally relevant activities and priorities as the 3rd Generation Balanced Scorecard methodology. The holistic structure of best-practice design promotes increased focus on the practical interventions required to trigger changes in behaviours and performance within an organisation. Once this type of Balanced Scorecard is in place, it automatically reveals the points of focus upon which individual goals should rest. By setting individual goals with reference to the local Balanced Scorecard, local relevance is assured. And because each objective on the local Balanced Scorecard will have measures and targets associated with it, the identification of factors to reward via an incentive scheme is also straightforward – most of the work is already complete.

---

[3] See "Third-generation balanced scorecard: evolution of an effective strategic control tool" by Gavin Lawrie and Ian Cobbold in the International Journal of Productivity and Performance Management, Vol. 53, No. 7 (2004).

How does it work in practice?

3rd Generation Balanced Scorecard designs are based on an agreed description of an attainable future that satisfies the interests of the organisation's stakeholders called a 'Destination Statement'. Divisional and functional management teams can use this information from a 'corporate' destination statement to create their own 'aligned' versions – called 'contribution statements' that each describes the impact of achieving the Destination Statement on their part of the organisation. These contribution statements can be reviewed, discussed and analysed before any work to identify measures and targets begins. Only once the organisation is satisfied that the various contributions do indeed 'add up' to the overall Destination for the organisation does this measure and target development begin.

Working from their agreed 'contribution statement' each management team identifies the key activities that need to be executed within their area of responsibility if the things described in their contribution statement are to be realised. Because the contribution statement they are working from has already been confirmed as being an effective contribution to the overall strategic goals of the organisation, in picking their priority activities a management team simply needs to demonstrate that their choices are the right ones to deliver their contribution statement – making it possible for each team to choose actions specifically relevant to their area or role. Likewise, measures and targets (the tangible part of their Balanced Scorecard) for these actions can be determined from the contribution statement, without the need for a whole-organisation review of measures and targets. Similarly once the measures and targets are in place, individual goals and incentives can be set and justified with reference to the local Balanced Scorecard, confident that such goals will explicitly contribute to the overall goals of the organisation.

How to find out more?

2GC Active Management is a research led consultancy expert in addressing the strategic and performance management issues faced by organisations in today's era of rapid change and intense competition. 2GC is acknowledged as a global thought leader concerning the application of 3rd Generation Balanced Scorecard. 2GC's web site includes a free to access resource section containing a wide variety of information concerning 3rd Generation Balanced Scorecard, along with recommendations for books and articles on the subject and links to other web sites. Visit the web site at **http://www.2gc.co.uk/** and click on the 'resources' tab.

2GC provides a wide range of services to support organisations working with Balanced Scorecards, including consultancy and training programmes. To find out more, contact me, Gavin Lawrie, or my colleagues at 2GC.

- appraising (or reviewing) performance;
- rewarding performance.

The omission of any of these stages will result in a process that is incomplete and ineffective. Figure 5.1 shows how performance management fits into the company as a whole.

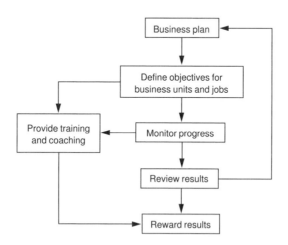

Figure 5.1 *The performance management process*

How to set objectives

The starting point for objective setting should be your mission and goals. This might sound over-elaborate or too much like management jargon, but it is important for a company of any size to have some view about its reason for existence, as this will help to focus on business priorities. It is also very helpful to your customers for them to know your business philosophy, which in turn will assist you in your marketing. For example, do you 'pile 'em high and sell 'em cheap' or do you provide quality at a price?

Your mission and goals will help you define your corporate or strategic objectives. Once you have established these you should incorporate them into a business plan and cascade them down the company so that there are objectives for each function and then for individual jobs. Overall objectives may then be broken down into more detailed targets.

There can sometimes be confusion over the differences between goals, objectives and targets. Generally goals tend to be broader in scope than objectives, which in turn are broader than targets. However, the particular terminology used is not important as long as everyone is clear about what is meant within the company.

When setting objectives for a particular job you should first consider the main purpose of that job, which should ideally be set out in the job description. From this, and the job's main accountabilities, you should be able to identify the outputs required, or key result areas (KRAs).

From these KRAs you should then be able to identify a number of objectives to be achieved for each KRA. These should be as specific as possible and linked to direct quantifiable outputs. Many objectives will be difficult to quantify, for example improving staff motivation, or giving high-quality advice, and in these cases a competency approach may be required (see below).

As far as possible the objectives you set should conform to what are generally described as SMART criteria (although there are different views about what the acronym actually stands for). This means they should be:

- specific;
- measurable;
- action-based (and achievable);
- realistic (and results-orientated);
- time-related.

An objective 'to improve sales performance' would not satisfy these criteria, but an objective 'to increase sales of widgets by 20 per cent by the end of the next financial year' would, provided the target was a realistic one.

As an example, suppose you want to increase your sales by 50 per cent during the coming year. Your KRA would be 'sales' and your objective would be 'to increase sales by 50 per cent by the end of the year'. You would then have to consider how you would achieve this, which could involve recruiting additional sales staff, training existing staff, or a combination of the two. To ensure that you achieve your aims, you would need to set specific targets and dates for reaching them. An example of a performance plan using this approach is set out in Figure 5.2.

You should also make objectives stretching but achievable. If they are unrealistic they are more likely to discourage than motivate the employee. It is also important that they are objectives that the employee can influence by her actions and behaviour.

Key result area	Objectives	The means	Targets
Sales	Increase sales by 50% in the next financial year.	1. Recruit additional sales staff. 2. Train existing staff in sales techniques. 3. Review sales incentives.	1. Recruit one additional salesperson by end of March. 2. Send three existing sales staff on training courses by the end of the financial year. 3. Develop new bonus scheme for sales staff by the end of the financial year.

Figure 5.2   *Performance plan*

The balanced scorecard

One of the complexities of setting objectives is deciding their number and scope. The balanced scorecard, designed by Kaplan and Norton, helps to overcome this problem by identifying four major areas in which objectives should be set. These can be applied, suitably modified, to virtually any type of organization. These areas and the type of questions they address are set out below.

Financial

- How are we managing the budget?
- What financial management processes need to be reviewed?
- How is our future income to be generated?

Customers

- How do our customers see us?
- Are we providing the services they require?
- Are we providing the best value?

Internal processes

- What improvements do we need to make to internal processes?
- What staff training and development is required?
- Do we have the right resources to provide the services required?

Innovation

- What future research is required?
- What services should we develop in the future?
- How do we continue to improve?

Analysing competencies

Particular problems arise when you try to set objectives and targets for jobs that do not have clearly identifiable outputs – for example, a secretary, a researcher, jobs providing counselling and advice, and so forth. For such jobs probably the best approach may be to try to identify those behaviours and skills that have been found to be the key to effective job performance in the past. These are generally described as 'competencies' or 'competences'. Once these have been defined, they can then be used as a framework for setting targets and measuring performance.

Some of the more common competencies that have been identified by various organizations are:

- communication skills;
- commercial or business awareness;
- leadership;
- problem solving;
- people management;
- planning and organization;
- initiative;
- self-confidence;
- flexibility and adaptability.

Each competency has to be precisely defined and then different levels identified, as in the example below.

Performance Management

John Brownbill, Chief Executive Officer of The Outsourced Training Company, explains why all organisations adopt performance management.

What is performance management?

Performance management is a method used to measure and improve the effectiveness of people in the workplace. The process involves creating a work environment or setting in which people are enabled to perform to the best of their abilities. Essentially, performance management is a whole work system that begins when a job is defined and ends when an employee leaves your organisation.

Many people use the term 'performance management' as a substitution for the traditional appraisal system. However, it is much more than this and is about managing the talent at your disposal.

Although often seen as time-consuming and complicated, performance management should be a real drive within a company as it brings benefits for employees and ultimately, the overall profitability of an organisation.

It is usually dealing with poor performance that places the biggest demand on managers and creates the most difficult challenges. The key to success is to recognise and manage performance issues quickly, to ideally stop people slipping in to poor performance.

Performance above standard rarely creates a management headache, but managing high performers is in itself a real issue that is a challenge to many organisations. One of the emerging trends is the use of some form of talent management system. Earlier models focused on graduate entrants or 'fast track' programmes 'for staff identified for senior or executive roles'. Increasingly talent management is being considered as an integral aspect of workforce development and an opportunity to 'harness diversity' effectively. Managing performance is therefore essential to deal with issues at both ends of the spectrum and to ensure all employees reach their true potential.

How does it work?

Performance management is most successful when individuals recognise that the process exists to support their performance and development and accordingly take ownership of the process. Senior managers should take the lead as performance management clearly begins at the top and if practised well is more likely to bring about an improvement in business outcomes. That said the employees, who are an integral part of the performance management initiative, really need to grasp the 'WIIFM' (what's in it for me') factor. That buy-in is also necessary 'bottom up' to ascertain the value, impact and most importantly the approaches that may appear to have a strategic value from a senior management perspective, but operationally are impractical and have no value to productivity or innovation from future leaders currently located at junior levels within the organisation.

Remember:

- Performance management is about people. It isn't about systems or processes or rules or computer systems
- Getting the best out of people is mostly about helping them to do a great job and making them feel that whatever their level, they are contributing to organisational objectives and growth
- Managers need to help their employees to clearly understand what is expected by providing explanation, clarification and agreeing performance expectations
- People also need help from their managers to meet these standards and expectations. A manager has to firstly identify what help they need, because it is different for everyone

- A large proportion of performance problems can be traced back simply to a failure to explain and agree expectations and a failure to understand and provide the help that the person needs. These are the responsibilities of the manager – not the employee
- Different aspects of performance and different tasks and responsibilities need treating in different ways, as do people according to their levels of experience, knowledge, capability, capacity and confidence
- The culture of the organisation will influence how people respond to performance management. If it is a positive and encouraging environment that attempts to engage people at all levels then it is likely that people will see the value in it

What are the benefits of performance management?

Performance management has two main drivers – a focus on business results and the fostering of engagement. Aligning individual performance with business and stakeholder needs, and making sure that the needs of both the organisation and the individual are clearly understood, are all key to success.

But surprisingly, in our experience the most important benefit organisations hope to realise is not financial. In fact, revenue growth often ranks further down among the benefits expected and it is alignment that it is the main benefit organisations hope to realise.

This alignment can take different forms:

1. Strategic and cross-departmental alignment – collaboration and accountability
2. Budgeting and planning process aligned with strategy
3. Resource alignment and optimisation.

It is estimated that billions are spent around the activity of performance management every year but that the biggest difficulty is still achieving strategic and departmental alignment. But why should organisations focus on alignment before revenue growth and financial transparency? First, revenue growth is certainly possible without performance management. However, alignment is essential to operational efficiency and effectiveness at the enterprise level. Goals and results established by departments, and not aligned to an overall strategy, can be achieved independently but might not necessarily advance the organisation as a whole.

Lack of alignment – often a symptom of the silo mentality – allows areas of the organisation to march to the beat of their own drummers and feel good about it.

It's a challenge to get departments to collaborate and share - to think about the greater good. But that's the reality: most organisations struggle with alignment issues such as collaboration, resource optimisation and tying planning to strategy so they look to good performance management initiatives to help.

Clearly, it does not take a performance management initiative to grow revenue. However, effective implementation of a performance management system which achieves alignment throughout the organisation can help achieve operational efficiencies to grow revenue.

How can I overcome resistance within my organisation?

The success or otherwise of performance management will depend on the prevailing culture. Cultural resistance is a primary obstacle to the success of performance management initiatives. This resistance is likely at the root of the second most notable obstacle which is the lack of collaboration and information sharing between departments.

This silo mentality is not atypical for organisations early in their performance management journey. Broad access to and use of information is new to many, and in the early stages of information evolution, individuals often act independently of others. Knowledge becomes an asset, which some are reluctant to share.

The best-built performance management systems in the world cannot address the culture hurdle. This is why Board-level sponsorship and an inclusive effort are important to the success of the initiative. Senior management must set the stage for an environment of measurement, sharing and collaboration.

For performance management to work there has to be an environment that encourages inclusion in the whole process. Management must effectively articulate the business strategy and employees need to understand the benefits of performance measurement. They need to know their roles in the effort and how that maps to the success of the organisation. In other words organisations need to do more to "sell" the concepts and the benefits to their people.

Executive management needs to actively manage the culture to break down resistance to measurement and encourage employees to collaborate and share. The effort must have employee buy-in. The most sophisticated technology cannot overcome employee resistance. Communication of strategy, clarification of roles, and assignment of accountabilities will help employees understand where their jobs fit in the scheme of things.

At The Outsourced Training Company, we have seen that the scope of performance management across an organisation varies, with significantly more effort occurring at a multi departmental level than in a single department. Involving key constituents – the finance area, operations, IT – will have a positive effect on the outcomes.

This inclusion helps break down some of the silos that impede sharing and collaboration. Assigning joint responsibility for performance management helps to ensure that the initiative is not too function-centric.

What should I do now?

Whether you decide to implement performance management in-house or engage with an external consultancy such as The Outsourced Training Company, an effective performance management system should include the following elements:

- Clear job descriptions for all employees
- An appropriate selection process
- Consistency of accomplishment-based performance standards, outcomes and measures
- Clarification of the purpose and process of performance management
- Effective orientation, education, and training
- On-going coaching and feedback using evidence
- Effective monitoring and evaluation
- Quarterly performance development discussions
- Effective and transparent compensation and recognition systems that reward people for their contributions and link pay with performance
- Clear effective communications cascade of company performance against a range of KPI's
- Career development opportunities provided for employees
- Exit interviews held to understand why valued employees leave the organisation

Performance management is an invaluable tool for today's organisations and the equation seems simple: Get your house in order first using the techniques above and the many rewards will follow.

For more information on how performance management can make a real difference to your organisation, visit **www.theoutsourcedtrainingcompany.com** or call **0800 169 3040**.

Example of team-working as a competency

Team-working – building and maintaining positive and open working relationships, co-operating and liaising with others to achieve goals. Understanding how teams work best and evaluating the motivation and needs of others.

1	2	3	4	5
Displays little ability in team-working. Tends to work in isolation and/or does not understand impact of own actions/role on others.	At times displays an awareness of the needs of others. Tends to be overly task oriented at the expense of achieving team goals or targets.	Shows an ability to take account of the needs of others. Keeps colleagues up to date with relevant information.	Demonstrates a very good insight into the motivation of others. Works positively with others to complete tasks, encouraging participation and adapting own style to suit different situations.	Displays an outstanding ability in all areas of team-working. Promotes an environment of cooperation and trust within and between teams, effectively overcoming resistance.

This approach is very useful both for managing performance and for recruitment because it provides a framework for deciding the core competencies required for a particular job – the minimum acceptable level for effective job performance, and the differentiating competencies (those that distinguish the superior performers from the acceptable ones).

There is a range of techniques for identifying competencies, the most common of which are:

- expert panels or focus groups that describe the competencies they think are required for average and for superior performance;
- surveys, and 360-degree ratings (involving jobholders, superiors, peers, clients) in which observers who know the job are asked to identify the specific behaviours defining competencies;
- an expert system database containing data from numerous competency models, which provides computer-generated competency definitions;
- behavioural event interviews (BEIs), which give detailed narrative accounts of how both superior and average performers thought and acted during critical incidents in their jobs, including successes and failures;
- observation, in which both superior and average performers are studied in actual or simulated work situations.

To try to determine the competencies required for a particular job you need to ask yourself the kind of questions about the job that are set out in the checklist below.

Competency analysis – interview checklist

- What is the main purpose of the job?
- What are the specific objectives the jobholder has to achieve?
- What are the positive aspects of behaviour that support the attainment of these objectives and what are the negative aspects of behaviour that hinder their attainment, considered under the following headings:
  - personal drive;
  - impact;
  - ability to communicate;
  - team management;
  - interpersonal skills;
  - analytical power;
  - ability to innovate (creative thinking);
  - strategic thinking;
  - commercial judgement;
  - ability to adapt and cope with change and pressure.
- What are the examples of effective and less effective behaviour?
- What type of experience and how much of it is required to achieve a reasonable level of competence?
- What type of education and training and level of qualifications are required to meet job objectives?

(Adapted from Armstrong, M (1993) *A Handbook of Personnel Management Practice*, Kogan Page, London)

An example of an objective-setting and staff development guide is set out in Appendix 1 at the end of this chapter and is reproduced with the kind permission of the Chartered Institute of Public Finance and Accountancy (CIPFA). Further examples of competencies are set out in Appendix 2, also at the end of this chapter.

How to manage performance

Managing performance means giving employees effective day-to-day support to enable them to carry out their roles effectively. You should:

- ensure that all necessary equipment and resources are provided;
- ensure that everyone is clear about the results required;
- provide any advice and guidance that may be required;
- give staff the training and development necessary for them to be able to do their jobs effectively and to equip them for larger roles;
- adjust targets, priorities and performance targets according to changes in markets, business aims, economic developments, and so forth;
- provide regular and positive feedback on performance.

As an overall aim you should encourage staff to take responsibility for their own performance.

How to appraise performance

Performance appraisal is something that happens throughout the year. Inevitably you will make judgements about how your staff are performing even if this process is not formalized. However, whatever process is used there will be a point or points in the year when you should sit down with each employee concerned and discuss that person's performance. Although there is no hard-and-fast rule, it probably makes sense to do this twice a year. To do it more often is likely to be too administratively time-consuming and less often may result in issues not being addressed quickly enough.

If you conduct an interim or progress review during the year there is probably no need to complete an appraisal form, although if the employee concerned is failing to achieve her objectives there may be a need to agree an improvement plan. You should keep a file note of any such agreement.

You should remember that the appraisal meeting is really only formalizing what should have been happening anyway, so there should be no real surprises, either for you or the employee. Remember also that the meeting is a two-way discussion.

Main objectives of performance appraisal

The main objectives of any performance review or appraisal process are to:

- review past performance;
- help improve current and future performance;
- identify training and development needs;
- assess potential and produce development plans;

- improve communications;
- improve motivation;
- give the employee the opportunity to raise issues or concerns.

Carrying out an appraisal discussion

Preparation

For appraisal to work effectively you have to prepare thoroughly. This means that you should:

- ask the employee to prepare for the discussion well before the meeting date, ideally using a form such as that set out below;
- ensure that enough time is set aside for the meeting and that it is held somewhere private and where you will not be interrupted;
- confirm the date, time and venue of the meeting;
- consult other managers who may have worked with the employee during the period under review;
- ensure that you have all the information you require readily available;
- consider whether there are external factors that might have influenced the employee's performance;
- plan the discussion.

Performance review scheme – employee preparation form

The purpose of the company's performance review scheme is to ensure that you are able to carry out your job as effectively as possible and to identify your training and development needs. Completion of this form before the appraisal discussion with your line manager will assist in this.

Name:
Review period:

1. Refer to your objectives for this period. How well do you think you have performed against these objectives?
2. What problems have you encountered in achieving these objectives? Are there any actions the company should take to minimize these problems in the future?
3. What do you consider to be your main strengths and weaknesses?
4. What training and/or development do you feel you need?

5. What overall performance rating best describes your performance over the period under review?

    A Exceptional   ☐
    B Excellent   ☐
    C Good   ☐
    D Satisfactory   ☐
    E Below standard ☐

6. Please insert any other comments below.

Conducting the discussion

There are rules and behaviours that will help to increase the chances of having a successful appraisal discussion. During the meeting you should:

- put the jobholder at ease with a few informal, friendly comments;
- state the purpose of the meeting;
- generally adopt a positive tone and encourage a supportive atmosphere;
- give praise where it is due;
- focus on facts and results, supported by examples where appropriate;
- encourage the employee to express her views, particularly about her performance;
- listen carefully, summarizing at frequent intervals;
- avoid surprises;
- in discussing less effective areas of performance stress the opportunities for improvement;
- obtain agreement over targets and try to ensure that these are as quantifiable as possible to reduce ambiguity about whether they have been achieved;
- consider and discuss development opportunities.

After the discussion

Following the appraisal discussion you should:

- note the points raised at the meeting;
- complete an appraisal form (see below);
- keep track of performance and ensure that agreed actions are taken.

Driving high performance

Jo Causon, director, marketing and corporate affairs at the Chartered Management Institute, examines why performance management is critical to organisational success. She outlines how employers can drive their staff to achieve business goals and personal targets.

'To aim is not enough. You must hit!' You would be forgiven for assuming these are the words of a sports coach but, in fact, they originate from central Europe as the backbone of a proverb designed to channel business thinking.

The point is a simple one; a business cannot survive, let alone thrive, if it consistently fails to achieve target. Yet hitting target is not just dependent on the ability to aim. If that was the case, surely it would be enough to produce a business plan with ambitious goals!

What really counts is the training, practice and experience that allows organisations – and the individuals within them – to perform. But even this is insufficient, because to succeed individuals need to be given direction. *Where are we now? Where do we want to be? How are we going to get there?* All of these questions have one thing in common – their answers need to be communicated by business leaders to create an understanding of why specific targets have been set. How they are shared will also provide the motivation that helps achieve them.

Of course, it does not always follow that targets will be reached simply because teams are constantly reminded about what is necessary to succeed. Good leaders don't just spend their time repeating goals in the hope they will be met. A more strategic approach involves outlining the broader issues and long-term goals? *Why do we want to do this? How will it affect my career? What impact will poor performance have on the company?* Successful leadership, whether the organisation is a large multinational or one of Britain's 4 millions SMEs, is about four key issues: ensuring individuals understand what they are doing in the context of their immediate environment; developing effective methods to motivate individuals, supporting and developing them; fostering a culture of where staff are empowered, accountable and take ownership to consistently hit high levels of performance; providing the right tools and techniques to deliver.

Framework for action: getting the best from staff

This means providing a framework for action; the ability to set targets, measure and review performance to give a clear indication about whether the organisation's key objectives are being met.

It sounds easy on paper, but there is almost always a difference between current levels of performance and where you, the business owner, would like it to be.

Individuals often try to reduce this gap by spending more time in the office or taking longer over a task to reduce the possibilities for error. But input doesn't always equate to output, which makes figures from a survey exploring the 'Quality of Working Life' in today's business environment all the more concerning.

Published by the Chartered Management Institute and Simplyhealth, the research revealed that only 36 per cent of respondents claim to be operating 'at or near peak productivity'. Worse still, 1 in 2 managers said they were not 'positively motivated' about work, with 54 per cent suggesting they worked beyond contract hours because of 'work volume' and 'deadlines'.

If the additional hours being put in are still not helping individuals meet their goals, the clear implication is that skills or competencies need to be examined and improved. Yet this is where many organisations – large and small, alike – appear to be falling down. Too much time is spent 'doing' with insufficient effort aimed at identifying shortfalls and room for improvement. Yet if business leaders are serious about aiming high – and actually reaching those targets – they need to consider issues around workforce capability. What, for example, are the skills that are needed right now? How can these be developed? And will they be sufficient for the longer-term?

Unless these issues are continually assessed and addressed the potential for failure and de-motivation remains high. Too often stories appear in the media about individuals plagued by a sense of regret, with many believing they have failed to reach their true potential. But why? The majority say they are held back by red tape, poor resources and, crucially, a lack of support.

It may sound like a 'hard luck' story, but what it means is that organisations are failing to get the best from their employees. Of course, some would argue that the onus is on individuals to 'make an effort' and utilise their strengths, but the reality is that performance management should be an integrated approach, with employer and employee agreeing on the steps needed to achieve success.

The last thing that you, as an employer would want is an unhappy employee; someone under-performing because they have not had the chance to develop the skills needed for their role. For the individual concerned it might become frustrating, but at the organisational level, it is a sign that performance processes and systems need to be challenged.

Performance enhancing: what can be done?

The key lies in continuous improvement, so the best place to begin is an assessment of current practice. Think about why performance issues may be arising. In the case of most SMEs the answer often lies in growth. No-one is suggesting that expansion is a bad thing for business! However, unless businesses development is managed well, problems can occur.

In part, the solution rests in establishing a culture in which employees are encouraged to both take responsibility for ongoing improvement and share expectations. On one hand managers and leaders can clarify exactly what they expect teams to do. Similarly those teams should not be afraid to share what support they need to perform well.

Clearly this means that performance management is less about 'telling' people what to do and more about joint decisions about how to move forward. But to work, it needs to be well planned. You cannot expect to get the best out of your staff if once a year you sit down for two hours and talk to them about the past. Rather, spend time together on a regular basis so that concerns don't become problems and solutions can be mapped out; the use of genuine ongoing dialogue is critical.

In an environment in which uncertainty is the only constant it is also often difficult for individuals and their organisations to deliver results, particularly when the demands of stakeholders or the needs of society fluctuate according to fashion, technological change or the wider economy. So it is a concern to note that research suggests innovation is a low priority amongst UK SMEs. Just 30 per cent argue that it is important in today's working environment. How can businesses grow if new ideas are not allowed to come to the fore?

Measurement is an essential tool for providing a framework to progress, a basis for feedback and a platform for organisational – and individual – growth. Measures need to be flexible to take into account the changing nature of the marketplace and the changing circumstances of your business. They also need to reflect your key objectives because there is little point measuring something if it has no bearing on the organisation's aims. The old adage of 'what gets measured gets done' rings true.

These objectives also need to be simple and realistic. Make your indicators something that is easy to collect data on and which give you a direct insight into whether efficiency and effectiveness is improving. For example, rather than demanding sales uplift of 10 per cent, which may be unrealistic given the size of the marketplace or economic climate, focus on numeric targets around new business leads, NPD and process improvements. There may be more targets that way, but they are all linked and can be used to indicate if and where different skills need to be improved upon.

Ultimately assessment is critical as it affords both employer and employee the opportunity to say 'we know where we're going and how to get there'.

Jo Causon, director, marketing and corporate affairs
Chartered Management Institute (www.managers.org.uk)

Managing performance – what to do:
- ☐ Identify where you currently are
- ☐ Outline and communicate where you want to be
- ☐ Link objectives to business goals
- ☐ Establish sensible measures
- ☐ Evaluate performance against measures

---

x Do not go for an 'all or nothing' approach. Performance management is about building skills/success

x Do not be rigid – involve individuals in the process

Performance review form

Name:
Job title:
Period covered by this review:
Name of manager:
Agreed objectives:

Results:
Rating:

(Comment on results achieved, taking into account business conditions, changes to objectives and any other relevant circumstances.)

To be completed by the line manager

For the review period:

What were the employee's main achievements or strengths?

What areas of performance need improvement or development?

What training and development does the employee need?

What is the overall performance rating?

A B C D E

A = performance that is exceptional and rarely attained
B = performance that is well above target in nearly all respects
C = performance that achieved all major objectives to the standard required
D = performance that fell just short of requirements in some key areas
E = performance that was not up to the standard required in most respects

Appraisee's comments:

Appraiser's comments:

Signature of appraisee:
Signature of manager:
Date:

To be completed by the reviewing manager

Comments on above review

*I confirm the performance rating above.
*I consider that, following discussion with the line manager, the performance rating should be changed to:

Signed:
Name:
Date:
*Delete as appropriate

Rating performance

A critical part of reviewing performance is rating the performance of the employee against identified objectives and targets. This rating will normally form the basis for decisions about promotion and bonuses. When rating performance you should:

- take into account overall objectives and individual targets;
- take account of both hard quantifiable measures, such as sales targets, and softer, more nebulous measures, such as customer relations;
- take into account factors that might have affected performance during the year;
- try to be objective and focus on outputs, setting aside personal feelings about the jobholder;
- weight objectives in favour of those that are more critical to the success of the business;
- use a rating scale as a basis for comparison, and possibly for deciding bonus levels and suitability for promotion (see below);
- consider using a forced distribution in which the percentage of staff receiving particular ratings is restricted (see Figure 5.3).

As part of the performance rating process you will need to develop some kind of measurement scale. It is difficult to be prescriptive about the form this should take, but generally you should avoid negative descriptions such as 'weak' as these could reinforce negative performance and attitudes. You should also be aware that with a five-point scale there is a tendency for most people to tick

Showing approximate percentages of staff receiving a particular performance rating in a typical company

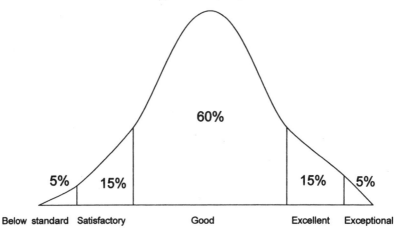

Figure 5.3 *Typical performance distribution*

the middle box, and that with a four-point scale the tendency is to place most people in the upper two boxes. An example of the former is set out below.

Example performance ratings

1. Exceptional – superior all-round performance achieving significant objectives that are critical to the success of the business.
2. Excellent – performance which generally exceeds job requirements with some notable achievements.
3. Good – performance which generally satisfies all job requirements.
4. Satisfactory – performance that is to the standard required in most aspects of the job but that requires improvement in some.
5. Below standard – performance where a significant improvement is required to satisfy job requirements.

Perhaps one of the more effective types of scale is one that describes performance as:

- above target;
- on target;
- below target.

This type of description is more factual and does not imply that someone is a weak performer just by being below target for the period under review. There may have been good business reasons for this.

Finally, where possible, it is probably advisable to have a two-tier approach in which someone more senior in the company reviews performance ratings by the employee's line manager, generally the manager's immediate manager. This helps to minimize the problems of personal attitudes affecting judgements and is essential in larger companies to ensure consistency between different functions.

Rewarding performance

The fact that you are bothering to assess performance implies that there will be some kind of a reward for good performance. Such rewards typically take the form of pay and/or promotion. As employees will see these rewards as a measure of their worth to the company it is important to ensure that they are allocated fairly, objectively, and in direct relation to the contribution made.

There is no one universal formula that can be applied to all organizations. When devising a scheme for paying for performance or contribution it is probably best to get external professional advice. The issues that need to be taken into account in such a scheme include:

- types of jobs involved – some jobs, such as those in sales, have outputs that are easier to measure and that are more directly related to performance than others;
- market practice – taking into account what your competitors are doing for similar jobs;
- the relative importance of different targets;
- the proportion of pay that is to be variable or 'at risk';
- the complexities of measuring performance;
- the extent to which performance should be recognized by permanent increases in pay or by one-off bonuses;
- the frequency of any bonus payments;
- the extent to which rewards are based on long-term or short-term objectives;
- the appropriateness of non-financial incentives;
- the extent to which rewards should be individual or team based;
- what the company can afford.

TRAINING AND DEVELOPMENT

A central reason for reviewing performance is to identify staff training and development needs. Specifically you will want to:

- help individuals develop their skills and abilities to improve job performance;
- help familiarize employees with any new systems, procedures and working methods;
- help employees and new starters become familiar with the requirements of a particular job and with the company (induction);
- build up a pool of expertise and skills in the company so that you will not be too adversely affected if you lose staff or if you need workers to cover for absent colleagues.

Effective training will help the company to be successful and avoid problems (such as health and safety problems) and it is therefore important that you develop a training policy. Any training policy will need to include the following stages:

1. an analysis of training needs;
2. a planned programme of training to meet those needs;
3. implementation of the training programme;
4. evaluation of the effectiveness of training provided.

Analysing training needs

When you are trying to assess the training required in the company you should do this for:

1. the company as a whole;
2. groups of staff or types of job within the company;
3. individual employees.

The need for training will arise when:

- you appoint new staff who will require induction training and training in job skills;
- you introduce new systems and processes;

Our future.
It's in our hands.

Leadership,
management,
collaboration...
it's these **skills** that really
start to make **numbers**
move for your
business.

You've employed the best people available for your business, but it's the skills you don't necessarily find on paper that can really help your company flourish. People skills like leadership and management allow the financial sector to really excel, but they can often be overlooked. Train to Gain offers the impartial advice and support your company needs to ensure your staff won't just have a head for figures; they'll have all the relevant skills to make those figures work even harder.

For more information visit
traintogain.gov.uk or call on 0800 015 55 45.

Train to Gain

Train to Gain gives even more businesses the help they need to succeed

When Prime Minster Gordon Brown said that "our challenge is to unlock all the talents of all of the people of our country", he was reaching out to every single person and encouraging them to take control of their future by improving their skills. Whatever sector you work in the need to consider training is vital if you want to shape the future of your business and your employees in the best possible way.

With this in mind, it is crucial that all employers take advantage of Train to Gain, the Government's flagship service to support businesses of all sizes and in all sectors in England improve the skills of their employees. Not only do better skills unlock talent and drive improved business performance, but there is an actual need to up-skill our nation. By 2014 it is estimated that two-thirds of all jobs in England will be held by people with at least Level 3 qualifications – yet, almost a third of the workforce in England is not currently qualified to this level.

From a wider perspective, an investment in skills is also an investment in the future of our economy as it will enable us to remain competitive in the global marketplace – especially in the face of rising markets such as Brazil, Russia, India and China. Already, Train to Gain has helped shape the future of almost over 73,000 businesses across the country. To help meet the needs of even more employers and individuals, the Secretary of State for Innovation, Universities and Skills, John Denham, recently outlined a massive expansion of the Service in 'A Plan for Growth'.

Within this, John Denham announced that funding for Train to Gain is expected to double to over £900 million by 2010/11 to ensure that a broader range of skills and funding opportunities are available to businesses of all sizes. This will support more qualifications as well as additional Skills for Life provision, enabling individuals to develop their basic adult literacy and numeracy skills. However, Train to Gain isn't just about qualifications; it provides high quality advice for businesses of all sizes to encourage them to take ownership of, and investment in, the skills of their workforce and the improvement of their business and gain access to a wide range of training and development solutions, from short courses to degree qualifications.

The expansion of Train to Gain will also help 60,000 senior small business leaders to access Leadership and Management funding and training over the next three years. This will involve a Leadership and Management Specialist visiting a company and carrying out a free and impartial Business Review. They will then help to develop a Personal Action Plan and find appropriate training courses – ranging from formal training, where managers work towards specific qualifications, to informal training, such as coaching and mentoring.

The Service is also supporting the new Local Employment Partnerships between employers and Jobcentre Plus to help unemployed individuals find sustainable employment with training.

Another way for businesses to demonstrate their commitment to training is by making the Skills Pledge. This is a voluntary, public commitment by the leader of a company or organisation to support all its employees to develop their basic skills and work towards relevant, valuable qualifications to at least

Level 2*. By making the Skills Pledge, employers are not only committing to training their workforce, but they are also able to ensure that their business has the edge it needs to succeed in the global market.

Through the Skills Pledge employers can access the independent advice of a Train to Gain skills broker who will visit a business at no cost to the employer. The skills broker will assess the businesses individual needs and will suggest appropriate training and funding opportunities available in a range of areas. This could include anything from first Level 2* and Level 3* and Skills for Life – like English for Speakers of Other Languages. Skills brokers also provide employers with a range of skills advice, discussing anything from Apprenticeships through to recruitment issues.

Skills brokers then work closely with their chosen training provider to ensure that relevant, high quality and flexible training is provided to meet the individual needs of the business and the employees. For example, they will look at whether or not training is best conducted on-site to minimise disruption and allow staff to practise their skills in real situations and there is also the option of out-of-hours training for shift workers. This partnership between all parties will help enable an even more effective learning system that's more responsive to businesses needs.

One business which is really benefiting from training is the Corby based construction firm Weldon Plant Ltd. HR Manager Bob Parkin had desperately been searching for training courses for over a year, but failed to find ones which would help improve the skills of their supervisors and construction workers. After an informative call with Train to Gain skills broker Allan Matthews, Bob decided to use Train to Gain.

Allan Matthews visited Weldon Plant and outlined their skills needs, advising on potential training and funding courses, which Weldon Plant quickly progressed. Allan sees that since training, Weldon Plant has been able to grow further as well as helping progress the careers of two members of staff.

We all need to recognise the challenges and embrace the changing needs of our society and economy: we all need better skills, more now than ever before. To take advantage of our opportunities and flourish both in life and in work, let's take on board the many training and financial opportunities available. Let's not get left behind - everyone can play a part: Our future. It's in our hands.

Jaine Clarke
Director of Skills for Employers
Learning and Skills Council

- To find out more about how Train to Gain and the Skills Pledge can help your business, please call **0800 015 55 45** or visit **traintogain.gov.uk**

Level 2 is the equivalent of 5 good GCSEs
Level 3 is the equivalent of two A level passes

- you reorganize or redesign jobs;
- there are changes in legislation;
- you require productivity improvements;
- you introduce flexible working arrangements;
- there are significant differences in productivity and performance between individuals and/or groups within the company;
- there are changes in your market;
- you need to ensure equality of opportunity.

Any organizational change will give rise to a training need. To identify other needs, such as those arising from productivity differences between different functions, you will need to maintain and review performance indicators such as sales levels, administration costs and lost productivity. The training needs of individuals should be identifiable through the performance management process.

Planning training programmes

When you are considering what training to provide you need to take into account:

- why you are carrying out the training;
- who is to receive it;
- what should be included in the content;
- the likely costs;
- the likely benefits;
- how the success of the training can be evaluated;
- the most appropriate training method;
- who will provide the training;
- whether it will be carried out in the company or at an external location.

When you are considering the costs of training, you should also consider the costs of not training. Failing to provide training when it is required is a false economy and could result in lowered productivity, more accidents and downtime, an inability to react to changing circumstances, infringement of legal requirements and lowered morale.

Implementing a training programme

When you draw up a training programme you should consider whether the training required is better provided internally through your own resources, or by an external provider. Generally, the training is better provided internally where:

- you are seeking to improve performance in some detailed aspects of an individual's job; and
- you have internal staff who can provide the required expertise and time; or
- the trainee requires practical hands-on experience; or
- you need to train staff in a new internal process or system.

External training may be more appropriate where:

- staff are required to learn about new ideas and approaches;
- you do not have sufficient internal resources and expertise to provide the training yourself;
- the training is of a highly specialized or complex nature that can only be provided by external experts;
- it is for staff development or the acquisition of a broad range of skills.

Training methods

Some of the more common methods of training are:

- On-the-job training – Training provided within the workplace. It is important to ensure that those providing the training are competent otherwise the trainee may learn bad habits.
- Coaching – Guidance provided by the line manager, supported by the performance appraisal process.
- Self-development – Using appropriate training resources such as CD ROMs, videos, workbooks, etc, to acquire knowledge and skills.
- Project work – Assigning the trainee to a practical problem or task designed to help the company.
- Job rotation – Moving staff into different roles to enable them to acquire a wide range of experience within the company.

- Secondment – Placing a jobholder in another function or department to enable that person to gain insight into its operations.
- Shadowing – Placing a jobholder alongside someone doing a different job so that she is able to learn from that person.
- Mentoring – Providing the employee with a mentor to provide advice on work issues.
- Training courses – Training courses can be internal or external and will typically be provided by specialist external trainers using a range of different training techniques.

Induction training

Every company should carry out some form of induction for new employees. The purpose of this is to:

- provide a smooth entry into the company and to promote a positive attitude about it;
- check that there are no matters outstanding following the recruitment process;
- confirm that the employee has all relevant information, including a statement of employment particulars;
- collect any information still required, such as the P45 or bank details;
- draw the employee's attention to the performance standards required and any other important points about working for the company, including health and safety and disciplinary rules;
- ensure that the employee knows how to operate any essential company procedures and equipment;
- ensure that the employee knows where all the basic amenities are located;
- identify any individual training and development needs;
- agree any more detailed induction programme, including meetings covering the company's various activities.

www.cityandguilds.com

Balance Your Workforce

City & Guilds offers over 500 qualifications in 28 industry areas, so there's likely to be one or more that will suit your organisation down to the ground. We can look at the sort of training you want to offer and advise you about whether we've already got a ready-made solution for you. Many of our qualifications attract Government funding, so there'll be even more reasons to smile.

For more information: **www.cityandguilds.com**

It's official: happy workers improve your bottom line

Five million workers dread going back to work after the weekend[1].

This means that five million people are less likely to be:

- happy at work
- motivated
- productive
- loyal

It's no coincidence that the happiest workers are those who feel supported in training and development needs, that the jobs they do are worthwhile and that the skills they have are utilised well, whilst the most unhappy workers feel the exact opposite.

At City & Guilds, we know how important it is for you to keep your staff happy and, more importantly, how this affects your bottom line. We have been working with employers, helping them to develop and improve their staff, for over 130 years.

The industry experts in our dedicated Business Unit provide a bespoke consultancy service, specialising in assessing training needs, evaluating programmes and providing innovative, tailor-made solutions appropriate to your individual business, sector and market.

We can assess, develop, improve and even accredit your own in-house training. We can even develop custom-made qualifications for your business, if necessary.

Moreover, our work with some of the country's biggest employers, such as Royal Mail, shows that it literally pays to train your staff and keep them happy. At Royal Mail, staff retention rose by an impressive 20% and staff sick days were reduced by 5%. Valued staff are more motivated, more productive and more loyal.

Giving employees access to training and actively encouraging the take-up of professional qualifications shows that you recognise the importance of the work they do, that they need certain skills to be able to do their jobs and that you want them to be able to perform their duties well.

From an employers' perspective, training your workforce also enables you to discover hidden talents and skills within your staff and spot potential not just for the now but also for the future.

We already work with high profile clients including Tesco, Honda, Orange Retail, Thames Water and Transport for London. To see what we can do for your business go to **www.cityandguilds.com/employers**

---

[1] According to the 2007 City & Guilds Happiness Index

An example of an induction training programme is set out below.

Induction programme

Day one

1. Introduction to immediate supervisor and colleagues.
2. Administration — completion of outstanding employment details.
3. Company information.
4. Tour of office.
5. Introduction to facilities (WC, coffee machine and so forth).
6. Products and services.
7. Employment terms — arrangements for payment of salary, pension and so forth, office hours, health and safety rules, first-aid arrangements, fire procedure, security arrangements, car parking, smoking policy, identity cards, disciplinary rules, sports and social activities.
8. Job duties — discuss main tasks and responsibilities.

During first week

1. Introduction to other internal contacts and main external contacts.
2. Company information — more detailed product and service information, business plan and strategy, organization structure, information about regular meetings, competitor information.
3. Employment terms — sickness absence reporting, time off arrangements, annual holiday arrangements, payment of expenses, confidentiality, use of telephone and e-mail, performance appraisal arrangements, explanation of other employment terms.

Evaluating training

Although it can sometimes be difficult to do, you should try to evaluate the results of any training provided. Some of the ways of doing this include:

- using questionnaires before and after the training, to test improvements in skills and knowledge;
- observing trainees while on the training programme and after their return from it;
- using tests of various kinds;
- interviewing trainees to assess what they have learnt from the training;
- measuring changes in a range of performance indicators, such as productivity, quality of delivery, and achievement of targets.

For certain types of training, such as management development, it may be particularly difficult to measure effectiveness directly. However, if the training has been successful you should notice longer-term improvements across a range of indicators such as lower absenteeism, fewer grievances, lowered staff turnover, improved motivation and higher productivity.

FURTHER INFORMATION

Cushway, B (reprinted 1999) *Human Resource Management*, Kogan Page, London

Kaplan, R S and Norton, D P (1992) The balanced scorecard – measures that drive performance, *Harvard Business Review*, January–February, pp 71–79

Megginson, D, Joy-Matthews J and Banfield P (2004) *Human Resource Development*, 3rd edition, Kogan Page, London

Spencer, L M, McClelland, D C and Spencer, S M (1992) *Competency Assessment Methods – History and state of the art*, Hay/McBer, Boston, MA

APPENDIX 1: CIPFA – OBJECTIVE SETTING AND DEVELOPMENT SCHEME. A GUIDE FOR STAFF

Guidance Notes

The Objective Setting and Development Scheme aims to encourage communication and generate open discussion between you, your manager (or reviewer) and your team. In addition to clarifying areas of responsibility, a key aim of the Scheme is to provide a systematic way of identifying training and development needs for all staff.

The Scheme will help you to:

- Become clear about your individual contribution to the products and services CIPFA offers and to the meeting of your department's business plan and objectives
- Carry out your role competently and confidently
- Understand what you are expected to achieve
- Have your contribution recognised and valued
- Review your work and plan ahead
- Discuss workload, timescales and approach to work with your manager

- Prioritise work and set targets
- Receive accurate and effective feedback on your performance at work
- Think about how you like to learn and what resources are available to you to enable you to learn and develop
- Identify training and development activities you need to become involved in to meet your objectives, improve the way you do things, expand your skills and knowledge or equip you to meet future requirements.

The Scheme will help CIPFA develop a staff able and willing to respond to change, and capable of adapting and learning, rather than being limited by the boundaries of existing skills.

Development is a two-way contract, based on business needs and individual motivation, ie a shared responsibility. It is not ideal for you to think that your development is the responsibility of CIPFA. Likewise, it is not ideal for CIPFA to believe development is entirely the responsibility of each individual.

There are three important stages/parts to the Objective Setting and Development Scheme:

Form to use?	What happens at this stage?	When does this happen?
Part 1	**Objective Setting and Development Plan**	**November–December**
	• You and your manager (or reviewer) will discuss and agree your work and personal development objectives for the coming year (or suitable period) • You and your manager will also identify training and development activities you need to become involved in to meet your objectives, improve the way you do things, and to expand your skills and knowledge	
Part 2	**Objectives and Development Review** **Mid Year**	**June–July**
	• A chance to reflect on what has gone well and, perhaps, not so well, hindrances to achieving objectives and how you have handled problems	

and overcome difficulties, the role of your manager and colleagues in helping you to achieve your objectives, improve performance and develop

- You will also discuss the training you have received and development activities you have participated in during the first half of the year, and how these have helped you meet your objectives and learn new skills and knowledge

Part 3	**Objectives and Development Review**	**December–January**

Full Year

- As Part 2, but for the whole year

Your **Mid Year Objectives and Development Review** should normally be six months from the date on which the objectives were initially agreed.

Your **Full Year Objectives and Development Review** should normally be one year from the date on which the objectives were initially agreed.

If you wish to have a review in a shorter time span, this should take place. Ask your manager for more frequent reviews.

New members of staff should agree their objectives with their manager within three months of joining CIPFA. For the interim period until these are set, appropriate work objectives for the former postholder will apply.

New members of staff can enter the Scheme at the most suitable time during the year. There is no need to wait until November/December to complete Part 1. Let's say you are a new member of staff and you join CIPFA in March. You would probably complete your Objective Setting and Development Plan (Part 1) in June, and have an Objectives and Development Review (Part 2) in December. This would enable you to fit into the Scheme with the rest of your colleagues at the end of the year.

Part 1, 2 and 3 – Before the Meeting

Part 1, 2 and 3 are discussions/meetings between you and your manager, not interviews. It is not something that happens to you; it is a process you need to participate fully in.

So how can you prepare?

Use the Scheme's Preparation Checklist

The Preparation Checklist has been developed to help you clarify your thoughts before each stage of the Scheme. You should receive a copy of this at least one month before the meeting, and it is important you make time to prepare thoroughly. If there is anything you are unclear about then check it out before the meeting.

Be as honest as possible when filling out the Preparation Checklist. One of the main aims of the Scheme is to help you to develop so the more fully you and your manager prepare for the meeting the more successful it will be.

Make sure you have read and understood your department's business plan

Once it has been finalised, your manager will distribute a copy of your department's business plan to all staff in the department. If this does not happen, please ask your manager for a copy. If you are unclear what any of it means or how it might relate to your work, then ask your colleagues or manager.

Attend the 'Preparing for Your Objectives and Development Review' course

This is a three hour event to help you get to grips with participating in Objectives and Development Reviews. The course will enable you to identify the skills of a good reviewee and you will get a chance to discuss what is expected of you before, during and after the review. There are a few courses throughout the year. After a year or so, it may be a good idea to attend again as a 'refresher'. Please contact Human Resources (HR) if you are interested in attending.

Part 1, 2 or 3 — At the Meeting

Practical arrangements

It is your manager's responsibility to ensure your Objective Setting and Development Plan meeting and your Objectives and Development Reviews take place where you can feel as relaxed as possible and where you will not be interrupted. It is important that you arrive on time and keep to the time you have set for the meeting. Two hours should normally be enough time.

Remember to take your Preparation Checklist, forms from your previous review(s), and a pen and paper in case you need to make notes during the meeting.

Who does what?

It is important to check and agree with your manager who will complete the appropriate form at the beginning of the meeting. You will also need to agree when it will be written up by, and when you will both be able to check and sign it. Make sure it is an accurate record of your meeting before signing it. If you disagree about any points it is important to try to sort things out at this stage. In the unlikely event that you or your manager just cannot agree or one of you feels unable to sign the form, then your manager's manager or, if necessary, HR will become involved.

Both you and your manager will be contributing to the meeting but it is important that you are prepared to do most of the talking. It is your manager's job to make sure that all the areas are covered and that you are as involved as possible in the setting of work objectives and personal development objectives, and the identification of your own development needs. It is important that you 'own' the agreed objectives, and should be willing to talk to your manager if you think certain objectives are unrealistic.

Once initially completed (and after each review) your manager will copy the Objective Setting and Development Scheme forms (Part 1, 2 and 3) to the appropriate director and also send to HR. HR will feed specific training needs into the training plan for the year. Your forms will be held confidentially in HR. You and/or your manager should also keep a copy of each form for reference.

Setting objectives

It is important to note that setting objectives is not the same as writing a job description. Your job description is a list of your tasks and responsibilities. In objective setting, your work objectives will encompass parts of your job description but will be measurable in some way and time bound.

The key point when setting work objectives is to identify areas of your work where achievement, improvement or performance will have the *most* impact. It is the main tasks or key result areas you should be concentrating on. We all carry out many tasks and have various responsibilities at work, but you don't need to translate *everything* you do into an objective.

Don't set too many or too few objectives. Aim for somewhere between 5 and 10, with a mix of work objectives and personal development objectives.

When you set objectives for the coming year, make sure they are **SMART**:

Specific, Measurable, Achievable, Realistic, Time Bound (see Appendix A for examples).

Don't agree to vague or 'woolly' objectives. 'Improve team meetings' is unhelpful. How could you possibly know if you have achieved this or not? A much better objective would be 'ensure all team members have an agenda of the team meeting one week before the meeting and minutes are circulated a maximum of one week after the meeting'. This way you would know exactly what is expected and whether you have achieved the objective or not.

Objectives need to be challenging to enable you to get some satisfaction from achieving them. Don't set objectives that are too easy to achieve, that involve no effort or creativity on your part. If they are too easy then you will have no sense of achievement when you have succeeded.

Be realistic about the time your objectives will take to complete. Are you being realistic if all your objectives are set for the same month?

It may be that you take on extra or different responsibilities in your job and as a result you may need to update your objectives. You and your manager should complete a fresh Objective Setting and Development Plan (Part 1), describing only the *updated* or *new* objectives and any development needs, and send to HR. There is no need to duplicate all the information from your original Objective Setting and Development Plan as we will already have this on file.

Try to revisit your job description before each of your Objectives and Development Reviews. It is important your job description is updated, if necessary, to reflect your current responsibilities.

Identifying your development needs

This is not just about courses or workshops you need to attend, but activities or experiences you need in order to meet your objectives, to improve the way you do things, and to expand your skills and knowledge.

Some development activities include projects, observation, discussion with your manager or colleagues, visits to other parts of CIPFA, asking questions, coaching and being coached, attending training courses, seminars, conferences, vocational qualifications, shadowing a colleague, books, journals, newspapers, video tapes, activities outside work.

Make sure your development needs are as specific as possible. If a training course is the most appropriate development activity, then we need to be sure that we are designing and organising training that actually meets those needs.

For example, 'communication' can mean different things to different people, so if this is an area you need to develop further, you will need to specify what aspect of communication you are meaning. Likewise, 'Microsoft Excel' doesn't give enough information. You may need to learn about absolute references, pie charts and macros. Please refer to the 'example' forms for more information.

Once the appropriate form has been completed, you and your manager will be able to start working on those development needs that require an activity/ response other than training courses. Information about any training courses planned in response to your needs will be made available as soon as possible to enable you and your manager to plan your workload, arrange cover etc. You should plan training courses into your diary like any other project, task or meeting.

Continuing Professional Development (CPD)

You may be a member of a professional body, society or institute (eg CIPFA, Institute of Personnel and Development, Chartered Institute of Marketing, Law Society) and are involved in their CPD scheme. To reduce duplication and save you time we may be able to accept their CPD scheme's documentation. However, we will need to check the suitability of the scheme and supporting documentation. Please contact HR for more information.

Appendix A — SMART Objectives

S	**SPECIFIC**	'To practise and receive monthly feedback on skills in setting work, reviewing performance and coaching'. Not 'improve management skills'
M	**MEASURABLE**	'Learn how to politely interrupt speakers when I am chairing a meeting with the intention of reducing meeting times by 15 minutes'. Not 'to be more effective in meetings'
A	**ACHIEVABLE**	'Increase membership of the Institute by 1% over x months'. Not 'increase membership of the Institute by 100% in 6 months'
R	**RELEVANT**	Relevant to your job, eg if you are a service purchaser: 'Reduce supplier costs by 10% per annum by negotiating discounts'. Not 'paint the outside of the building at weekends'
T	**TIME BOUND**	'Produce the annual report on training costs by 18 December'. Not 'produce a report on training costs soon'

APPENDIX 2: ABC UK — COMPETENCY LEVELS AND DEFINITIONS

1. Communication

Being able to express themselves clearly, effectively and persuasively, verbally and in writing and to understand clearly given communications. Demonstrating an ability to tailor the communication style and content to different situations, objectives and audiences. Being able to win the commitment of others to a decision, view or course of action.

1. Does not communicate effectively with others. Is unable to establish rapport. Fails to give required information at appropriate time. Information given lacks clarity. Fails to listen attentively or understand communications received.

2. Generally communicates clearly but sometimes lacks clarity in presenting views. May sometimes not fully understand clearly given advice and/or instructions.
3. Communicates information clearly, accurately and concisely and at the right time. Information is presented in a confident and structured manner. Listens well and seeks clarification where necessary.
4. Is able to communicate complex information clearly and concisely taking into account the type of recipient and using appropriate verbal and visual aids to reinforce the message. Is aware of, and takes into account non-verbal signals. Listens attentively and is able to recognize implicit as well as explicit messages.
5. An exceptional and highly persuasive communicator. Is quickly able to draw the right conclusions from hints and non-verbal signals and adapt behaviour appropriately.

2. Analytical thinking/problem solving

Being able to resolve complex problems and devise original solutions.

1. Shows little ability to process information and to arrive at logical conclusions through analysis.
2. Is generally able to resolve routine problems and knows where to find any required information. More complex problems would be referred to others.
3. Is able to deal with problems in an organized and systematic way and can analyse both written and numerical data. Seeks advice on complex problems and applies that advice.
4. Is able to deal with complex problems in a structured and organized way and identify the key issues in most situations, using information from a variety of sources.
5. Is able to resolve highly complex problems requiring original thinking, research and analysis. Identifies key issues and analyses the implications of various courses of action.

3. Planning and organizing

Being able to devise and apply systems to take account of relative priorities. Planning, and organizing a variety of resources to meet objectives in a changing environment.

1. No evidence of an ability to plan ahead or to understand priorities. Tends to miss deadlines. Needs to be closely managed.
2. Is generally able to plan and organize work to meet routine targets and deadlines but may need guidance in responding to changes in priorities or routine.
3. Identifies priorities and plans and organizes work to meet these. Monitors progress and takes appropriate action to achieve targets. Can be trusted to seek support when required.
4. Successfully plans and coordinates major and complex projects. Focuses attention on key objectives and makes optimal use of resources, redirecting effort as required. Consistently meets deadlines and targets.
5. Displays outstanding planning and organizing skills. Creates, monitors and reviews policies and plans to meet overall business priorities. Anticipates and plans for changes to priorities. Always meets deadlines and targets.

4. Adaptability

The ability to meet, anticipate and deal with new challenges.

1. Generally unaware of and not interested in new developments. Fears change.
2. Aware of new developments and is prepared to change working methods to accommodate these, following guidance or direction.
3. Shows an enthusiasm for new developments and takes steps to keep up-to-date on these. Happy to try new ideas and approaches and to adapt working arrangements as necessary.
4. Maintains a keen awareness of new developments in the sector and the company and takes all steps necessary to ensure that you are kept fully aware of these. Embraces change and acts as a champion for new ideas and approaches.
5. Actively seeks new challenges and opportunities, constantly striving to develop approaches that will give the company a competitive edge. Fully aware of new developments in the sector. Drives change but also takes steps to ensure that implementation is effective.

5. Teamworking and relationships

The ability to work well with others and to deal effectively with both colleagues and customers.

1. Tends to work in isolation and shows little appreciation of impact of own actions on others. Tends to be formal and cool with team members and external customers and contacts.
2. Is generally cheerful and courteous to other team members and external contacts. Tends to put individual aims above team goals. May be overly task-oriented at the expense of team motivation and morale.
3. Shows a clear appreciation of the needs and objectives of others and adapts behaviour accordingly. Enjoys working as part of a team and contributes to the attainment of common goals. Keeps colleagues informed of developments and offers assistance and guidance to others.
4. Shows good insight into the needs of others, exercising tact and diplomacy where necessary. Works positively with others to encourage the attainment of common goals, adapting own personal style to suit different situations. Viewed as a key team member.
5. Shows outstanding ability as an effective and essential team member. Promotes an environment of cooperation and trust within and between teams and team members, setting and achieving stretching goals and effectively overcoming obstacles while maintaining motivation and morale. Actively develops team members. Able in all situations to tailor words and actions to promote a positive effect on others.

6. Commitment

The desire to achieve the best possible outcome for all parties and being prepared to take all required actions to ensure that targets are achieved on time, within budget and to a high standard.

1. Shows little commitment to the work of the company or interest in customers. Does what is required, but no more. Prefers to play safe by not taking action where this is an option.
2. Shows some interest in the work of the company and the problems of customers but prefers to refer problems to others, rather than attempt to resolve them. Generally works effectively showing concern for quality of own work.
3. Shows a keen interest in the work of the company and the problems of customers. Takes all necessary action to resolve a problem within the scope of his/her own responsibilities. Sometimes suggests improvements to systems and processes.

4. Shows enthusiasm for and a commitment to the work of the company. Takes a keen interest in problems of customers and other external contacts. Is prepared to go the extra mile in resolving problems and will commit himself /herself to resolving an issue rather passing the problem on. Prefers to take action with all associated risks rather than do nothing. Regularly shows a concern for improving systems and processes.

5. Demonstrates a consistently positive attitude and the highest level of enthusiasm for the work of the company and colleagues. Keeps fully up-to-date with developments and seeks to enthuse others about these. Takes a keen interest in problems of customers and other external contacts and is prepared to suffer personal inconvenience to resolve problems. Prefers to take action with all associated risks rather than do nothing. Consistently looks for improvements to working methods, systems and processes.

7. Technical awareness

The requirement to understand and carry out tasks and responsibilities to the required standard and to keep abreast of new developments.

1. Does what is required in terms of the job, but no more, to a reasonable standard. Requires guidance on some aspects of the work. Shows no awareness of or interest in external developments.

2. Carries out job duties effectively requiring little guidance. Is aware of new products changes to work processes.

3. A very effective performer who is technically proficient in all areas of the job. Knows about and understands the implications of technical developments affecting products and processes.

4. A highly effective performer who demonstrates considerable technical competence in all aspects of the work. Regarded as an expert in his or her field and will be consulted by others on technical issues. Understands the implications of the latest technical developments affecting products and processes and is able to advise others about these.

5. A top performer who is regarded as the top technical expert in his or her field within the company. Promotes understanding throughout the company of the latest technical developments affecting products and processes in the sector. Consulted by others requiring definitive information in the field.

8. Leadership

The ability to achieve aims and objectives through others by providing them with focus and direction and by motivating and inspiring them though the use of interpersonal skills such as persuasion, enthusiasm, diplomacy etc. This includes individuals and teams.

1. Displays little leadership ability. Is unable to define goals effectively or to motivate others to meet them. Shows little influencing skill. May panic or fail to respond under pressure.
2. Tries to influence others but lacks the self-confidence to be fully effective or does not adapt personal style to suit the situation, such as being overly dogmatic or directive where this is not appropriate. May rely too much on authority rather than influence and fail to take account of the needs of individuals. Tends to be irritable under pressure.
3. Is able to define goals and objectives and influence others to achieve these. Takes into account the aims and aspirations of others and adapts behaviour and style accordingly. Expresses confidence in the ability of others. Remains calm under pressure.
4. Encourages ownership of team goals and consistently achieves results through others. Adapts style and behaviour to meet the aims and aspirations of others. Encourages the development of individual and team potential through effective coaching and makes the best use of individual skills and abilities. Deals calmly with conflicting priorities under pressure.
5. Demonstrates an outstanding level of leadership. Formulates goals into an understandable set of plans and objectives and obtains complete commitment to these. Builds multi-skilled teams to meet business needs, modifying roles and responsibilities as necessary. Adapts style and behaviour to meet the aims and aspirations of others and encourages the development of individual and team potential through effective coaching. Recognized as someone who brings out the best in people and commands total loyalty. Adept at dealing with complex high-pressure situations, giving an air of calm assurance and conveying that to others.

9. Commercial awareness

Being aware of ABC's products and services, taking an interest in commercial developments in the sector, the position of ABC within it and of the financial and profit implications of actions taken.

1. Displays little awareness of or interest in ABC products and services or in the market generally. Does not understand impact of own actions on finances.
2. Aware of ABC products and services but has limited interest in market developments. Only vaguely aware of financial implications of own actions.
3. Fully aware of and shows an interest in ABC products and services. Also aware of developments in the wider market and among competitors. Understands financial implications of own actions.
4. Very interested in, and fully up-to-date on, all ABC products and services, both existing and planned (as far such information is available). Shows a keen interest in the external market and is fully aware of developments in it and their potential impact on ABC. Fully aware of the financial implications of own actions and takes into account the impact of these on others and the business.
5. Shows extensive awareness of ABC products and services (existing and planned) and of their impact on finances. Researches the external market to maintain a full awareness of the actions of competitors and their implications for the commercial success of ABC. Possesses considerable commercial insight and applies this for the benefit of the company to exploit business opportunities and reduce internal costs.

10. Customer service

Providing a high level of service to customers to ensure that their experience is a positive one and to encourage them to develop a long-term relationship with the company.

1. Displays little understanding of customer needs. Has difficulty in establishing rapport with others and lacks confidence in dealing with customers.
2. Generally shows an awareness of customer needs and some interest in addressing these. Not always able to translate those needs into solutions acceptable to the customer.
3. Displays a clear understanding of customer needs and expectations and responds effectively to these to fully meet customer expectations in terms of results and timing.
4. Displays an ability to understand and anticipate customer needs and expectations and to respond effectively to these so that these expectations are exceeded and the company's reputation enhanced. Will take action to resolve any issues even where this may go beyond job requirements.

5. Displays an exceptional ability to understand and anticipate the needs and expectations of even the most difficult customer and to respond effectively to these. Takes action to resolve any issues even where this goes beyond job requirements and may involve significant personal inconvenience. Will regularly receive customer accolades. Encourages a customer focus in others.

11. Self-motivation

Seeking to enhance own skills and job effectiveness and achieving personal satisfaction through self-development. Demonstrating a drive to achieve.

1. Does no more than is asked. Shows no interest in learning new skills or in improving existing ones. Not prepared to exercise initiative.
2. Occasionally does more than is required without being asked but generally does only what is required. Prepared to put in extra work when asked. Prepared to learn new skills or receive training if asked to do so. Occasionally exercises initiative in resolving problems.
3. Demonstrates enthusiasm for the work, anticipates what needs to be done and generally takes action without being asked. Does more than the minimum required. Seeks opportunities to learn new skills or improve existing ones.
4. A highly-motivated and enthusiastic worker who can be relied to do all that is necessary to achieve results and who regularly exceeds basic job requirements. Actively seeks new challenges and opportunities. Enthusiastic about learning new skills and developing existing ones and proactive about putting himself/herself forward.
5. Demonstrates the highest level of motivation and ambition. Strives for excellence in everything he/she does and is strongly focussed on meeting and exceeding all targets, whilst maintaining quality. Actively seeks new challenges and opportunities. Consistently seeks opportunities to learn new skills and develop existing ones and commits time to this.

6

Dealing with absence

The absence of staff from work causes obvious problems of productivity, especially when such absences are unplanned. The smaller the company, the greater the effect. Reducing unplanned absence should therefore be a priority of any company.

PLANNED ABSENCES

Many absences are legitimate contractual and legal entitlements. These include:

- annual holidays;
- public holidays;
- attendance on training courses;
- maternity and paternity leave;
- parental leave;
- adoption leave;
- time off to care for dependants;
- time off for jury service;
- time off for public duties;
- time off for trade union duties and activities;
- reserve training;
- attendance at health and safety committees or works councils;

We can't
solve all work-related problems.

We can
help resolve the issues of absence, wellness and health protection.

Norwich Union's Employer Solutions makes it easy to get the most out of a workforce. As well as offering a range of tools to help reduce staff absence levels, it includes products and services that aim to keep them healthier and happier overall.

Employer Solutions offers three modules – Absence, Wellness and Health Protection Solutions. Each one provides a comprehensive range of services from health screening to PMI to rehabilitation. And they can be mixed and matched to meet the specific needs of any enterprise. So whatever the health issues are, we'll ensure every business can enjoy the sweet smell of success.

For more information about our complete list of products and services, visit www.nuemployersolutions.com or call 0800 142 142. Alternatively if you would like an adviser to visit please call 0800 015 0404.

Calls to and from Norwich Union Healthcare may be recorded and/or monitored.

NORWICH UNION
an AVIVA company

We just make it easier.

Employer Solutions from Norwich Union Healthcare

Founded in 1990, Norwich Union Healthcare offers employers the best of both worlds. The strength and experience of one of the UK's most trusted financial service companies with the freshness and vigour of a dynamic company. Employer Solutions is an example of our continued commitment to the health, protection and insurance markets and our desire to provide relevant and timely solutions for all our clients needs.

At Norwich Union Healthcare we understand the needs of our clients are varied and changing. From militating against short-term employee absence to improving bottom-line productivity, for most employers ensuring staff are healthy and happy at work is a key priority. That's why we've developed Employer Solutions.

Employer Solutions is a range of health, insurance and protection-based options that work together, or as stand-alone solutions helping to meet a range of employer needs. At its heart, Employer Solutions offers:

- **Absence Solutions** – three modules that form the basis of an integrated absence management programme that can work on their own or as part of a broader solution that includes existing occupational health programmes.

  Absence Solutions includes:
    - o Absence Manager
    - o Absence Rehabilitation
    - o Audit and Consultancy

- **Wellness Solutions** – a range of preventative health products and services that aim to identify any potential employee health risks early on and enable employers to put in place a range of options that keep employees in tip-top condition.

  Wellness Solutions includes:
    - o Health Vision
    - o Health and Fitness Club Membership
    - o Health Screening
    - o Employee Assistance Programme
    - o Personal Health Manager

- **Protection Solutions** – a range of options that includes traditional Private Medical Insurance, Income Protection and Group Risk products combined with a selection of Occupational Health services to enable employers to mitigate short and long-term absence and help ensure that regulatory liabilities are met.

  Solutions, our flexible **Private Medical Insurance** product is designed especially for small to medium sized businesses. You start with Core Cover and can choose to bolt on up to 4 extra cover options and/or select up to 4 options to reduce your premium, such as member excesses. You can adapt the level of cover for up to three different groups of 3 or more employees, reflecting the needs of each group and helping to make private health cover even more affordable and a better fit for your business.

- bereavement or compassionate leave;
- layoffs or short-time working;
- suspension on medical grounds.

You should have policies covering most absences and including:

- what time off is allowed;
- which absences will be paid and which unpaid;
- the procedure for agreeing time off;
- how much time off will be given for particular events;
- actions that will be taken if the facilities given are abused.

Time off for dependants

You must give any employee reasonable time off to deal with an emergency involving a dependant, such as when a dependant falls ill or has an accident. This is to enable the employee to deal with the emergency and to make longer-term arrangements but it would also apply to attendance at a funeral and making funeral arrangements. A dependant is the partner, child or parent of the employee or someone who lives with the employee as part of the family, or someone who reasonably relies on the employee for assistance. There is no set amount of time allowed and no limit to the number of occasions this time off is given. If you have reason to believe that this right is being exercised more than is reasonable and/or it is causing problems for the company, you should warn the employee about it.

Public duties

Employees have a legal right under the Employment Rights Act 1996 to a reasonable amount of time off to carry out public duties such as being a magistrate, a local authority councillor, or a member of certain statutory and public bodies. This does not have to be paid but the main problem is deciding how much time off is reasonable.

Jury service

You have little choice but to give someone time off for jury service, unless there are convincing reasons why they may be excused, such as serious damage to the business. This time off does not have to be paid.

Trade union activities

You must allow employees who are officials of an independent trade union reasonable paid time off to carry out duties related to industrial relations in the company or to undergo training.

Since the Employment Act 2002 you must also allow time off to Union of Learning Representatives (ULRs), who are union members appointed to advise members about their training and education needs.

Safety representatives

You must allow paid time off to safety representatives to allow them to carry out their functions and to undergo training.

Redundant employees

You must give reasonable paid time off to any employee made redundant, and with two years' continuous service, to allow that person to look for a new job.

Reservists

Reservists are required to undertake annual training and it is up to you to decide whether to grant unpaid leave for this purpose (reservists get allowances and pay) or to insist that it is taken as part of the annual leave entitlement. If the reservist is called out for active service you will have little option but to allow this as you will have been required to sign an agreement to this effect. You must keep the reservist's job open for him.

Bereavement or compassionate leave

Employees have a legal right to a reasonable amount of unpaid time off following the death of a dependant (see above). You can, however, also develop a policy on this, which will then become a contractual entitlement.

Other time-off rights

There are also rights to time off for maternity and paternity (see Chapter 7) and to parental leave (see Chapter 8).

REDUCING UNPLANNED ABSENCES

To manage absence effectively and to keep unplanned absences to a minimum you need:

- information about the numbers and frequencies of absences;
- procedures to ensure that all necessary processes are in place to enable you to control absences;
- policies to encourage high levels of attendance.

Information

You should keep the following information:

- number of days of absence of individuals;
- number of spells of absence;
- reasons for absences;
- whether absences are certificated or uncertificated;
- employee details.

You should note that, following the Data Protection Act 1998, you need to make employees aware that you will keep records of sickness absence and get their express permission for you to keep such records.

How to calculate absence frequency

Work out the total number of available working days in a specific period. This is the total number of days multiplied by the total number of employees. For example, if the period under review is a working week (five days) and there are 100 employees, then the total number of days available for work is 500 (100 multiplied by 5).

Work out the number of days missed by individuals. Calculate the percentage absenteeism rate by: taking the total number of days of absence, dividing by the total number of days available, multiplying by 100. For example, if there are 50 days' absence during a period in which there are 500 days available for work then the percentage rate for absenteeism is $50/500 \times 100 = 10$ per cent.

Calculating individual absences

The Bradford Factor

Calculating the overall level of absence alone is unlikely to give you all the information you need to decide on future action. Frequent short-term absences are likely to be more disruptive to the business than longer-term absences that can be planned for. However, these may not always show up in the absence figures. One way round this is to use a calculation method generally known as the Bradford Factor (having been devised by Bradford University), which takes into account both the length of absences and the frequency of them.

The formula is $S \times S \times D$ where S = the number of specific spells of absence in the last 52 weeks, and D = the number of days of absence in the last 52 weeks.

Example

Under this approach: one absence of 20 days is $1 \times 1 \times 20 = 20$; 10 absences of two days is $10 \times 10 \times 20 = 2,000$.

Having collected information about absences you should look for particular patterns, such as higher sickness levels following bank holidays or weekends, and whether absences are higher for particular groups of staff, for certain types of job, or in certain locations.

You should also have trigger points that activate processes once absences have reached a predetermined level. These can be either a number of days, or a number of spells of absence, or a combination of the two. The main danger with having a trigger point, such as 10 days annual absence, for example, is that any such target can soon become known to employees and can come to be regarded as the level of absence that management is happy to tolerate.

Procedures to reduce absence

There are a number of procedures that you should introduce and actions that you should take as a manager to keep unplanned absences under control. You should:

- produce clear written guidelines to employees for reporting absences (see example below);
- train managers and supervisors in handling absences;
- ensure that those managers and supervisors take responsibility for controlling absence;

- set targets for absence levels;
- interview those returning to work after absence;
- try to identify likely poor attendees during the selection process.

Absence reporting procedure

On the first day of absence:

If you cannot attend work you must notify your manager as early as possible, and by no later than 10.00 am on the first day of absence. You must speak to your line manager and not to one of your colleagues. You should telephone personally, and only in exceptional circumstances should a friend or relative do this for you. If you do not have a telephone, you should make this known to your line manager so that alternative arrangements can be made. You should explain the reason for your absence and say when you expect to return to work. You should complete a company self-certification form on your return to work.

On the fourth working day:

You must let your manager know of your continued absence and say when you expect to return.

By the eighth calendar day:

You must get a doctor's certificate and send it to your manager no later than your eighth calendar day of sickness. You need to keep your manager informed during your period of sickness. Continued absence must be supported by medical certificates otherwise you may lose your right to any sick pay.

Return to work interviews

One of the most effective ways of controlling absence is the return to work interview. You should:

- make a point of discussing any absence with the employee on his return to work;
- make it clear that he was missed;
- adopt a friendly and interested tone;
- if any problems arise from the meeting try to ensure that these are addressed.

The purpose of the meeting is to:

- find out the reason for the absence;
- find out whether there are any particular problems and, if so, what action is being taken to address them;
- find out whether the employee has consulted a doctor (if the reason is sickness);
- review any other recent absences;
- welcome that person back and inform him about work developments;
- offer support where appropriate;
- agree any necessary actions.

A meeting is also valuable during sickness when an employee has been off sick for some time as it is important to show that the company continues to take an interest and to try to find out when a return to work can be expected. Generally your tone at any such meeting should be supportive, unless clear problems or a particular pattern have emerged, in which case you may need to be more formal.

The whole emphasis is on getting the employee to reduce the level of absence, or to return to work at the earliest opportunity, but you should not allow someone to return before being fit to do so, as all employers have a duty of care to their employees.

Policies to encourage good attendance

There are a number of policies that should be introduced, and actions taken by you, to try to ensure that attendance levels are kept high. You should:

- provide good physical working conditions;
- ensure that health and safety rules and procedures are followed;
- ensure that all staff receive the appropriate training, especially when working with machinery or in a hazardous environment or when undertaking physical activities;
- review working arrangements where there are high levels of absence;
- ensure that there is adequate training of supervisors and line managers, particularly in relation to maintaining motivation and morale;
- ensure that, where possible, there are opportunities for promotion and/or development;

- where possible encourage team-working, as peer group pressure can help to encourage good attendance;
- operate flexible employment policies such as flexible working hours and job-sharing;
- focus on outputs and performance targets, rather than just attendance hours;
- where possible provide crèche or childcare facilities;
- agree reasonable absences for emergencies and medical appointments, bearing in mind that some of these rights are enshrined in statute;
- consider the introduction of programmes to promote good health;
- consider redesigning jobs to relieve people of high levels of monotonous routine or stress.

Incentives to encourage good attendance

You could consider financial incentives to encourage good attendance. However, there is little firm evidence that these have a long-term effect and they can result in staff complaining that they are penalized for being ill. Probably the best type of incentive is something along the lines of a full attendance draw, in which employees with full attendance over a certain period may be entered into a draw for a prize, such as a holiday or cash. This has the merit that it stresses the importance the company places on good attendance and it cannot really be said to penalize those who are sick.

Developing a sickness policy

You should produce a written policy for managing sickness. Without this there will be confusion about the rules applying to sickness, leading to inconsistent and possibly unfair treatment of employees. The policy should cover:

- what an employee should do if unable to come to work, including who should be contacted to report the absence and how that contact should be made;
- whether a self-certificate is required (see example on page 188);
- at what stage a medical certificate will be required;
- the intervals at which medical certificates should be provided;
- the action to be taken on returning to work;
- to whom the policy applies;
- entitlement to sick pay and any conditions attaching to it, such as length of service;

- any rules relating to sickness such as the requirement to have a medical examination;
- action that may be taken if the rules are not followed;
- the actions that will be taken by the company to keep in touch with the employee;
- the right to statutory sick pay (SSP);
- what will happen when the sick pay entitlement expires.

An example of a sickness policy is set out below.

Sickness absence policy

Introduction

It is recognized that from time to time staff may be unable to attend work because of ill health. This document sets out the procedure to be followed by all staff and the entitlement to sick pay in the event of such absences.

Notification of absence

If you are unable to attend work because of sickness or injury you must notify your line manager by telephone of the reason as soon as possible on the first day of absence and, ideally, within one hour of your normal start time.

Notification can be by you or by someone on your behalf.

You must maintain regular contact with your line manager on any subsequent days of absence.

If you are absent for more than seven days you must get a doctor's certificate for the entire period of absence and send this to your line manager.

The company may, at its discretion, request a doctor's certificate for periods of absence of less than seven days. The company will reimburse any cost of getting a certificate in these circumstances.

For long or frequent periods of absence the company may require you to be examined by the company's medical adviser.

Returning to work

On your return to work you must report to your line manager, who will interview you.

If you return to work within seven calendar days you must complete a self-certification form, which is available from your line manager, on your first day back.

Sick pay

The company will pay you sick pay, provided you comply with the notification arrangements, on the following scale:

Years of employment	Full pay	Half pay
Less than 1 year	SSP only	SSP only
One to two years	one month	one month
Two to five years	two months	two months
Over five years	three months	three months

Payment is in relation to any period of 12 months, starting with the first day of sickness. Anyone starting part-way through the calendar year will be paid in proportion to his or her length of service. Similarly, part-time staff will be paid on a pro rata basis.

When you have exhausted your entitlement to sick pay the company will continue to pay you SSP, provided you have an entitlement to it. The company will offset any other payments received for the sickness or injury against company sick pay.

Withholding sick pay

The company may withhold sick pay if:

● you do not comply with the company's requirements for the notification of sickness absence;
● you refuse to undertake a medical examination at the company's request;
● you work for another employer during your period of sickness absence, in which case the company will also take disciplinary action.

Accidents at work

Any accident at work must be reported to your line manager as soon as possible, and an accident report completed.

Sickness absence and annual leave

If you fall sick while on annual leave and you produce a doctor's certificate relating to the period of sickness, the company will treat this as sick leave and not annual leave.

Long-term sick leave

If you are on long-term sick leave, which is a period of 13 weeks or more, you must keep your manager informed of your progress on a weekly basis. You must produce medical certificates to cover the absence.

Benefits

All the benefits to which you are entitled will continue to be paid during your period of sickness absence and your annual leave entitlement will continue to accrue during this period.

Frequent or prolonged absence

The company reserves the right to terminate your employment because of frequent or prolonged absences.

PAY DURING ABSENCE

You do not have to pay for any unauthorized absence. For sickness absence there is a statutory entitlement to statutory sick pay (SSP). It is for you to decide whether you wish to pay anything above this legal minimum with a company sick pay scheme. If you do so, you should ensure that the scheme is not so generous that it encourages staff sickness and you should make it clear that abuse of the system is a disciplinary offence.

Many company sick pay schemes apply a sliding scale of entitlement (see example sickness absence policy).

Statutory sick pay (SSP)

Employees are entitled to SSP once they have been sick for four days in a row (including Sundays, holidays and rest days). No payment is due for the first three days, which are known as 'waiting days'. Any sickness absence is described as a 'period of interruption of work', abbreviated to 'PIW'.

Any day of absence has to be a 'qualifying' day for payment of SSP – a day on which the employee would normally have been expected to work if he had not been sick.

Periods of absence that are less than eight weeks apart are linked to count as one period of sickness, or PIW, for payment of SSP. This means that if someone is sick for a second time during this eight-week period, and the total absence is four days or more, SSP would have to be paid from the first day of that second absence. The maximum entitlement is to 28 weeks of SSP in any PIW.

Statutory sick pay is treated as part of normal earnings and is subject to tax and National Insurance.

Reclaiming SSP

If you experience a relatively high level of sickness absence you can claim back the amount of SSP paid in a tax month that exceeds the percentage of your gross NI contributions. This is currently 13 per cent.

Employees not entitled to SSP

There are some employees who are not entitled to SSP including those:

- whose earnings are below the Lower Earnings Limit for National Insurance contributions;
- who are pensioners;
- who have received certain state benefits within the preceding 57 days;
- who have not worked under the contract of employment;
- who fall sick during a stoppage arising from an industrial dispute, unless they did not take part and had no interest in it;
- who are in legal custody or in prison;
- who are sick during the maternity pay period (see Chapter 7).

Notification of absence

There are rules about how absence should be notified and you can withhold payment of SSP if notification is late without a good reason. However, you must:

- make the rules about notification clear to employees;
- indicate how notification must be made;
- accept notification by someone else on behalf of the employee;
- not require notification earlier than the first day of sickness or by a specific time on that day, or more than once a week;
- accept any written notification that the employee is sick, even if this is not on a form provided by you.

Although you can accept any reasonable written notification, you can use a self-certification form such as that set out below, or use one that is available from the local social security office.

Self-certification form

This form must be completed after any absence from work because of sickness or injury. It must be completed on the first day back.

If you have been away for more than seven consecutive days you will need a medical certificate. Failure to produce one could result in loss of sick pay.

Name:
Job title:
Date of first day of absence:
Date of last day of absence:
Reason for absence (please state as precisely as possible the nature of the illness or injury):

Did you visit your doctor or a hospital during your absence? Yes/No

I confirm that the above details are correct and that I have not worked during my period of absence.

Signed:
Date:

Manager's statement

To be completed by your line manager

I confirm that the above information is correct.
Signed:
Date:
Position:

Records

You are required to maintain records of SSP payments for at least three years after the end of the tax year they relate to.

Withholding SSP

You are entitled to withhold SSP from the employee if you feel that:

- the employee's incapacity is not genuine; or
- you have not been correctly notified; or
- evidence of incapacity has not been provided.

If you do withhold SSP the employee has the right to ask you for a written statement of the reason for refusal, which you must provide.

DEALING WITH PERSISTENT ABSENCE

Short-term sickness absences

When dealing with short-term absences you should:

- obtain an explanation from the employee about the reasons for these absences;
- where there are frequent short-term absences not supported by medical evidence, ask the employee to consult a doctor, as there could be a serious underlying medical condition;
- if there are no good reasons for the absence, deal with the matter under the company's disciplinary procedure (see Chapter 12);
- consider whether the absences are likely to be temporary and whether the company can help in any way;
- tell the employee what improvement in attendance is required and what is likely to happen if no such improvement is forthcoming.

If the absences continue and you decide to take disciplinary action you should take full account of the employee's past performance, age, length of service and the likelihood of improved attendance in the future.

Poor attendance is a legitimate reason for dismissing someone, but only after you have investigated the matter thoroughly, and the employee's circumstances, as well as the effect on the business and your other employees, have been taken into account.

Long-term absence through ill health

Where an employee has been absent with a long-term illness, before taking any decision to dismiss you should:

- maintain regular contact with the employee;
- obtain the employee's written agreement if you intend to seek medical advice;
- notify the employee of any action you propose to take, particularly if his employment is at risk;
- consider whether suitable alternative work might be available;

- consider how much disruption is being caused by the employee's absence;
- consider whether the work can be covered in some other way;
- consider whether there is an alternative to dismissal, such as early retirement;
- consider whether the employee has a disability, in which case you may need to make reasonable adjustments, as required by the Disability Discrimination Act 1995;
- take into account the employee's age, length of service and so forth;
- discuss the position and possibilities with the employee.

You have to get the employee's permission to obtain any medical records and the employee has the right of access to any reports about him (see example consent form below). The employee can also refuse to allow any reports to be provided. However, where the employee refuses to cooperate by providing medical evidence, a decision can still be made on the basis of the information available and the employee should be notified of this.

If the illness persists and there is no likely prospect of an early return to work, you may have no option but to dismiss the employee.

Consent to medical report

This form is a request for your consent to a medical report. Under the Access to Medical Reports Act 1988 you have the right to:

- withhold your consent for an application to be made to a doctor;
- ask your doctor to let you see the report and to amend any part of the report you consider to be inaccurate or misleading;
- attach your written objections to the report if the doctor refuses to amend it;
- withhold your consent to the report being supplied to the company.

Employee declaration

Having been made aware of my statutory rights I give my consent to a medical report being obtained from my doctor or medical specialist by the company. I understand that the clinical details in the report will be treated as confidential, but that the content will be used by the company management as part of the information required for deciding on future action.

I understand that if I wish to see the report before it is sent to the company I must arrange to do so with my doctor or medical specialist within 21 days of making the application.

I do not wish to see the report before it is sent to the company.*
I wish to see the report before it is sent to the company.*

Signature:
Date:
Doctor/specialist's name and address:

*Delete as appropriate

FREQUENT LATENESS AND UNAUTHORIZED ABSENCES

In considering what action should be taken about persistent lateness and unauthorized absences, account should also be taken of the circumstances surrounding these, such as current travelling difficulties. However, actions that can be taken to reduce these problems include:

- monitoring attendance records for individuals and groups;
- asking employees to telephone by a particular time on every occasion they are absent;
- having return-to-work interviews;
- restricting overtime.

Finally, there may be a need to take disciplinary action.

COMPANY HEALTH CHECK

You might wish to check how healthy your company is in its approach to managing absence levels. The checklist below may help in this.

- Do you have sickness records that show:
  - the number of days off for each employee;
  - the reasons for the absence;
  - numbers and duration of each absence for individual employees, different functions and the company as a whole?
- Are these records sufficiently comprehensive to enable you to identify patterns?
- Is the information computerized with built-in trigger mechanisms?
- Do you calculate the costs of absence?
- Are there clear procedures for reporting absences?
- Are any such procedures clearly notified to employees?
- Are targets set for absence levels at company and functional levels?

- Is there top management commitment to the encouragement of good attendance?
- Are line managers and supervisors made responsible for managing absence?
- Are managers and supervisors trained in handling absence?
- Are checks built in to the recruitment process to try to identify probable poor attendees?
- Are employees made fully aware of the importance the company attaches to good attendance?
- Are return-to-work interviews held?
- Are other strategies used for encouraging good attendance, such as health programmes, team-working, incentives, job redesign, or performance management?

FURTHER INFORMATION

Access to Medical Reports Act 1988
Data Protection Act 1998
Disability Discrimination Act 1995
Employment Relations Act 1999
Employment Rights Act 1996
Essential Facts – Employment (2001) Gee Publishing Ltd, London
Huczynski, A A and Fitzpatrick, M J (1989) *Managing Employee Absence for a Competitive Edge*, Pitman, London
Personnel Manager's Factbook (2001) Gee Publishing Ltd, London
Reserve Forces Act 1996
Statutory Sick Pay (General) Regulations 1982

7

Maternity and paternity rights

This chapter describes the maternity and paternity rights applying to all employees, which include:

- time off for antenatal care;
- medical suspension during pregnancy;
- maternity leave;
- paternity leave;
- maternity pay;
- paternity pay;
- the right not to suffer a detriment or be dismissed because of pregnancy, maternity or paternity;
- adoption leave;
- adoption pay.

TIME OFF FOR ANTENATAL CARE

Any pregnant employee is entitled to paid time off, during working hours, to receive antenatal care. This applies irrespective of the employee's length of service or working hours. After the first appointment you can ask for written proof that she is pregnant and that an appointment has been made.

MEDICAL SUSPENSION DURING PREGNANCY

You must assess the risks to the health and safety of any new or expectant mother and change her working conditions or hours of work if any such risk exists. This includes offering alternative employment. If none of these changes are possible then you must suspend her on full pay for as long as the risk remains.

MATERNITY LEAVE

With effect from 1 April 2007 all pregnant employees are entitled to 26 weeks Ordinary Maternity Leave (OML) and 26 weeks Additional Maternity Leave (AML), starting at the end of the OML period, regardless of length of service or hours of work. There are some differences between the statutory rights applying during these two periods.

You can give an employee rights to maternity leave in the contract of employment and then either these contractual rights, or the statutory rights, whichever are more favourable, will apply. The same rule applies to maternity pay.

An example form for an employee going on maternity leave is set out below.

Example form for employee going on maternity leave

Please complete this form and return it to your line manager as early as possible, and no later than the end of the 15th week before your expected week of childbirth.

If you are unable to give this notice, please notify us at the earliest practicable date.

You must attach your Mat B1 certificate, or other evidence of pregnancy, signed by a midwife or doctor.

Name:

1.   Please state your expected week of childbirth.
2.   What date will your maternity leave begin?
3.   Will you be taking additional maternity leave following the birth of your child?
4.   What date do you intend to return to work?

I confirm that I am pregnant and that I will be taking maternity leave as set out above.

Signed:

Date:

Ordinary maternity leave

A pregnant employee must let you know when she intends to begin her ordinary maternity leave by the 15th week before the EWC. She is required to confirm:

- that she is pregnant;
- the date her ordinary maternity leave is to begin;
- the expected week of childbirth (EWC).

You should ask her to produce evidence of the EWC in writing (although you are not required to do so) and this will normally be produced on form Mat B1.

If she is unable to give the required notice, as long as she lets you know as soon as reasonably practicable, she will have satisfied the notification requirement. A woman can also change her mind about when she wants her leave to start, provided she gives you 28 days' notice, if reasonably practicable. You must respond to this notification within 28 days. An employee who does not comply with these requirements might have to forfeit her maternity leave and could lose her right to statutory maternity pay (SMP). However, you should be very cautious about taking action in these circumstances. A model letter recommended by the BERR to acknowledge notification of maternity leave is set out below.

Model letter for employers to acknowledge notification of maternity leave

This letter should be used when only the statutory levels of leave and pay are provided. (Employer must respond within 28 days of receipt of employee's notification.)

Date: ....

Dear ......

Congratulations and thank you for telling me about your pregnancy and the date that your baby is due. I am writing to you about your maternity leave and pay.

As we have discussed, you are eligible **for 26 weeks' ordinary maternity leave and 26 weeks' additional maternity leave**, ie 52 weeks in total.

Given your chosen start date of [*insert date*], your maternity leave will end on [*insert date*].

If you want to change the date your leave starts you must, if at all possible, tell me at least 28 days before your proposed new start date or 28 days before [*insert date leave starts*] (your original start date), whichever is sooner.

If you decide to return to work before [*insert date leave ends*], you must give me at least 8 weeks' notice.

As we discussed, you are eligible for **39 weeks' Statutory Maternity Pay/not eligible for Statutory Maternity Pay** [*delete as appropriate*].

Your maternity pay will be £[*insert amount*] from [*insert date*] to [*insert date*] and £[*insert amount*] from [*insert date*] to [*insert date*].

or

The form SMP1 (enclosed) explains why you do not qualify for Statutory Maternity Pay. You may, however, be entitled to Maternity Allowance. If you take this form to the Jobcentre Plus or Social Security Office at [*insert local details*], they will be able to tell you more.

As your employer I want to make sure that your health and safety as a pregnant mother are protected while you are working, and that you are not exposed to risk. I have already carried out an assessment to identify hazards in our workplace that could be a risk to any new, expectant, or breastfeeding mothers. Now you have told me you are pregnant I will arrange for a specific risk assessment of your job and we will discuss what actions to take if any problems are identified. If you have any further concerns, following this assessment and specifically in relation to your pregnancy, please let me know immediately.

If you decide not to return to work you must still give me proper notice. Your decision will not affect your entitlement to SMP.

If you have any questions about any aspect of your maternity entitlement please do not hesitate to get in touch with me. I wish you well.

Yours sincerely,

Premature birth

If an employee gives birth before the EWC, the ordinary maternity leave period starts on the date of childbirth.

Pregnancy-related illness

If a pregnant employee is absent from work wholly or partly because of pregnancy during the four weeks before her EWC, the ordinary maternity leave period will begin from the first day of absence.

Compulsory maternity leave

You must not allow a woman to work during the two-week period immediately following childbirth. This period extends to four weeks if she works in a factory.

Contractual rights during ordinary maternity leave

During ordinary maternity leave (and also during additional maternity leave) the employee's contract of employment continues to exist. This means that you must apply to her all the terms and conditions of employment that would have applied had she not been absent, with the exception of wages or salary. In effect, this means treating her as though she had not been absent, apart from in relation to remuneration. Remember that when calculating the entitlement to maternity pay during the maternity leave period you must include any pay rises given to your employees during that period, and during the period used to calculate the rate of maternity pay to be applied.

Particular problems can arise where bonus payments are involved. Whether or not the employee is entitled to such payments will depend on the wording of the conditions relating to payment. You will generally need to take advice about whether they should apply.

Returning to work after ordinary maternity leave

If the employee does not wish to take additional maternity leave she would be expected to return to work at the end of the ordinary maternity leave period. She does not have to notify you about this return but can just turn up for work on the due date. However, if she wishes to return before the end of the ordinary maternity leave period she must give you at least 8 weeks' notice of her intention to return. If she does not give this notice, you can postpone the date of return until this notice provision has been satisfied.

You should bear in mind that the employee cannot return during the compulsory two-week leave period referred to above.

If she is unable to return at the end of the ordinary maternity leave period because of sickness, this should be treated as normal sickness absence.

The employee must be allowed to return to the job she was doing immediately before her period of maternity leave began and on the same terms and conditions of employment.

Additional maternity leave

In addition to ordinary maternity leave, an employee is entitled to an additional 26 weeks' leave, beginning immediately after the period of ordinary maternity leave.

Contractual rights during additional maternity leave

The employee's contract of employment continues during additional maternity leave, although the protection of her employment rights is more limited than during the ordinary maternity leave period. She is entitled to retain your implied contractual obligations of trust and confidence and also any terms and conditions of employment relating to:

- notice of dismissal;
- compensation for redundancy;
- disciplinary and grievance procedures.

In practice, this means that if you dismiss her during her additional maternity leave period you would have to pay normal wages or salary for the notice period, or give pay in lieu of notice. Similarly, you would need to pay her any redundancy payments to which she was entitled. She would remain entitled to bring claims under the disciplinary and grievance procedures.

One issue that sometimes arises is whether entitlement to annual leave continues to accrue during additional maternity leave. The position is that there is no entitlement to the annual leave provided in the employment contract or in any staff handbook, but there is entitlement to statutory leave in accordance with the Working Time Regulations. In practice the simplest approach is to allow contractual annual leave to accrue rather than do two different calculations.

Return to work after additional maternity leave

The provisions for returning to work after additional maternity leave are the same as those applying to ordinary maternity leave. All the employee needs to do is to turn up for work after the leave period. You must give her the job she was doing before she went on maternity leave, or another job that is suitable and appropriate in the circumstances. If you offer her another job, it must be of a similar or better status and on equal or better terms and conditions than the old job.

You should give her the same terms and conditions (except pay) she would have been entitled to if she had not been absent. However, absence on additional maternity leave does not count for seniority (unless her contract of employment provides for this).

If she wishes to return before the end of the additional maternity leave period she must give you 8 weeks' advance notice.

Refusal to allow the employee to return to work

If you do not allow an employee to return to work after either ordinary or additional maternity leave, she may make a claim to an employment tribunal that she has been unfairly dismissed for reasons relating to the maternity leave. You would have to be able to satisfy the tribunal that there was a valid reason for dismissal, or redundancy, which was unrelated to the exercise of maternity rights. In practice, this is likely to be difficult to prove.

Dismissal during maternity leave

You must not dismiss any woman for reasons connected with pregnancy or childbirth. Any dismissal will be automatically unfair if it is because of:

- pregnancy;
- the fact that an employee has given birth;
- suspension from work on maternity grounds;
- the fact that the employee took maternity leave;
- the fact that the employee tried to take advantage of the benefits applying during the maternity leave period.

Similarly, if you make an employee on maternity leave redundant without having first offered her suitable alternative employment, in preference to her colleagues if need be, this will also be automatically unfair.

It is possible for you to dismiss an employee who is pregnant or on maternity leave for legitimate reasons, but in practice it is likely to be very difficult to prove that it was not because of the pregnancy or maternity leave. There are also other practical difficulties in that any dismissal would need to be preceded by a meeting with the employee and if she is on maternity leave this might prove difficult to arrange. Dismissal without any such meeting is likely to be procedurally unfair.

STATUTORY MATERNITY PAY (SMP)

Statutory maternity pay applies for up to 39 weeks during the maternity leave period.

To qualify for SMP the employee must:

- have been employed continuously for at least 26 weeks by the start of the 15th week before the EWC, known as the 'qualifying week';
- have average earnings of at least the Lower Earnings Limit for payment of National Insurance;
- still be pregnant at the 11th week before the EWC or have given birth earlier;
- provide you with evidence of the expected date of childbirth;
- have stopped working.

Statutory maternity pay comprises: a higher rate equivalent to 90 per cent of the employee's normal weekly earnings for the first six weeks, and a lower rate for the remainder of the period (£117.18 per week from April 2008).

Recovery of SMP

You can recover 92 per cent of the gross amount of SMP paid by deducting that amount from the total of employees' and employer's National Insurance contributions payable.

If you qualify for small employers' relief (your gross National Insurance contributions in the preceding year were less than £45,000) you are able to claim 104.5 per cent of the SMP paid out.

Keeping in Touch days

Up to 1 April 2007 a woman would lose a week's SMP if she did any work (however little) in a maternity pay week for the employer paying her SMP. From that date, however, the government has introduced 10 'Keeping in Touch' (KIT) days, which allow a woman to do a limited amount of work for her employer during the maternity pay period and still retain her SMP for that week. However, *any* work done on any day, for example attending a one-hour training session, will count as a whole KIT day. There are no restrictions on when KIT days can be used for SMP, though the maternity leave regulations prohibit a woman from working for two weeks after childbirth. Once those days have been used up, the woman will once again lose a week's SMP for any week in which she does any work for her employer.

A woman is entitled to be paid for any KIT days worked, but the rate will need to be agreed and must be at least equivalent to the SMP rate.

MATERNITY POLICY

An example of a company maternity policy is set out below.

Maternity policy

The following document sets out the company's policy on maternity leave, maternity pay and all other issues relating to pregnancy and maternity.

This represents the law at the date of this handbook and may have to be amended in the light of future changes to the law.

The policy is designed to be as comprehensive as possible. However, if you have any questions about the policy please contact your line manager.

Time off for antenatal care

If you are pregnant you are entitled to take time off during your normal working hours to receive antenatal care. This should be at times agreed with your supervisor or line manager and preferably at the start or end of your working day. Antenatal care includes appointments with your GP, hospital clinics and relaxation classes.

Procedure for notifying absence for antenatal care

You should advise your line manager that you will be absent as far in advance of your appointment as possible, and you may be asked to produce your appointment card.

Pay

There will be no deduction of salary for attendance at authorized antenatal appointments.

Maternity leave

Entitlement

All pregnant employees are entitled to take 26 weeks' ordinary maternity leave and 26 weeks' additional maternity leave, giving 52 weeks in total, no matter how long they have been employed by us and no matter how many hours they work each week, subject to the rules set out below.

When does your maternity leave start?

You can choose to start your maternity leave at any time after the start of the 11th week before the week in which your child is due except in the following cases:

(a) If you are absent because of an illness related to your pregnancy at any time during the four weeks before your child is due, the company reserves the right to require you to start your maternity leave on the first day of that absence.

(b) If your child is born earlier than your planned date of starting maternity leave, then the maternity leave starts on the day the child is born. You should write as soon as possible to notify the company, enclosing Form Mat B1, unless you have already handed this over by then.

Note: if your child is stillborn after the 24th week of pregnancy you retain your maternity leave rights (and your right to statutory maternity pay subject to the SMP rules stated below).

Notification requirements

At least 28 days before you start your maternity leave you must give notice in writing addressed to your line manager. That notice must state:

- that you are pregnant;
- the week in which your child is due (note that for these purposes a week begins on a Sunday);
- whether you intend to take ordinary or additional maternity leave (which depends upon your entitlement as set out above); and
- when you want your maternity leave to start.

You should enclose a Form Mat B1 signed by your GP or midwife with your letter, unless this has been given to the company earlier.

If you are unable to give 28 days' notice because you have to start your maternity leave sooner than you anticipated, provided that you give notice as soon as you can, you will not lose your right to take maternity leave.

Keeping in touch

You are allowed to work for up to 10 days during your maternity leave without losing your entitlement to maternity pay. These 'Keeping in Touch' (KIT) days need to be discussed and agreed with your line manager.

Returning from maternity leave

If you return to work at the end of your maternity leave period you need not formally notify us in advance of your return and you will return to work in the same job that you left before you started your maternity leave. If, for health and safety reasons, you were doing a different job from your usual one while you were pregnant, you may be required to return to that different job for a short time if you are still at risk when you return to work.

You may wish to return to work before the end of your maternity leave period, but if you choose to do so you must give us 8 weeks' advance warning of the date of your return.

If you cannot return to work because you are ill you should notify your line manager, who will advise you how much, if any, sick leave you are entitled to. Please note that in some circumstances if you cannot return to work at the appointed time you will lose your right to return to work altogether.

If you decide not to return to work at the end of your maternity leave period you must notify your line manager at once in writing of your decision.

Maternity pay

To qualify for statutory maternity pay you have to be pregnant (or have given birth) at the start of the 11th week before the baby is due. If you have at least 26 weeks' service by the end of the 15th week before the expected week of childbirth you will be entitled to receive statutory maternity pay (SMP) whether or not you intend to return to work. (Note that if your normal weekly earnings are less than the lower earnings limit for National Insurance contributions for the previous eight weeks then you will not qualify for SMP). If you do not qualify for SMP you may be entitled to claim maternity allowance. Your local Benefits Agency office will be able to advise you how to claim this.

Statutory maternity pay is payable for a maximum of 39 weeks, for the first 6 weeks at the higher statutory rate of nine-tenths of your salary followed by the lower statutory rate for the remaining period. You will be given a statement of your exact entitlement when you start your maternity leave.

To claim SMP you must give 28 days' notice in writing of your absence on maternity grounds and you must give the *original* Mat B1 form, not a photocopy, to your line manager. You can only receive SMP once you have stopped work.

Once you start your maternity leave, your maternity pay will be paid into your bank account on the same date when you would have received your salary, and will be subject to deductions for income tax and National Insurance.

Contractual benefits

You will continue to receive your contractual non-remuneration benefits for the first 26 weeks of your maternity leave period.

Holidays

While you are absent on ordinary maternity leave you will continue to accrue holiday entitlement in the usual way for the first 26 weeks. You must take this additional holiday within 12 months of your return to work. Alternatively you may, if you wish, receive pay in lieu as long as you inform your line manager within four weeks of your return to work. During any additional maternity leave you will accrue holiday entitlement in accordance with the provisions of the Working Time Regulations.

Pension contributions

Your maternity leave period will be treated as pensionable service and the company will therefore continue to make contributions on your behalf into the pension scheme based on the maternity pay you receive rather than your usual salary.

Health and safety

If you are employed in a job that has been identified as posing a risk to your health or that of your unborn child you will be notified immediately and arrangements will be made to eliminate that risk.

For this reason you are required to notify your line manager as soon as you are aware that you may be pregnant. Arrangements will then be made to alter your working conditions, or if this is not possible, you will be offered a suitable alternative job for the duration of your pregnancy.

If there is no alternative work, the company reserves the right to suspend you on full pay until you are no longer at risk.

These alternative arrangements may continue after the birth of your child if you are still considered to be at risk.

If you have any concerns about your own health and safety at any time you should let your line manager know immediately.

PATERNITY LEAVE

In addition to the 13 weeks' parental leave, any new father is entitled to 2 weeks' paid paternity leave provided he has at least 26 weeks' continuous service with you by the 15th week before the expected week of childbirth. This leave must be taken within a period of 56 days beginning with the date on which the child is born.

The employee has rights on returning from paternity leave similar to those applying to women returning from maternity leave. This means that he has the right to return to the same job and must not be subject to any detriment, or be unfairly dismissed for reasons connected with the taking of this paternity leave.

STATUTORY PATERNITY PAY

Statutory Paternity Pay may be paid to any employee who meets the 26-week service qualification and whose average weekly earnings are above the Lower Earnings Limit for National Insurance contributions. The rate of Statutory Paternity Pay is determined by Regulations, but in 2008 is the lesser of £117.18

per week or 90 per cent of the employee's average weekly earnings. This should be administered in the same way as Statutory Maternity Pay and amounts paid out reclaimed in the same way.

ADOPTION LEAVE

Rights to adoption leave are similar to those for maternity leave. Adoptive parents have the right to take ordinary adoption leave for a period of up to 26 weeks, with a right to a further period of additional adoption leave of 26 weeks, giving a total of up to one year's leave. This right is in addition to the right to parental leave.

As with statutory paternity leave, the employee has the right to return to the same job following absence on ordinary adoption leave, and must not suffer any detriment or be unfairly dismissed for reasons relating to adoption leave.

STATUTORY ADOPTION PAY

Statutory Adoption Pay is paid to any employee who meets the 26-week service qualification and is earning at least the Lower Earnings Limit for National Insurance contributions. It is paid for a period of up to 39 weeks and the rate is determined by Regulations, but in 2008 is the lesser of £117.18 per week or 90 per cent of the employee's average weekly earnings. This should be recovered in the same way as that applying to Statutory Maternity Pay and Statutory Paternity Pay.

FURTHER INFORMATION

Employment Rights Act 1996
Essential Facts – Employment (2006) Gee Publishing Ltd, London
Maternity and Parental Leave etc Regulations 1999
Personnel Manager's Factbook (2001) Gee Publishing Ltd, London
Statutory Maternity Pay Manual (CA29)
Trade Union Reform and Employment Rights Act 1992

8

Working hours and holidays

WORKING TIME REGULATIONS 1998

Working time limits

The Working Time Regulations 1998 limit a worker's average working week, including overtime, to a maximum of 48 hours over seven days. The average figure for working hours is calculated over a reference period of 17 weeks.

In calculating the reference period certain days are 'excluded'. These include days when the worker was on sick leave or maternity leave or any periods for which the worker agreed to work more than 48 hours per week. However, where such excluded days arise, the reference period must be extended by a number of days equal to the number of excluded days to get the total of 17 weeks. These additional days must be from the period immediately following the reference period.

For example, if the worker has one week of sickness during a 17-week reference period the number of hours worked in the one week immediately following the reference period would be added to the calculation to get to the total of 17 weeks (see Figure 8.1).

The formula used to calculate working time is A+B/C, where A = the number of hours worked in the reference period, B = the number of hours excluded from the reference period and C = the number of weeks in the reference period.

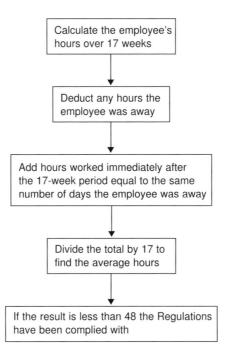

Figure 8.1 *Working time calculation*

Exclusion

The working time limits do not apply to any workers who can decide their own working hours.

Opting out of the Regulations

Workers can agree to work longer than the 48-hour limit by signing an 'opt-out'. This must be in writing and signed by the worker (see example in Chapter 2). You need to keep a record of all employees who have signed such an opt-out.

Workers can cancel this agreement at any time but they must give you seven days' notice or any longer period you agree with them, although this cannot be more than three months.

As an employer you are obliged to take all reasonable steps to ensure that workers are not required to work more than an average of 48 hours per week unless they have signed an 'opt out'.

The meaning of working time

Working time includes all those hours that the employee is required to be working for you, including lunch breaks, travelling, undertaking job-related training, and working abroad. It does not include routine home-to-work travel, rest breaks, or training that is not job related.

Time off

You must ensure that workers are given the time off that they are entitled to during the working period. Workers are entitled to a rest period of 11 uninterrupted hours between each working day and one day a week off (which can be averaged over a two-week period).

Young workers

A young worker is a worker who is over school leaving age but is not yet 18. Such workers are entitled to 12 uninterrupted hours off in each 24-hour period of work. They are also entitled to two days off each week, but this cannot be averaged over two weeks.

Rest breaks

Any worker required to work for more than six hours without interruption is entitled to a rest break of 20 minutes, which must be taken during the six-hour period.

If a young worker is required to work more than 4.5 hours at a stretch he is entitled to a rest break of 30 minutes.

Annual leave

All workers, including part-time workers, are entitled to 4.8 weeks' annual leave. The number of days' leave is related to the number of days normally worked. For a five-day week, therefore, the entitlement will be 4.8 × 5 = 24 days' annual leave, but for a three-day week it will be 4.8 × 3 = 14.4 days per annum. All public holidays count towards the annual leave entitlement.

Leave accrues at the rate of one-twelfth of the annual entitlement per month during the first year of service. A full-time worker with three months' service would be entitled to three-twelfths of the annual entitlement of 24 days' leave (ie six days). A part-time worker working three days a week with one month's service would accrue 1.2 days (24 days × three-fifths = 14.4 days × one-twelfth).

You should agree with the workers concerned how and when notice of their intention to take leave should be given.

If there is no such agreement the notice that the worker must give you should be at least twice the period of leave to be taken. You may in turn refuse the worker permission to take the leave but must respond within a period equal to the period of leave requested.

Calculating a week's pay

For workers paid a fixed wage or salary, a week's pay is that which is due for the basic hours worked. It excludes overtime unless this is a guaranteed part of the contract.

If the worker is a piece worker or receives variable bonuses or commission related to output, a week's pay is the average hourly rate multiplied by that worker's normal working hours (see also Chapter 3).

To calculate the hourly rate, the weekly pay over the previous 12 weeks should be divided by the number of hours worked during that period. If no pay was received for any of those weeks, then this should be replaced by a week before the 12-week period to make it up to the total of 12 weeks.

A week's pay is the total eligible pay (excluding voluntary overtime but including relevant bonuses) over the 12-week period divided by 12.

Common issues relating to working time

Signing opt-out agreements

You cannot force a worker to sign an opt-out agreement and any action taken against a person for not doing so is likely to be unfair.

Workers with second jobs

If you know that a worker has a second job you should agree an opt-out with that person if the total time worked is likely to be more than 48 hours a week. It may be a wise precaution to insert a clause in the employment contract requiring employees not to take on other employment without the agreement of the company. However, if a worker does another job without your knowledge it is unlikely that you would have any liability in the event of the Regulations being breached.

Rest breaks

You do not have to pay for rest breaks but this is a matter to be agreed with your employees or their representatives.

Employees voluntarily working longer hours

If employees voluntarily wish to work more than 48 hours a week you would have no liability under the Regulations, provided you made it clear to the employees that they are not required to work longer than 48 hours.

TIME OFF IN LIEU OF OVERTIME (TOIL)

Some organizations have employees who are required to travel or work outside normal working hours. Compensation for these hours, where given, may be payment of overtime or by giving time off in lieu (TOIL). How to implement a TOIL policy is set out below.

Implementing a TOIL policy

1. Review existing contracts to ensure that there are no provisions preventing the introduction of time off in lieu, eg any commitment to give paid overtime.
2. Review past practice in relation to overtime and time off to ensure that there are no precedents that could give rise to any contractual entitlement.
3. Ensure that any members of staff who may be required to regularly work more than 48 hours per week sign an opt-out agreement. This will have normally been carried out under the Working Time Regulations anyway.
4. Consult staff about the proposed agreement, especially in relation to the number of hours to be carried over and the period in which any time off may be taken.
5. Ensure that the policy is coordinated with any other time off provisions, including those required by UK statute, so that the company can meet operational requirements.
6. Arrange for the recording of TOIL on existing timesheets.

Example policy for time off in lieu of overtime

The company recognizes that the nature of its work means that staff may often have to work or travel outside recognized office hours. The company also recognizes its duty to protect the health and safety of its staff by ensuring that they do not work too many hours and that they are recompensed for any extra time that they do have to work.

What is lieu time?

Lieu time is time off which you are allowed to take in lieu of overtime pay, for hours worked beyond the working day (ie evenings and weekends). Overtime is compensated only in time off, not in any addition to base pay, and all references to 'overtime' in this document mean unpaid overtime.

Accrual of lieu time

1. If you need to attend an evening or weekend meeting or event in the course of your work, or have to travel outside normal working hours you should ensure that your line manager is aware of this, preferably before the date concerned, and you should record the hours worked on your time sheet.
2. Time off must be equal to time actually worked, ie there is no provision for time-and-a-half, double time, etc — if you work two hours, you can claim two hours' lieu time, regardless of the day or time that the work is actually carried out.

Redemption of overtime

1. Lieu time should be taken in the same month that it is accrued, and not carried forward from month to month. If this is not possible, it must be taken within the following two months. Lieu time accrued and not redeemed as outlined will be lost.
2. No more than 15 hours' lieu time may be accrued in any one month.
3. Use of lieu time must be clearly marked on your time sheet.
4. Reasonable notice should be given to your line manager when lieu time is to be taken, and it is your responsibility to ensure that the proposed time off fits with your work commitments, etc.
5. Line managers have the discretion to vary these arrangements to suit operational requirements.

ANNUAL HOLIDAYS

Apart from the requirement under the Working Time Regulations to give all employees a minimum of 4.8 weeks' paid holiday a year it is for you to decide the company's policy on annual holidays. You can also decide the arrangements for booking holidays. If you are likely to require staff to take their holidays at certain times of the year you should take care to ensure that this is specifically referred to in the employment contract.

Employees do not have any legal right to carry over unused annual holiday from one holiday year to another, or to receive payment in lieu of holidays, except when leaving the company.

PARENTAL LEAVE

Employees with at least one year's service and who are parents of children born or adopted on or after 15 December 1999, or who were five years of age at that date, are entitled to 13 weeks' unpaid leave up to the child's fifth birthday for each child. You can agree with the employees the amount of leave to be taken at any one time, but if you do not have any such agreement you will have to apply what is called the 'fallback' scheme. Under this scheme employees can take parental leave in blocks of one week or more, subject to a maximum of four weeks in any one year. Any such request for leave should generally be made 21 days before the date on which it is due to begin. You have the right to postpone the leave for up to six months if the business is likely to be unduly disrupted by the employee's absence.

During the period of the absence the employee maintains full employment rights and is entitled to return to the same job.

You are entitled to ask for reasonable evidence of an employee's responsibility for a child and the date of birth of that child.

Parents of disabled children have the right to 18 weeks' leave.

SUNDAY WORKING

Staff working in shops, including betting shops and racecourses, cannot be forced to work on Sundays. If they have previously agreed to do so they can opt out by giving you three months' notice in writing of their intention not to work on Sundays. Any disciplinary action by you against employees protected in this way, or who have opted out of Sunday working, would be automatically unfair.

EMPLOYMENT OF SCHOOL CHILDREN

You may not employ any child:

- under the age of 13;
- during school hours;
- before 7.00 am or after 7.00 pm;
- for more than two hours on a school day;
- for more than two hours on a Sunday.

FLEXIBLE WORKING ARRANGEMENTS

Flexible Working Regulations

Under the Flexible Working Regulations 2002, effective from April 2003, an employee who has 26 weeks' continuous employment can request a change in hours of work, working times or place of work to be able to care for a child under the age of 6, or a disabled child under the age of 18. From 1 April 2007 the right to request flexible working has been extended to carers. A 'carer' is an employee who is, or expects to be, caring for their husband, wife or partner, or for a close adult relative or for an adult who lives at the same address.

The right is to request the flexible working arrangements, not to receive them automatically. You can refuse the request if there are good business reasons for doing so. These reasons could include the following:

- the burden of additional costs involved;
- a possible detrimental effect on customer service;
- difficulty in reorganizing work among other staff;
- a possible detrimental impact in work performance or quality;
- inability to accommodate the request because of planned changes to company structure.

If you receive such a request, which must be in writing, you must arrange to meet the employee within 28 days and give your decision within 14 days of that meeting. The employee can take the matter to an employment tribunal if you fail to follow a correct procedure or make a decision based on incorrect facts. Compensation would be two weeks' pay at the statutory rate.

Part-time workers

A part-time worker is any worker who does not work as many hours as your full-time workers. The general rule is that you should treat part-timers no less favourably than full-time workers. This means that they should receive exactly the same pay and benefits as full-time employees in comparable jobs, applied on a pro-rata basis where appropriate. They should also be given the same opportunities for promotion and training and development.

Job-sharing

Job-sharing arises when two employees voluntarily share the responsibilities of one full-time job.

Contracts

In preparing a contract for job-sharers you will need to incorporate the following additional clauses:

- that an offer to one person is conditional on the other also accepting it;
- the days and hours to which the job-share relates;
- how entitlement to public holidays will be decided;
- that if one job-sharer leaves and a replacement cannot be found the remaining job-sharer will have to convert to full-time working or may instead be dismissed.

Terminating employment

If one job-sharer leaves, any dismissal of the remaining job-sharer will only be fair provided:

- the remaining job-sharer is consulted about the action to be taken;
- that person is offered the additional work;
- an attempt is made to find a replacement job-sharer;
- an assessment is made of whether the business requirements are such that full-time coverage is necessary;
- you consider whether the work undertaken by the person who has left can be carried out in some other way;
- you try to find alternative work for the remaining employee;
- dismissal is the last resort, once all other arrangements have been explored.

Table 8.1 *Implications of home-working on employment policies and procedures*

Policies and procedures	Implications
Equal opportunities policy	You need to ensure that all staff are given the option of home-working, not just those with family responsibilities. You need to ensure that all staff have equal access to promotion, training and bonus opportunities, especially if one particular group, for example women, is over-represented. Good opportunity for using staff who may acquire a disability.
Disciplinary rules	Will generally be the same but some may not apply, for example dress code, and others may need to be inserted.
Disciplinary procedure	Generally, no change.
Grievance procedure	Generally, no change.
Maternity leave	This is a statutory right so will apply as normal. You need to ensure that there is a formal process for notifying return to work. You need to ensure that no work is done in the two weeks following childbirth.
Maternity pay	This is a statutory right so will apply as normal.
Holidays	Generally, no change.
Hours of work	You need either to ensure that staff do not work more than 48 hours per week or that they sign an opt-out. They must also be given breaks at least every six hours. Home-workers may have to provide time sheets.
Paternity leave	This is a statutory right applying equally to home-workers.
Statutory paternity pay	This is a statutory right applying equally to home-workers.

Table 8.1 *(Continued)*

Policies and procedures	Implications
Adoption leave	This is a statutory right applying equally to home-workers.
Parental leave	This is a statutory right applying equally to home-workers. Office-based employees may view this as unduly generous to home-workers.
Time off for dependants	This is a statutory right applying equally to home-workers.
Other time off	Generally, no change. Again may be viewed as generous by office-based staff.
Sick pay	Generally, no change.
Job descriptions	May need to be modified as certain duties and responsibilities arise from working in an office environment.
Person specifications	Will need to be modified to reflect characteristics required of someone who may be deemed suitable for home-working. Different competencies are likely to be required.
Selection process	Selection tests will need to establish suitability for home-working.
Pay	If office staff receive luncheon vouchers or benefit from a subsidized canteen should home-workers be given a commensurate allowance? Regional weighting allowances are likely to need adjusting. Where overtime or shift pay is given there will need to be processes for managing these. Bonuses and PRP will need to be applied equally to home-workers and office staff but with greater emphasis on IPRP with the former. Performance

Table 8.1 *(Continued)*

Policies and procedures	Implications
	measures may need to vary (for example team-working will not apply to home-workers but may be part of an incentive scheme for office staff). Job evaluation factors and related grades/pay ranges may be affected. There is a need to ensure that there are no equal value problems.
Benefits	Most benefits should be unaffected, although some will not apply to home-workers, for example season ticket loans.
Union membership	Arrangements must be made to ensure that home-workers have equal rights in terms of union membership. This is mainly the responsibility of the union but it could become critical in the event of a dispute about union recognition where the 'appropriate bargaining unit' is in dispute.
Employee relations	Similar considerations to above, but where partnership arrangements are in place processes will need to be introduced to ensure active participation of home-workers.
Health and safety	There will be a need to carry out an initial health and safety audit to ensure that the working conditions and equipment are suitable and there are minimal risks to health. You will need to check that insurance cover is adequate for any equipment used and that there are no mortgage or local authority restrictions. You must keep lists of outworkers and send this information to the local authority twice a year and to the Health and Safety Inspector if requested (Factories Act 1961).

Holidays

One of the main complexities with job-sharing is how to deal with public holidays, especially when one job-sharer works all Mondays when most public holidays occur. Probably the simplest option is to allocate each employee an additional amount of annual holiday equivalent to the total number of public holidays, with the job-sharer who would usually be working on the day the bank holiday falls having that day deducted from the annual entitlement.

Home-workers

Working from home has become more common in recent years and it can offer employees a lot more flexibility, particularly if they have family responsibilities. If you are considering employing home-workers there are a number of key issues to be addressed:

- How will you ensure that home-workers are given equal opportunities for promotion, training and bonuses?
- How will you measure and reward performance?
- How will you ensure participation in company and union activities?
- What changes do you need to make to the contract of employment?
- How will you monitor working hours, holidays, sickness and time off?
- Do you need to change any of your employment policies and procedures to ensure equal access to these?
- What are your health and safety responsibilities to home-workers and what actions do you need to take to cover yourself?
- How do you need to modify your recruitment and selection processes to ensure that you select staff with the appropriate skills and attitudes?

You have to ensure that all your employment policies and procedures are sufficient to provide statutory safeguards and to ensure continued employee motivation and performance. The implications of home-working for your policies and procedures are summarized in Table 8.1.

Employer's checklist on home-working

The following checklist might help ensure that you have taken all appropriate actions when considering the employment of home-workers.

Checklist on home-working

Equal opportunities

Do you have systems and procedures that ensure that office and home-based staff have the same conditions of employment and equal access to opportunities for promotion, training and development?

Recruitment

Have you adapted your recruitment and selection processes to ensure that those selected for home-working have the required skills, attitudes and competencies?

Hours of work

Have you introduced procedures to ensure that the hours of work of home-workers are monitored?

Reward structure

Have you developed reward systems that reflect the differences between home-workers and office-based staff, and that provide home-workers with incentives and participation in company bonus schemes?

Disciplinary rules

Have your disciplinary rules been adapted for home-workers?

Union recognition

Have you identified the appropriate bargaining unit for home-workers for the purposes of union recognition? How are home-workers catered for in your participation arrangements?

Health and safety

Have you undertaken a risk assessment and health and safety audit of your home-workers' working environment? What guidance have you issued?

Insurance

Is the appropriate home insurance in place?

Notification

Have you notified the local authority?

FURTHER INFORMATION

BERR website: www.berr.gov.uk
Working Time Regulations 1998

9

Writing a staff handbook

Most companies will want to produce a staff handbook that gives details of all the terms and conditions and benefits applying to staff. Much of this information is often too detailed and lengthy to be included in any offer letter or written statement of particulars of employment.

This chapter describes some of the main areas that are usually included within any staff handbook and gives extensive examples of what this content would typically look like. This is not intended to be a comprehensive summary of everything that could be included in a staff handbook, as this is primarily a matter of choice for the company in question.

The subjects most frequently covered in staff handbooks are:

- welcome and introduction to the company;
- mission statement and values;
- product or service information;
- terms and conditions of employment;
- the induction process;
- ethical considerations, for example gifts, confidentiality and conflicts of interest;
- limits of authority, particularly in terms of finance;
- holiday and leave provisions;
- termination of employment;

- outside employment;
- disciplinary and grievance procedures;
- pay and benefits, including bonuses, loans, cash awards and so forth;
- car policy;
- share options;
- pension scheme;
- travel and business expenses;
- performance appraisal;
- staff development;
- intellectual property;
- use of computers and e-mail;
- equal opportunities policy;
- harassment policy;
- whistle-blowing policy;
- health and safety, including policies on smoking, fire safety, first aid, AIDS, use of drugs and so forth;
- personnel records;
- employee communications;
- trade union membership;
- dress code;
- charitable giving;
- names of relevant persons in the company.

WELCOME TO THE COMPANY

The first section of any handbook should comprise some kind of welcoming note, a description of how the handbook should be used and the name of the person in the company whom the employee should contact for further information or assistance. The wording could be along the following lines, although it should obviously be adapted to suit your circumstances:

> I am pleased to welcome you to the company and hope that your association with ... is a long and happy one. This handbook is provided for your guidance and information and describes the terms and conditions applying to your employment with the company. These, together with your letter of appointment and written statement of particulars, form part of your contract of employment. You will be notified in writing of any changes to these terms and conditions.
>
> If you require any further information, or would like anything explained in more detail, you should contact ...

BACKGROUND INFORMATION

The next section of the handbook should contain information about the company. In particular, you may wish to include information about:

- the company's history, including how and when it was formed;
- the company's mission statement and values;
- the company's climate and culture (what it is like to work in the company);
- how the company is organized;
- company size, location and associated ventures;
- key personnel in the company;
- future aims.

TERMS AND CONDITIONS OF EMPLOYMENT

Salaries

In this section you should set out, more or less, the same information set out in the offer letter or written particulars of employment (apart from the precise salary offered to an individual). The wording is likely to be similar to this:

> Salaries are paid monthly in arrears, on the 25th of each month, by direct transfer to your bank/building society account.
>
> Your salary will be reviewed on a regular basis, and at least annually. Any such review is entirely at the company's discretion. In carrying out any review we will take account of your performance and that of the company as a whole, as well as any other relevant factors. However, there is no guarantee that salaries will be increased at any particular time.

Expenses

You should include any rules about expenses. A typical clause is as follows:

> The company will reimburse you for reasonable expenses incurred by you arising from your employment. Claims must be authorized by your line manager and supported by the production of valid receipts or such other documentary evidence as the company may require from time to time. You must also comply with the company's procedure for claiming expenses.

Benefits

You need to describe the main benefits provided by the company such as a pension, company car, share options, bonuses, medical insurance, and any conditions attached to them. In the case of a pension you may have to refer the employees to the pension provider for more information.

Mobility

You may need to give more information about any mobility requirements contained in the job. An example of the type of wording that might be appropriate is as follows:

> Your normal place of work is set out in your contract of employment.
>
> The company has the right, as a term of your employment, to change your normal place of work to any other company premises. If we do so, you may, at our discretion, be entitled to financial or other relocation benefits.
>
> You may from time to time be required to work at other locations throughout the UK and Europe depending on business requirements. Appropriate travel and accommodation arrangements will be made in such circumstances. We may also need you to work outside the UK for periods of more than one month, and if we do so, we will let you know the length of your stay abroad, the currency in which you will be paid, any benefits in kind you will receive while abroad and the terms and conditions of your relocation package. We will also give you details of the terms and conditions applying to your return to the UK.

Hours of work

You should explain in detail any rules and regulations applying to hours of work. An example of a section of this kind is set out below:

> The normal working week is 35 hours and the hours of work are from 9.00 am to 5.30 pm, with a one-hour break for lunch. However, you are expected to work such additional hours as are reasonably necessary to perform your duties, without additional pay.
>
> The Working Time Regulations provide that average working time, including overtime, must not exceed 48 hours for each seven-day period (to be averaged over a period of 17 weeks) unless you agree that this provision should not apply to your employment. You will usually be asked to agree that this provision should not apply to your employment with the company.
>
> At any time during your employment either you or the company may give three months' notice in writing that the opt-out from the 48-hour limit shall cease to apply with effect from the expiry of that notice.

The company will monitor your working time, in accordance with the requirements of the Working Time Regulations and to ensure that your health and safety are protected. It will monitor working time primarily by when you enter and leave the company's offices. For the purpose of these Regulations:

The meaning of 'working time' is all the time between you entering and leaving the company's offices.

You must let us know if there is any other time that you consider should be treated as 'working time' and you must keep records of it.

You must comply with any requests made, or measures imposed, to enable the company to monitor your 'working time', which will be primarily through our existing time sheet and office systems. Failure to do so will be a disciplinary offence.

If you have any concerns about the number of hours you are working, this may be raised with your manager, on a completely confidential basis, who will take whatever steps are necessary to address the situation.

Holidays

You should describe the holiday entitlement for employees and particularly any rules relating to the taking of holidays, payment in lieu and the carry over of any entitlement from one year to the next. The section should also cover how any entitlement to outstanding holiday not taken will be dealt with on termination of employment. An example is set out below:

Your holiday entitlement is 20 working days in addition to public and bank holidays in any calendar year. You also earn an additional day of holiday for every completed year of service up to a maximum of 25 days. Your holiday accrues at the rate of 1.67 days per month.

If you joined part-way through the year you will only be entitled to holiday that accrues in the remainder of that holiday year.

If you leave part-way through the year, holiday entitlement will be calculated on the basis of the part of the year worked, and you will either receive pay in lieu of those days that are untaken at the date of leaving or, alternatively, if you have exceeded the amount of holiday to which you are entitled, pay in lieu of the excess days will be deducted from your final salary or repaid by you.

Holidays cannot be carried forward from one year to the next, without the company's written consent.

All requests for holidays should be approved in advance by your line manager. All holiday requests should be approved at least one week in advance.

If you are ill while on holiday the days of absence will only be treated as sick leave, rather than holiday, if you produce medical certificates as evidence of your illness.

Time off for dependants

There is a statutory entitlement to time off to care for dependants. You should describe the company's arrangements for administering the rules relating to this time off. An example is set out below:

Although all employees have an entitlement to paid holidays it is recognized that there may be occasions when unpaid leave, with or without notice, may be required to deal with an emergency involving a dependant. We will give you a reasonable amount of time off when such an unexpected or sudden problem arises, for example when a dependant falls ill or if a childminder fails to turn up.

You should notify your supervisor as soon as possible about any such absence, including the reason for it and how long you expect to be away from work.

Parental leave

There is a statutory entitlement to parental leave. You should set out the company's rules relating to the taking of this leave. An example is set out below:

Once you have completed one year's service you are entitled to a maximum of 13 weeks' unpaid parental leave. This is subject to the production of a birth certificate in the parents' names or other evidence of parental responsibility.

You may take this leave at any time in the year, up to a maximum of four weeks in any one year, and you must give at least 21 days' notice of the required dates. The company reserves the right to postpone the leave for up to six months for operational reasons, although we will try to be as flexible as possible.

For adopted children (subject to the production of documentation) there is an entitlement to 18 weeks' leave to be taken within the first five years after the date of adoption or until the child's 18th birthday.

On recruitment, where it is known that there is a child or children under five (or adopted) you must declare how much parental leave has been taken with any previous employer in respect of each child. This will be checked with them.

Any abuse of this benefit is likely to be treated as gross misconduct and could lead to dismissal without notice.

Bereavement leave

Any entitlement to compassionate or bereavement leave should be described. An example is:

You are allowed a day off with pay to attend the funeral of a close relative (such as a parent, grandparent, husband/wife, brother or sister) plus an additional three days' compassionate leave with pay. Any other compassionate leave must be agreed with your supervisor and will be unpaid.

Absence

You should describe in this section any rules relating to the reporting and control of sickness absence. An example is set out below:

If you have to be absent from work for any reason, you should contact your supervisor as early as possible, preferably within one hour of your normal start time, and no later than 10.30 am, on the first day of absence, to let him/her know.

If you are absent because of illness, you should give an indication of the nature of your illness and how long you think you are likely to be away from work. You should contact us yourself, but if, exceptionally, you are unable to do so you should get someone to telephone on your behalf as soon as possible. If you are away for more than one day you should contact us on a daily basis.

You are required to provide a certificate for any period of sick leave in excess of four days. Where the illness is no more than seven days in total this may simply be a statement from you that you have been ill. Beyond seven days, you must provide us with a medical certificate from your GP. When deciding what sort of certificate you need to provide us with, you should bear in mind that weekends and bank holidays count as days of absence.

You will receive statutory sick pay, in accordance with the statutory rules during any period of sickness absence. Any additional payment will be at the company's discretion and will depend on your individual circumstances.

The company may require you to be examined by a doctor of our choice and at our expense and you will be required to agree that the company can have access to the medical report produced as a result of that examination.

Maternity and paternity

You should set out details of any maternity and paternity policies. There are legal requirements about the amount of maternity and paternity leave and pay to which employees are entitled, but employers often give more than the minimum entitlement. Your company's policy, and any conditions attached to it, should be set out in this section. An example of a maternity policy is set out in Chapter 7.

DISCIPLINARY PROCEDURE

The disciplinary procedure will usually be too lengthy to be contained within the written statement of employment particulars and should therefore be described in detail in the handbook. An example of a disciplinary procedure is set out in Chapter 12.

GRIEVANCE PROCEDURE

Any grievance procedure should be set out in the staff handbook if it is not already fully contained within the written statement of particulars. For small companies this procedure can frequently be summarized in one sentence and can therefore easily be contained within the written statement. An example of a grievance procedure is set out in Chapter 13.

CONFIDENTIAL INFORMATION

Any company will have a certain amount of commercial and other information that it will want to safeguard. The rules relating to the treatment of such information can be set out in the handbook. An example is set out below:

During your employment with the company you will acquire or have access to information in written, verbal or electronic form relating to the company, its customers, suppliers, employees, and so forth, and to products and processes. Some of this information will be confidential in nature, and although this will depend on the circumstances, if you are in any doubt you should treat any such information as confidential. Examples of the type of information that the company will generally consider to be confidential are set out below, although this list is not intended to be exhaustive:

- Technical information relating to the company's products and processes or arising from the company's research and development activities.
- Information relating to the company that will not be generally known to the company's competitors such as any business plans, pricing information, customer data, etc.
- Personnel information relating to the company's staff.
- Any internal incidents or conversations relating to company staff, customers, directors, suppliers, guests, visitors, and so forth, which you might hear about or witness during your employment and which could potentially damage the company or anyone associated with the company.
- Information described as confidential by the company.

Information about the company's business dealings must be kept confidential unless you have express permission from a company director to disclose the information. You will also be required, if requested by the company, to sign an agreement with a customer or potential customer not to disclose any confidential information relating to that customer if they make such a request.

You must not disclose any confidential information in any form about the company, its directors, employees, contractors, customers or any other persons or organizations connected with the company to any third party either during your employment or afterwards without the written agreement of the company.

Any breach of this policy during employment will be treated as gross misconduct.

INTELLECTUAL PROPERTY

Any invention by an employee belongs to that employee unless it arose directly out of the work that person was required to do. You may therefore wish to make it clear that any inventions arising in the course of employment belong to the company. The following example seeks to do this:

> While you are employed by the company it is a term of your employment that the work you produce belongs to the company. You must disclose and deliver to the company all information developed or discovered by you working alone, or with others, during the course of your employment.
>
> You must also waive any rights to such material and give the company control over how it is used in the future, without any further reference to you. This obligation continues following the termination of your employment for whatever reason.

RESTRICTIONS DURING AND AFTER EMPLOYMENT

Exclusive employment

You may wish to discourage your employees from taking second or other jobs while they are in your full-time employment, not least because they might then end up working more than the 48-hour limit set out in the Working Time Regulations. An example of a clause aiming to do this is set out below:

> You are a full-time employee of the company and must therefore devote the whole of your working time and energies to the company's business. You should not take on any employment outside the company without the express permission of one of the directors.

Restrictive covenant

Most companies will wish to protect their commercial interests following the departure of an employee. This most commonly means trying to prevent that person from setting up in competition or using company products and information for the benefit of a competitor. The main problem with any such restriction is that you cannot seek to prevent someone from earning a living and so any restrictions should be no more than is reasonable to protect your interests. These particular restrictive covenants or restraint of trade clauses are often contained in the written statement of employment particulars, particularly for senior jobs. An example of a restrictive covenant is set out below:

> The company will require you to agree that you will not: 1. During your employment, and for a period of six months after the date of termination of your employment, for any reason, have any commercial involvement in any capacity in any business which competes with the company without the written consent of a director of the company. 2. For the six months following the date of termination of your employment for any reason, solicit or offer employment to any of the company's employees. 3. For the six months following the date of termination of your employment for any reason, directly or indirectly, try to solicit or entice away anyone who has been a customer of the company and with whom you have had personal dealings during your employment, or to try to persuade them to cease, reduce or adversely affect their business with the company.
>
> You will also be required to agree that you will not: (a) During or after your employment with the company make or publish any derogatory or disparaging statement about the company, or any of its officers or employees. (b) Without the company's prior written consent, at any time during or after your employment with the company, disclose information obtained from a third party and which you know to be confidential, or use any material for which the company or its customers or suppliers owns the copyright.
>
> You must also agree to notify any new employer of the restrictions contained in this agreement and the company reserves the right to do so in any case.
>
> You are required to agree that the restrictions set out above are reasonable and necessary for the protection of the company. If any restriction on its own is considered by a court to go beyond what is reasonable to protect the legitimate business interests of the company, but would be considered reasonable if amended, these clauses will still apply with those amendments.

COMPANY PROPERTY

You may wish to incorporate a clause relating to the return of company property on leaving the company. The following is an example:

You are responsible for any company property issued to you and must ensure that you take all necessary precautions to prevent loss or damage. You should immediately report any such loss or damage to the company.

When you leave the company you must return all company property including any confidential information, equipment, lists of customers, internal procedures, correspondence and any other information relevant to the business, in whatever form it is held. You must return any company vehicle together with keys, and any car telephone and any personal or notebook computers that are the property of the company. You must not keep any copies of any company documents or information received or created during and in connection with your employment, in whatever form held, and must not allow them to be used by any other person.

GIFTS

A satisfied customer will often want to give some small gift as a token of satisfaction with the service provided and equally, a potential contractor may wish to give a gift as an inducement. It is wise to have a clear policy on this so that staff know how to react in either circumstance. An example is set out below:

You must not accept any gifts, entertainment or other favours, other than those that it would be discourteous to refuse and which are of nominal value, from any third party with which the company has had business dealings. You should report any such offer to your line manager.

EQUAL OPPORTUNITIES POLICY

There are strong legal safeguards against discrimination on grounds of sex, race, religion or belief, age, or disability. To ensure that you do not infringe the law and that you treat all staff fairly, you should have an equal opportunities policy. An example is set out in the extract below:

Equal opportunities policy

It is the policy of the company to give equal opportunity in employment regardless of sex, marital status, sexual orientation, race, ethnic origin, religion or belief, age, or disability. This applies to recruitment, training, pay, conditions of employment, allocation of work and promotion.

Implementation

As an equal opportunity employer our key criterion for selection, promotion, training and reward is ability to do the job to the required standard. For this reason we will not discriminate on any grounds unrelated to performance, regardless of whether these are prohibited by law.

It is your personal responsibility as an employee to ensure that this policy is followed. Any questions or doubts about the application of the policy should be referred to your line manager.

The policy applies not only to our staff but also to our relationships with our customers and suppliers.

If you feel that you have been discriminated against you should raise the matter through the grievance procedure.

Discipline

Your cooperation is essential in ensuring the success of this policy. Discriminatory actions or behaviour by employees will be treated as serious misconduct and could lead to dismissal.

HEALTH AND SAFETY POLICY

The staff handbook is the ideal place to describe your health and safety policy. What you actually put into the policy will depend largely on the nature of your business, with those companies working in a manufacturing or similar environment, or operating potentially dangerous machinery, plant and processes requiring much more detail in their policy than would apply in a typical office environment. Generally, however, it might typically contain information and procedures relating to first aid, accidents at work, fire safety, and so forth.

SMOKING AT WORK

Smoking at work is illegal in Scotland, Wales and England. A policy on smoking at work can be contained within that on health and safety, but making it a separate document highlights it. An example is set out below:

Smoking is not permitted in any of our offices or other premises.

This applies to staff at all levels in the company and regardless of their office location.

Visitors to the company, including actual and potential customers, should be asked to observe the company's rules in this respect.

Any infringement of this policy could lead to disciplinary action.

HARASSMENT POLICY (see also Chapter 13)

Harassment of staff, which primarily means sexual or racial harassment, can potentially be very serious for the business, as well as for any employee concerned. One of the main problems is likely to be in deciding when mere banter goes beyond what may be considered to be reasonable bounds. For this reason it is a good idea to have a written policy so that there should be little doubt about what is, or is not, acceptable. An example is set out below:

Example harassment policy

Introduction

Sexual or racial harassment at work is unlawful, and both the company and the harasser may be held liable to pay damages for such unlawful actions.

The following sets out the company's policy on harassment.

Policy

The company deplores all forms of sexual or racial harassment and will seek to ensure that the working environment for staff is free from such actions. The following section gives examples of the type of behaviour that is unacceptable to the company.

You are expected to comply with this policy.

Examples of harassment

Sexual harassment can take many forms, from mild sexual banter to actual physical violence.

It is not always obvious what behaviour might constitute sexual harassment but it is up to you to try to recognize that what is acceptable to one employee may not be acceptable to another.

Sexual harassment is unwanted behaviour of a sexual nature by one employee towards another. Examples include:

- insensitive jokes;
- provocative comments about appearance;
- threat of dismissal, loss of promotion and so forth for refusal of sexual favours.

Racial harassment can also take many forms, from relatively minor abuse to actual physical violence. Examples of racial harassment include:

- insensitive jokes related to race;
- deliberate exclusion from conversations;
- racial abuse.

233

The examples above are not exhaustive. Depending on the circumstances, some types of harassment may constitute gross misconduct, punishable by summary dismissal under the company's disciplinary procedure.

Informal remedy

If you consider that you are, or have been, a victim of minor sexual or racial harassment or other intimidation you should make it clear to the alleged harasser that the behaviour is unacceptable and must stop. If you or a colleague feel unable to do this by word of mouth, then a written request (explaining the distress that the behaviour is causing) handed to the harasser may be effective. You may also discuss your complaints with your line manager, in total confidence.

Formal procedure

Where informal methods fail, or serious harassment occurs, employees should bring a formal complaint under the company's grievance procedure. The complaint should be made in writing to the Managing Director and state:

- the name of the harasser;
- the nature of the harassment;
- dates and times when harassment occurred;
- names of witnesses, if any, to any incidents of harassment;
- any action already taken by the complainant to stop the harassment;
- any suggested remedy.

The Managing Director will carry out a thorough investigation as quickly as possible, and in any event within two weeks, and if there is a case to answer action will be taken against the harasser under the company's disciplinary procedure.

Harassment outside work

A recent decision of the Employment Appeal Tribunal upheld a ruling that employers can be held liable for incidents of sexual harassment which take place at work-based social events whether or not they are outside the workplace. Accordingly, the company may take disciplinary action against anyone who subjects a member of staff to harassment outside the workplace.

OTHER MATTERS

There are number of other policies and terms of employment that could be included in any staff handbook. For further information on any particular aspect you should consult the appropriate chapter of this book. You may wish to include general information that you do not intend to be part of the employee's contract, and where this is the case, it should be made clear. This might apply, for example, to information about sports and social facilities. You should remember that written policies and agreements made collectively are all part of an employee's contract of employment.

When you are preparing a handbook it is probably a good idea to produce a draft that can be discussed with managers and staff. When you are happy that the content is appropriate and readily understood, the handbook can then be suitably bound and circulated. Once it has been produced, you will need to ensure that it is kept up to date, and for this reason, it is probably sensible to keep it in a loose-leaf binder.

FURTHER INFORMATION

Essential Facts – Employment (2006) Gee Publishing Ltd, London
Personnel Manager's Factbook (2001) Gee Publishing Ltd, London

10

Personnel records and data protection

PERSONNEL RECORDS

Every company needs to keep records of its employees. Not only are these in many cases a legal requirement, but without personal information about employees it would be extremely difficult for you to manage a company. You need to keep such information to:

- provide a store of personal information about individual employees;
- assist in planning the company's future people requirements;
- help in the recruitment and selection process;
- provide training and development information;
- provide information to help in performance appraisal;
- provide information for pay purposes;
- provide general employment information for dealing with such issues as changes to terms and conditions of employment, relocation, redundancy and disciplinary procedures;
- provide information for health, safety, and welfare;
- provide information for statutory returns.

The main information you should keep for each employee includes:

- personal details of the employee including address and contact details, next of kin, National Insurance number, etc;
- the employee's employment history;
- details of the job, including job title, function, location, grade, and so forth;
- the terms and conditions attached to the job;
- the employee's absence record;
- the employee's disciplinary record;
- any training given to the employee;
- any performance appraisal information;
- job evaluation data.

You should be able to analyse the information in various ways, for example by age, length of service, pay rate and gender. You should also keep information on the ethnic origin of employees and whether any are registered as disabled. You should also be able to summarize information about labour turnover, retention rates, absence, time-keeping, salary and wage costs, and accidents.

You should, of course, keep personal files confidential and although the Data Protection Act 1998 gives employees the right of access to personal information held about them, this does not necessarily mean that they can have unrestricted access to the whole personal file (see below).

DATA PROTECTION

The Data Protection Act 1998 came into effect on 1 March 2000. The Act regulates the use of personal data and gives individuals the right of access to that data as well as requiring the holders of such data to be open about the use of it and to follow certain principles in how that information is obtained, used and stored. Whereas the previous 1984 Act related only to data held on a computer, this later Act applies to manual records as well.

Those about whom information is held are referred to as *data subjects*, whereas those who hold and control the data are described as *data controllers*. As an employer you will be a data controller, although it is common for companies to appoint one person who has responsibility for implementing the Act.

Personal data comprises any information held about an individual. This need not be particularly sensitive information and could just be a name and address to fall within the definition.

Personal files

As an employer, the two most important considerations for you to bear in mind are that employees have a right to any information held about them and also that those employees must have given permission for such information to be held. Although it is not entirely clear that an employee has an automatic right of access to his personal file, it is probably wise to assume that he does.

Data protection principles

Any personal data you hold must conform to the following eight principles:

- the data must have been obtained fairly and lawfully and the employee must have agreed to data being held and processed;
- the data must be held only for specific and lawful purposes and not processed in any manner incompatible with those purposes;
- the data should be relevant, adequate and not excessive for the purposes for which it is used;
- it should be accurate and kept up to date;
- it should not be kept for any longer than is necessary;
- it should be processed in accordance with the rights of people under the Act;
- measures should be taken to guard against unauthorized or unlawful processing of personal data and against accidental loss, destruction or damage to it;
- personal data should not be transferred to a country or territory outside the European Economic Area, unless that country or territory provides an adequate level of protection.

Individual right of access

An employee has the right to be given a copy of any personal data held and processed by the employer and can ask for the removal or correction of any inaccurate data. You must respond within 40 days of receiving such a request providing that:

- the request is in writing;
- any fee requested (up to a maximum of £10) has been paid;
- the employee has supplied any information that is required to confirm his identity and the location of the relevant information;

- you have not already complied with an identical or similar request by the same individual, except after a reasonable interval has elapsed.

Exemptions

There are some exemptions from these provisions including:

- references given by you;
- references received if disclosure would give information about another individual, unless that third party had consented to the disclosure;
- where the disclosure of data might be likely to prejudice the conduct of your business, such as if there are proposed redundancies or mergers;
- if disclosure would be likely to give away your negotiating position, for example in relation to salary negotiations;
- personal data disclosed for the purpose of legal proceedings in relation to legal rights;
- data that might compromise national security or hamper detection of crime and tax evasion, etc.

As indicated above, for information about individuals to be legitimately held you need to get the permission of those individuals to the holding of this data. Probably the best way of doing this is to incorporate an appropriate clause in the contract of employment (see the example written statement of particulars in Chapter 2).

Sensitive personal data

Some information is categorized as sensitive personal data. This includes any data relating to:

- ethnic or racial origin;
- political opinions;
- religious beliefs or other beliefs of a similar nature;
- trade union membership;
- physical or mental health;
- sex life;
- the commission or alleged commission by the employee of any criminal offence;

- any proceedings arising from a criminal offence or alleged offence or the result of such proceedings.

Sensitive personal data such as those itemized can only be held with the express consent, ideally in writing, of the employee concerned, unless you need the information to comply with a statutory requirement. If you require this sensitive personal data to be held you must be very clear about explaining the reasons for doing so and ensuring that you get the individual's consent.

Ensuring compliance with data protection principles

To ensure that you comply with the requirements of the Data Protection Act you should:

- decide what information needs to be kept in personnel records;
- notify employees of what information is held and the reasons for holding it;
- appoint someone as data controller;
- clarify the rules about access to data;
- ensure that confidentiality is maintained;
- ensure that information that is kept is accurate and up to date;
- review existing forms such as application forms to ensure that the information requested is justified;
- make unauthorized disclosure of confidential information a disciplinary offence;
- train line managers in the implications of data protection.

Notification

If you keep personal information about living individuals on a computer it is likely that you will need to notify the Information Commissioner. You can check whether you need to do so with the Commissioner either through the internet or by telephone (enquiry line: 01625 545745).

Data protection policy

It is a good idea to have a written policy on data protection, which could be included within the staff handbook. An example policy is set out below:

Example data protection policy

It is a legal requirement for the company to comply with the Data Protection Act 1998. It is also company policy to ensure that every employee maintains the confidentiality of any personal data held by the company in whatever form.

Data protection principles

The company needs to keep certain information about its employees, customers and suppliers for financial and commercial reasons and to enable us to monitor performance, to ensure legal compliance and for health and safety purposes. To comply with the law, information must be collected and used fairly, stored safely and not disclosed to any other person unlawfully. This means that we must comply with the Data Protection Principles set out in the Data Protection Act 1998.

These principles require that personal data must be:

- obtained fairly and lawfully and shall not be processed unless certain conditions are met;
- obtained for specified and lawful purposes and not further processed in a manner incompatible with that purpose;
- adequate, relevant and not excessive;
- accurate and up to date;
- kept for no longer than necessary;
- processed in accordance with data subjects' rights;
- protected by appropriate security;
- not transferred to a country outside the European Economic Area without adequate protection.

In processing or using any personal information you must ensure that you follow these principles at all times.

Data protection coordinator

To ensure the implementation of this policy the company has designated the company secretary as the company's data protection coordinator. All enquiries relating to the holding of personal data should be referred to him in the first instance.

Notification of data held

You are entitled to know:

- what personal information the company holds about you and the purpose for which it is used;

- how to gain access to it;
- how it is kept up to date;
- what the company is doing to comply with its obligations under the 1998 Act.

This information is available from . . .

Individual responsibility

As an employee you are responsible for:

- checking that any information that you provide in connection with your employment is accurate and up to date;
- notifying the company of any changes to information you have provided, for example changes of address;
- ensuring that you are familiar with and follow the data protection policy.

Any breach of the data protection policy, either deliberate or through negligence, may lead to disciplinary action being taken and could in some cases result in a criminal prosecution.

Data security

You are responsible for ensuring that:

- any personal data that you hold, whether in electronic or paper format, is kept securely;
- personal information is not disclosed either verbally or in writing, accidentally or otherwise, to any unauthorized third party;
- items that are marked 'personal' or 'private and confidential', or which appear to be of a personal nature, are opened by the addressee only.

You should not use your office address for matters that are not work related.

MONITORING OF E-MAILS AND TELEPHONE CALLS

You have the right to monitor telephone calls made and e-mails sent by your staff, provided you notify them that you intend to do so. It may be advisable to incorporate a clause in the contract of employment stating this fact.

You can also monitor or record communications without the caller's consent for the purposes of:

- recording evidence of transactions;
- ensuring compliance with regulations or rules;

- gaining routine access to business communications;
- maintaining the effective operation of your systems;
- monitoring standards of service and for training purposes;
- combating crime and the unauthorized use of the system.

Developing an e-mail policy

You may consider it a wise precaution to develop an e-mail policy. If you do so, any such policy should:

- make it clear that the company owns the system;
- notify employees that they do not have an individual right to privacy when using the system;
- notify them that e-mails are likely to be monitored;
- set out permissible uses and those that are prohibited;
- prohibit the use of unauthorized passwords;
- notify employees that they must report any inappropriate use of the system.

All employees should be given a copy of the policy and be asked to sign a declaration that they have read and understood it.

An example of an e-mail and internet policy is set out below.

Example e-mail and internet policy

The use of e-mail and the internet is important for the maintenance of efficient operations and effective communications. However, their inappropriate use could lead to a loss of efficiency, personnel problems and also possible legal claims against the company. This policy sets out how these systems should be used by all employees, describes your individual responsibility and states how the company will respond to inappropriate use.

Appropriate use

When using e-mail or the internet you must comply with the following rules:

- the system must only be used on authorized company business;
- the style and content of any e-mails must conform to those applying to written correspondence;
- e-mail should not be used as a substitute for other forms of communication that may be more effective;

- where the content of any e-mail is confidential, the sender must ensure that all steps are taken to protect this confidentiality, by specifying that it is confidential and to be read only by the addressee;
- passwords should be memorized and not written down;
- only authorized passwords should be used;
- all necessary steps must be taken to ensure that no other person has unauthorized access to your computer;
- you should ensure that there is backup storage for any critical information, so that data is not lost in the event of a system failure.

Failure to follow these rules will be likely to lead to disciplinary action and could result in dismissal.

Inappropriate use

The system is not to be used for any of the following purposes:
- any messages which could be construed as bullying or harassment or as sexually or racially discriminatory;
- accessing or downloading pornography;
- online gambling;
- excessive personal use;
- downloading or distributing copyright information;
- disclosing confidential information about other employees;
- making derogatory comments about the company or its management, its customers or suppliers;
- accessing information using another person's password.

The system is the property of the company and its use will be monitored. Any misuse of the system will be subject to disciplinary action and could lead to summary dismissal. Hard copies of e-mail messages will be used as evidence.

Any employee who has a complaint about the use of the system should raise the matter informally through his line manager or formally through the company's grievance procedure.

FURTHER INFORMATION

Data Protection Act 1998
Website: www.dataprotection.gov.uk

11

Handling organization change

An inevitable consequence of running a business is the need to make changes from time to time. These may be to reflect changes in markets and the demand for products, developments in technology and production methods, the loss or acquisition of employees, and so forth. Whatever the reason, you will at some stage find yourself having to make changes to the company's structure, processes, procedures or people, and perhaps all of them simultaneously. Any change can be unsettling for people, creating uncertainty and suspicion, and therefore has to be handled carefully.

Some of the main issues to be taken into account when implementing any organization change are set out in this chapter.

CHANGES IN RESPONSIBILITIES

You will often wish to change the responsibilities of employees, perhaps to give them additional roles reflecting changes in business requirements and the individual's own development, or possibly to transfer someone to a role to which she may be more suited. Where responsibilities are increased you need to:

- ensure that any person who is given extra responsibility is also given any necessary training;
- ensure that the person concerned is clear about the requirements of the new role;
- provide any necessary support in the early stages of the change, including reviewing the employee's pay package to ensure that the changes to the job are appropriately reflected;
- consider the effect of this change on other jobs.

You need to keep an eye on the situation to ensure that the new responsibilities do not create too much stress for the person concerned, because as an employer you have a duty of care to your staff, and higher levels of stress are likely to lead to higher levels of absence and staff dissatisfaction.

The other side of the coin is that you may wish to reduce someone's responsibilities, possibly because you feel that she is not up to the job or because she is overloaded. The main points to bear in mind when doing this are:

- Significant reductions in responsibility, which lower the status of the individual concerned, might be viewed as a breach of contract serious enough to allow the individual concerned to resign and claim constructive dismissal (see Chapter 14).
- You may have to maintain the employee's current level of earnings for a less responsible job unless that person voluntarily agrees to a pay reduction. Imposing the changes might again be seen as a breach of contract by you.
- Where such changes are proposed for performance reasons you should ensure that you have adequate evidence to support your conclusions.
- Finally, you should ensure that any change to responsibilities does not result in an overlap or duplication with other jobs and also that no vital responsibilities are neglected in the transition.

CHANGES TO ORGANIZATIONAL STRUCTURE

When you make any changes to the structure and reporting lines in the company you should bear in mind that changing someone's reporting line, for example from reporting directly to the managing director to reporting instead to another director, might diminish the status of the individual concerned and could possibly be a breach of contract. Similarly, flattening the structure by increasing spans of control may be more efficient and lead to improved communication and swifter decision making, but it will inevitably lead to fewer promotion opportunities.

Any restructuring needs to ensure that all main responsibilities are covered but not duplicated. One way of ensuring this is to plot the main areas of responsibility against the jobs you have, perhaps by using a matrix such as the one shown in Figure 11.1. This identifies the jobs that have the main or prime responsibility for delivering key business objectives, and those that have a supporting or shared role.

Job	Operations Director	Finance Director	Sales Director
Accountability			
1. Achieve production targets	P	S	S
2. Maximize sales	S	S	P
3. Research new products	S	S	P
4. Develop new markets	S	S	P
5. Maintain customer relations	S	S	P
6. Control company finances	S	P	S
7. Train and develop staff	P	S	S

P = Prime accountability, S = Shared accountability

Figure 11.1 *Accountability matrix*

CHANGES TO PROCESSES AND PROCEDURES

When you make changes to any of your internal procedures, working methods or processes you should bear in mind that:

● any proposed changes should be first discussed with those who will be most affected by the changes and who have detailed day-to-day knowledge of how they work;

- the changes will need to be effectively communicated to anyone affected by them;
- the staff and supervisors will need to be given the appropriate training;
- where the changes affect working methods and the use of plant and equipment the safety implications of the changes need to be fully considered;
- if you have full consultation processes the appropriate staff representatives will need to be consulted about any proposed changes;
- the impact on productivity and earnings will need to be fully taken into account;
- the changes will need to be monitored and modified if necessary.

OBTAINING COMMITMENT TO CHANGE

Any change creates uncertainty and may be seen as threatening. To obtain commitment to change you should:

- consult staff as far as possible about the proposed changes;
- explain the reasons for them;
- demonstrate how they will improve matters;
- highlight the advantages to the company and the people affected;
- give safeguards to ensure that no one is adversely affected by the changes, for example by guaranteeing existing status and pay levels where possible;
- involve people as fully as possible in the change process, so that they feel that it is their process.

INTRODUCING PARTICIPATION

You may wish to consider giving your employees more involvement in the running of the company, a process generally described as 'participation'. If you involve them in making decisions about the company you are likely to gain a greater degree of commitment to any changes you might propose.

To introduce participation successfully you should adopt the following approach:

- agree the aims and objectives of participation;
- consider how these affect your policies, procedures, jobs, and management generally;
- show your full support for participation by both your words and actions.

Where you are involving unions in the process try to ensure that they are seen to support it. If they do not, you may have to exclude them. If they are support-ive then you can use any existing consultative machinery as a means of communication.

Be prepared to commit the time and resources necessary for its successful introduction and to provide any necessary training.

RELOCATION

There is sometimes the need to relocate staff, for example because of plant closure, centralization or decentralization of operations, to reduce accommo-dation costs and so forth.

Where such relocation is within the same local area there may be few prob-lems, although you may need to consider reimbursing staff for any additional travelling costs for a certain period. However, where the relocation is to prem-ises that are some distance away, and there is no hard and fast rule for gauging whether such a relocation is significant, you will have to discuss the change with the staff affected, taking into account their domestic circumstances, and offer them a comprehensive relocation package. Such a package would typically include:

- reimbursement of all costs associated with moving, such as legal and estate agent's fees, survey fees, insurance and removal costs;
- reimbursement of indirect costs such as new carpets and curtains or telephone installations up to a fixed limit;
- assistance with arranging a mortgage;
- payment of any excess housing costs;
- payment of a disturbance allowance;
- reimbursement of any house-hunting costs.

There are a number of relocation agencies that can assist with such a move. Staff who are unwilling or unable to relocate are, in effect, redundant, and should be offered the appropriate redundancy package.

BUSINESS TRANSFERS

The Transfer of Undertakings (Protection of Employment) Regulations 2006

These Regulations have superseded the Transfer of Undertakings (Protection of Employment) Regulations 1981 (TUPE). They are critical if you are thinking of acquiring the whole or part of another business, or if you are the target of a takeover or merger. They apply to any situation where there is a transfer of business ownership and this can include not just the sale and purchase of businesses, but also contracting out, licensing, franchising, and granting of concessions.

The two broad categories are business transfers and service provision changes, although some transfers will be both a business transfer and a service provision change.

Where a business transfer takes place the key question is whether there is a transfer of a 'stable economic entity' that will retain its economic identity after the transfer.

To decide if there is a stable economic entity that is capable of being transferred you should consider the following factors:

- Is the type of business being conducted by the transferee (incoming business) the same as that of the transferor (outgoing business)?
- Has there been a transfer of tangible assets such as buildings and moveable property? (Not essential.)
- Have the majority of employees been taken over by the new employer?
- Have the customers been transferred?
- Is there a degree of similarity between the activities carried on before and after?

If the answer to all or several of the above questions is 'yes', it is safe to assume that there has been a transfer of a stable economic entity. The absence of a profit motive is not a determining factor.

A service provision change occurs when a client who engages a contractor to do work on its behalf is either:

- reassigning such a contract, or
- bringing the work 'in-house'.

It will not be a service provision change if:

- the contract is wholly or mainly for the supply of goods for the client's use, or
- activities are carried out in connection with a single specific event or a task of short-term duration.

The Regulations provide that where a business is transferred:

- the employment contracts of employees of the former employer (the transferor) are automatically transferred to the new employer (the transferee), as are any relevant collective agreements;
- all the transferor's rights, duties, liabilities and powers connected with the employees pass to the transferee;
- dismissal of any employee for a reason connected with the transfer is automatically unfair, unless it can be shown that the dismissal was for an economic, technical or organizational (ETO) reason entailing a change in the workforce;
- elected employee representatives or recognized trade unions have the right to be informed and in most cases consulted, prior to the transfer taking place.

This is a complex area of law that has not been made any easier by contradictory decisions arising from the various courts. The main difficulty concerns the meaning of what constitutes an economic entity and the stage at which an employee's link with the previous company can be said to have been broken, thus enabling the new employer to change terms and conditions. Most interpretations suggest that the Regulations only apply where there has been a significant transfer of assets or a major part of the workforce. The question appears to be whether the identity of the previous company has been taken over. The Regulations would not apply, for example, to a transfer arising from a change of share ownership. If you are contemplating such a takeover the safest course would be to assume that you will not be able to change the terms and conditions of employment, including pay, of the staff transferring. From 6 April 2006 transferors have been obliged to give the transferee written information about the employees who are to transfer and all the associated rights and obligations relating to them. This information includes the identity and age of the employees who will transfer, information contained in the employees' written particulars of employment and details of any claims that the transferor reasonably believes might be brought.

If the transferor does not provide this information, the transferee may apply to an employment tribunal for such amount as it considers just and equitable. Compensation starts at a minimum of £500 for each employee in respect of whom the information was not provided or was defective. Further information is available from www.acas.org.uk and www.berr.gov.uk. In view of the complexity of this area you should ensure that you obtain professional advice before making any final decisions.

Disclosure of information in the transfer of an undertaking

If you are proposing to transfer the ownership of your business to a third party or to take over another business, or to merge companies, you have a duty to inform and consult 'appropriate representatives' of any of the affected employees. These are employee representatives elected by the employees, or representatives of any recognized trade union. However, you must consult any recognized trade union.

You must let them know, well before any transfer takes place:

- the fact that a transfer is to take place;
- the approximate date of the transfer;
- the reasons for the transfer;
- the 'legal, economic and social implications' of the transfer for the affected employees;
- what actions you intend to take in relation to the employees (if no action is to be taken, they must be told of that fact).

If you are the transferor you must indicate what action the purchaser intends to take in relation to transferred staff. If the purchaser does not intend taking any action, you must notify the employees of that fact. If you are the purchaser you must give the transferor the information needed in sufficient time to be able to comply with this requirement.

You must undertake any consultation with a view to achieving an agreement. This means that you should enter full discussions to try to seek consensus about the way in which the transfer will be carried out and how it will affect employees. You must consider any representations made by appropriate representatives, reply to them and state the reasons for rejecting any of them.

In common with the consultation on redundancy, you can argue that there are special circumstances that make it not reasonably practicable to carry out consultation. However, you must take all reasonable steps to consult and the onus would be on you to prove that special circumstances prevented you from doing so. In practice, such circumstances are likely to have to be exceptional, for example where a transfer has to be kept secret to avoid commercially damaging the company.

FURTHER INFORMATION

Cushway B, and Lodge, D (1999) *Organizational Behaviour and Design*, 2nd edition, Kogan Page, London

Department of Trade and Industry (2006) Employment rights on the transfer of an undertaking: a guide to the 2006 TUPE Regulations for employees, employers and representatives. London: DTI. Available at: http://www.berr.gov.uk/files/file20761.pdf.

The Transfer of Undertakings (Protection of Employment) Regulations 2006 (2006) SI 2006/246. London: HMSO. Available at: http://www.opsi.gov.uk/si/si200602.htm.

12

Handling disciplinary issues

There will invariably be times when you have to take disciplinary action against staff, either because of their conduct or because of their work performance. This chapter describes what disciplinary rules should be applied, the procedure to be followed, and the actions you can take.

As an employer you have an obligation to set the required standards of behaviour and performance, to ensure that these are brought to the attention of employees and to inform them what will happen if these standards are not reached.

It is also a legal obligation under the Employment Rights Act 1996 and the Employment Act 2002 for any employer to include within the written statement of employment particulars (see Chapter 2) details of any disciplinary rules that apply to the individual (or where such rules can be found – for example, in a staff handbook), to whom any appeal against disciplinary action should be made, and the procedure for doing so. Finally, it is important for any employer to comply with the Statutory Dispute Resolution Procedures introduced from 1 October 2004 and described later in this chapter.

DISCIPLINARY RULES

Disciplinary rules govern the behaviour of employees in the workplace and help to make employees aware of the acts and omissions that might lead to disciplinary action. Once rules have been established it is important to ensure that they are applied fairly and consistently.

You should set out disciplinary rules that make it clear what standards of behaviour are required of your employees. You cannot hope to cover everything that might require disciplinary action, but you should have rules relating to:

- absence, including the rules relating to sickness absence and the arrangements for reporting absences;
- health and safety, including the requirements for the use of safety equipment, protective clothing, smoking, alcohol, health and hygiene, etc;
- gross misconduct, including the types of offence that the employer considers serious enough to warrant summary dismissal, ie instant dismissal without notice;
- use of company facilities and equipment, such as the extent to which employees can use the office telephone and e-mail facilities for personal reasons;
- discrimination, such as any rules describing what constitutes discriminatory behaviour or harassment;
- performance standards, such as any specific targets that might have been made as part of the job requirements;
- activities that are prohibited.

You must also ensure that, whatever rules are drawn up, employees are made aware of them and have easy access to them. They should be made particularly aware of the likely consequences of breaking the rules and particularly of actions or omissions that might constitute gross misconduct (see below).

Drawing up disciplinary rules

Disciplinary rules apply in any workplace and often these may have grown up through custom and practice and be passed on by word of mouth. However, this can lead to uncertainty and it is therefore preferable that they are written down as this makes it easier to ensure that employees are notified of them and to prove when any breaches have occurred. The aim of these rules is not to form the basis for disciplinary action but to ensure that such action is avoided in the first place.

enlightenHR Q&A

Tell me Alison, why 'enlightenHR'? – There are lots of small to medium sized businesses with hugely talented Directors focused on maximising business opportunities and revenues; constantly changing and often complex Employment Legislation isn't their primary focus and they often see it as a "dark art"! Our job is to enlighten and advise employers in a flexible and affordable way to ensure they avoid all pitfalls, some of which can be very costly, whilst achieving their business objectives.

What about your background, is it pure HR? – I actually grew up in the family hotel business, so small business is in my blood! I then spent the first half of my working career, 12 years, in business operational management, firstly with a major hospitality chain followed by a leading High Street retailer before progressing into HR management with a number of blue chip companies. This I believe enables me to see the bigger, business picture, not only from the people perspective.

Would you say you specialise in any particular areas? – Whilst we can and often do assist with virtually any and every HR and training issue, our primary work streams broadly encompass Employee Legislation/Relations and associated documentation, together with specialist coaching and training around all employment related concerns. Our website gives full details of these services.

What would you say are the principal challenges facing your consultancy today? – To continue to be considered as a true business partner in delivering appropriate, flexible and affordable HR solutions to our customers, whilst growing our client portfolio. We specialise in working for SMEs and have as clients organisations which employ from 5 to 250 employees in different sectors, some without any HR resource, some with an established HR team seeking specialist help or advice. I'm delighted to say that the quality and success of our work is reflected in the fact that almost all our new business comes via referral from satisfied customers.

What makes your service offering different, special perhaps? – Each of our specialist team members is a CIPD qualified and experienced HR professional, each one only handling a small select number of business owners or managers. That way they get to quickly develop a full understanding of all the business issues, as a true business partner and adviser, feeling very much a part of the team, able to give specialist help and advice when and where it is needed most. Some employment law advisers simply tell you the law and leave it there. We not only know the law, we use our knowledge to deliver the total solution for your business. We also provide an invaluable Support and Advice Line between 8am and 8pm six days a week available on annual subscription.

So, Alison, in summary? – Being on the wrong side of Employment Law can be very damaging in more ways than pure cost, think of the organisation's reputation – both internally and externally – for example. So don't be in the dark and struggle, let us enlighten you and give you peace of mind.

Alison Benney, Director of enlightenHR was talking to Paul Stokes, Regional Director of Versutus Recruitment Communications.

When drawing up a set of rules you should follow the following principles:

- Ensure that the rules are written down and that employees are made fully aware of them. It is important to be able to demonstrate that a breach of the rules has occurred, especially if the result is disciplinary action.
- Ensure that all rules are non-discriminatory and are applied equally regardless of sex, sexual orientation, marital status, race, religion, disability, age, etc.
- The rules should be readily available to all employees and managers should ensure that they are made aware of and understand them.
- An explanation of the rules should be given to all new employees as part of the induction process.
- Particular care should be taken to ensure that the rules are fully understood by employees with limited knowledge of English or who have little work experience.
- When it is intended to change a rule, to introduce a new one or to remove an old one, employees should be consulted in advance and notified of any agreed changes.

Gross misconduct

You should give examples of what the organization considers to be gross misconduct. This is misconduct that is considered to be so serious that it is likely to lead to summary dismissal, which is dismissal without any prior notice or warning.

Common examples of gross misconduct are:

- theft, fraud and deliberate falsification of records;
- fighting at work;
- serious bullying or harassment;
- wilful damage to the employer's property;
- misuse of an organization's property or name;
- bringing the employer into serious disrepute;
- drunkenness or drug abuse;
- serious breaches of health and safety rules;
- serious insubordination;
- serious breaches of confidentiality (excluding whistle-blowing under the Public Interest Disclosure Act, 1998).

You should state that the breach of any of these rules could render the employee liable to dismissal. This is preferable to stating that any breach *will* lead to dismissal as this could imply an element of pre-judgement.

While the above events would be regarded as gross misconduct in most companies, there may be other matters that should also be included for your own company. An increasingly common problem where employees have access to the internet is the downloading of pornography. This could be another area that the company might regard as gross misconduct. If so, employees' attention should be drawn to this fact.

You should make it clear that any list of examples of gross misconduct is for guidance and is not intended to be comprehensive.

Reviewing disciplinary rules

It is important that you review disciplinary rules periodically, especially in the light of changes to employment legislation or work practices to ensure that they continue to be relevant and effective. Any changes to the rules should only be introduced after giving reasonable notice to employees and, where necessary, consulting employees representatives.

You should also review disciplinary records to ensure that rules and procedures are being applied fairly and consistently and to identify any problems to be addressed. Managers and supervisors who are required to apply the disciplinary rules should be thoroughly trained in their application, the reasons for them and how to deal with any breaches.

DISCIPLINARY PROCEDURE

A disciplinary procedure describes how breaches of discipline will be dealt with. The ACAS Code of Practice describes the essential components of a fair disciplinary procedure. The Code states that the procedure should:

- be in writing;
- specify to whom it applies;
- be non-discriminatory;
- provide for matters to be dealt with without undue delay;
- provide for proceedings, witness statements and records to be kept confidential;

- indicate the disciplinary actions that may be taken;
- specify the levels of management that have the authority to take the various forms of disciplinary action;
- provide for an employee to be informed of complaints against him and to be given an opportunity to state his case before a decision is reached;
- provide an employee with the right to be accompanied by a trade union representative or fellow employee;
- ensure that, except for gross misconduct, no employee is dismissed for a first breach of discipline;
- ensure that disciplinary action is not taken until the case has been investigated;
- ensure that individuals are given an explanation for any penalty imposed;
- provide a right of appeal and specify the procedure to be followed.

Although the ACAS Code only recommends best practice and does not by itself have the power of statute, any failure by an employer to follow the Code would put him at a distinct disadvantage in the event of any case being brought against the company.

You should provide a copy of the disciplinary procedure to all employees, perhaps as part of the staff handbook. It is generally not considered a good idea to make the procedure part of the contract of employment because this would mean that any breach of it in dismissing an employee would be a breach of the contract, which might enable that employee to bring a claim of wrongful dismissal. However, the Employment Act 2002 makes the provision of a disciplinary procedure an implied term of the contract, so failure to provide one would be a breach of that implied term.

The general aim in any disciplinary process should be to try to avoid taking formal disciplinary action. This means that, as far as possible, matters of concern should be dealt with informally, with the employee being told what behaviour is unacceptable, or how his performance falls short of the standards required, and what he must do to remedy the position. No formal records should be kept of any informal warnings, although it is clearly sensible for any manager to keep a diary note as a reminder.

The original ACAS Code of Practice, superseded by the new one effective from 1 October 2004, recommended a staged disciplinary procedure with the first stage being a formal verbal warning followed by a first written warning, a final written warning and finally dismissal. Any of these stages could be omitted provided the offence was serious enough, so, for example, the employer could start the process with a written warning. Going straight to dismissal, however, would only be justified for offences constituting gross misconduct. The verbal, or oral, warning stage involved warning the employee verbally and then making a written file note of the warning. The new Code, however, omits completely the verbal or oral warning stage and the first stage of the formal procedure now becomes the written warning.

This means that you can still have a verbal warning stage in a disciplinary procedure, but as including it merely lengthens the formal process, there seems no point in doing so.

Another key difference between the new Code and the former one is that an employee now has to be informed *in writing* of the complaint against him.

To summarize, any disciplinary action must comprise three stages to be legally compliant. These stages comprise:

Step 1 – a letter setting out details of the aspects of the employee's behaviour that are causing concerns and inviting the employee to a meeting.
Step 2 – a meeting to discuss the issue and to enable a decision to be taken.
Step 3 – an appeal against any action taken.

Failure to follow these stages could result in a Tribunal increasing the compensation payable to an employee in any unfair dismissal case by up to 50 per cent.

Implications for small businesses

The ACAS Code recognizes that it may not be practicable in small organizations to adopt all the good practice guidance set out in the Code. It adds that employment tribunals will take account of employer's size and administrative resources when deciding if that employer has acted reasonably (the experience of some employers, however, is that this does not always happen in practice). Nevertheless, the Code recommends a number of core principles that should be followed by any employer. These are:

- Use procedures primarily to help and encourage employees to improve rather than just as a way of imposing a punishment.
- Inform the employee of the complaint against him, and provide him with an opportunity to state his case before decisions are reached.
- Allow employees to be accompanied at disciplinary meetings.
- Make sure that disciplinary action is not taken until the facts of the case have been established and that the action is reasonable in the circumstances.

- Never dismiss an employee for a first disciplinary offence, unless it is a case of gross misconduct.
- Give the employee a written explanation for any disciplinary action taken and make sure he knows what improvement is expected.
- Give the employee an opportunity to appeal.
- Deal with issues as thoroughly and promptly as possible.
- Act consistently.

An example of a disciplinary procedure based on the Code's recommendations is set out below.

Disciplinary procedure

The company recognizes that it is essential to maintain high standards of performance and behaviour. This procedure seeks to ensure fair treatment for anyone whose performance or conduct falls below those standards.

The procedure sets out the process to be followed when disciplinary action is taken. The procedure may be activated at any stage, except that the company will only proceed directly to Stage 3 – Dismissal in cases of gross misconduct.

It is our intention that wherever possible any shortcomings will be dealt with informally by your line manager and we will provide any assistance, advice or training required to achieve the necessary improvement.

General guidelines

1. You have the right to be accompanied by a colleague or a trade union representative at any meeting held under this procedure.
2. Except in more serious cases, the formal procedure will normally only be activated once the informal process has failed to achieve the desired results.
3. Any complaint will be thoroughly investigated under this procedure before any action is taken, and you will be notified in writing of the nature of any such complaint and will be given the opportunity to respond.
4. You will be fully informed of the stages of the procedure and the possible consequences, and of your right of appeal.
5. If dismissal (including dismissal on grounds of capability, conduct, redundancy, non-renewal of a fixed-term contract, or retirement) or other disciplinary action short of dismissal (excluding warnings under this procedure) is contemplated, you will be notified in writing of the basis for this.

Stage 1 – Written warning

If your conduct or performance does not improve following any informal warnings, or for more serious cases, you will be informed in writing of what you are alleged to have done and why this is not acceptable. You will be invited to a meeting with your line manager to discuss the position. Any allegations will be explained to you and you will have the opportunity to respond, to ask questions, present evidence, call witnesses and raise any points about information provided by witnesses.

Following this disciplinary meeting you will be sent a letter describing the outcome of the meeting. You will be asked to sign a copy of any warning letter to confirm your understanding of the content. The letter will clearly state what has to be done to remedy the position, a deadline date by which any improvements must be made, and the likely consequences of failure to achieve the desired results. A copy will be held on your personal file but this will be disregarded for disciplinary purposes after six months.

Stage 2 – Final written warning

If your conduct or performance does not improve following the written warning given at Stage 1, or for more serious cases, the company may have to consider issuing a final written warning. You will be invited in writing to a meeting with your line manager to discuss the position. Any allegations will be explained to you and you will have the opportunity to respond, to ask questions, present evidence, call witnesses and raise any points about information provided by witnesses.

Following this disciplinary meeting you will be sent a letter describing the outcome of the meeting. You will be asked to sign a copy of any warning letter to confirm your understanding of the content. The letter will clearly state what has to be done to remedy the position, a deadline date by which any improvements must be made, and the likely consequences of failure to achieve the desired results. A copy will be held on your personal file but will be disregarded for disciplinary purposes after 12 months.

Stage 3 – Dismissal

If your conduct or performance does not improve following the final written warning given at Stage 2, or for more serious cases, the company may have to consider dismissal. You will be invited in writing to a meeting with your line manager to discuss the position. Any allegations will be explained to you and you will have the opportunity to respond, to ask questions, present evidence, call witnesses and raise any points about information provided by witnesses.

Any decision to dismiss you must have the prior agreement of the Managing Director. The decision will be confirmed to you, together with details of the appeal process and the name of the person to whom any appeal should be made.

Summary dismissal

Where there has been gross misconduct the company may consider that summary dismissal may be the only reasonable option. Gross misconduct includes serious breaches of discipline such as striking another member of staff or a manager, theft or fraud, substance abuse in the workplace, etc. Summary dismissal is dismissal without notice, or pay in lieu of notice.

If the company has reasonable grounds for suspecting gross misconduct, you may be suspended on full pay for a period of up to five working days while the circumstances are investigated. This investigation will be conducted by a manager not previously involved and with no direct line management responsibility for you, to ensure impartiality. This investigation will include a meeting with you and any relevant witnesses. Following the initial investigation you will be asked to attend a meeting with the manager concerned, where the findings will be reviewed and a final conclusion reached. If the case of gross misconduct is upheld you will be summarily dismissed. The decision will be confirmed to you in writing and this letter will also give details of the appeal procedure.

Appeals against disciplinary action

1. You have the right to appeal against disciplinary action taken at any stage of this procedure.
2. You have the right to be accompanied by a colleague or trade union representative at any appeal hearing.
3. Any appeal against disciplinary action must be made in writing within two weeks of the disciplinary action.
4. An appeal against any disciplinary action or dismissal should be made to the Managing Director stating the grounds of your appeal. He will carry out a full review of the facts, which may include a further meeting with you and the relevant line manager. Following this review, he will reply in writing within five working days.

Applying disciplinary rules and procedures – general guidelines

There are a number of general guidelines you should follow when applying disciplinary rules and procedures. These are as follows:

- Make sure that any disciplinary rules are set out in writing and that copies are made available to all new employees.
- Ensure that any rules are clear and unambiguous and where there is any danger that they may be misunderstood they should be clearly explained to the employees affected.
- Disciplinary rules must be applied fairly and consistently and without discriminating against any particular employee group.

- Although it is important to be consistent when applying disciplinary rules, they should not be applied too rigidly, especially where observance in the past has been relatively lax.
- Where there is believed to have been a breach of the rules the circumstances in which this has occurred should be thoroughly investigated before any action is taken.
- Any written warning should make it very clear what improvement is required and the likely consequences if this does not occur. The wording should be specific and avoid vague injunctions.
- Employees should be clear about what constitutes gross misconduct.
- Bear in mind that warnings may sometimes be implied, for example by failing to give someone a pay rise, but where it is intended that this is part of the disciplinary procedure this should be made clear in writing and the employer is obliged to follow the full written process.
- No employee should be dismissed without the sanction of a senior manager.
- Ensure that all managers and supervisors responsible for the discipline of staff are trained in applying the disciplinary procedure and in conducting disciplinary investigations and hearings.
- Review procedures regularly to ensure that they still meet the needs of the company and are being applied fairly.
- Ensure that any disciplinary investigations are carried out as quickly as possible. Where it is decided that disciplinary action is justified, you do not have to be clear beyond any doubt about the employee's guilt but must act reasonably in the circumstances.
- Any employee subject to an investigation should be notified in writing of what he is accused of, be made aware of any evidence against him and be given a chance to explain.
- Employees have the right to be accompanied at any disciplinary meeting that might result in a disciplinary sanction.
- Any disciplinary procedure should provide a right of appeal to a more senior manager and set out the process for lodging the appeal.

The right to be accompanied

All employees have the right to be accompanied by a fellow employee or a trade union official at certain disciplinary or grievance hearings they are invited to by the employer. This right applies to any disciplinary meetings held as part of the statutory dismissal and disciplinary procedures or which could result in:

- a formal warning being issued to the employee;
- some other disciplinary action, including, for example, suspension without pay, demotion, dismissal, etc;
- the confirmation of a warning or other disciplinary action, such as at an appeal hearing.

This right to be accompanied does not apply to any informal discussions or counselling sessions, or meetings to investigate any incidents that could lead to a disciplinary hearing. If it becomes clear during any investigation or informal meeting that disciplinary action may be required, then the meeting should be discontinued and a hearing arranged at which the employee will have the right to be accompanied.

It is up to the employee to make a request to be accompanied, although the employer has an obligation to make the right known, and any request made must be reasonable. It would not be reasonable, for example, for an employee to ask to be accompanied by someone who might prejudice the discussions, or who might be based at a geographically remote location, when there is a suitably qualified person on-site.

Employees cannot generally ask to be accompanied by someone other than a fellow employee or trade union official, such as a legal representative, unless there is provision for this in the company's disciplinary procedure. The trade union official can be from any union, whether or not recognized by the employer, but should be appropriately trained in the role.

Any employee who agrees to accompany a colleague employed by the same employer is entitled to take a reasonable amount of paid time off to do so. The companion is allowed to address the hearing to put the employee's case, sum up the employee's case, and to respond on the employee's behalf to views expressed at the hearing. However, the companion has no right to answer questions on the employee's behalf if the employee does not wish this.

Investigating disciplinary complaints

When a disciplinary issue is raised you should thoroughly investigate the matter before taking any action. This includes making full enquiries into the circumstances and giving the employee an opportunity to provide an explanation. Following this investigation you should consider whether there is a case for taking disciplinary action, whether the matter can be dealt with informally, or whether there is no reason for any further action. In particular, you should consider:

- what the employee is alleged to have done or not done;
- the circumstances in which this took place;
- the consequences arising from this;
- the employee's job;
- the employee's age and length of service;
- the employee's past performance and disciplinary record;
- the evidence of any witnesses;
- any records or other information that can shed light on the situation;
- any changes that may have recently occurred in the job or working environment;
- if there have been previous incidents related to this one;
- whether the employee has received the appropriate counselling or training.

While it is accepted that you cannot hope to investigate every single aspect of allegations against an employee, it is critical that any such investigation is reasonable in the circumstances. What is reasonable depends on the facts of the case and clearly where an employee readily admits an offence, no further investigation may be necessary.

Having taken into account all of the above, you then need to consider whether:

- there is a case to answer;
- there is an alternative to disciplinary action, eg training or redeployment;
- the matter is serious enough to require a disciplinary hearing.

Who should conduct any investigation is clearly a critical consideration and ideally it should be a relatively senior manager who has had no direct involvement relating to the allegations. In a small company it may not always be easy to find such a person but it would still be expected that any investigation should at least be conducted impartially. The role of the manager carrying out the investigation is to assemble the facts and any supporting information, to decide whether there is a case to answer and then to notify the employee of the allegations. Depending on the nature of the alleged misconduct, there may be a need to interview other staff, and sometimes members of the public, to gather evidence. The decision about the next step to take will need to be decided on the balance of probabilities.

Holding a preliminary interview

Before taking any disciplinary action you will need to hold a meeting with the employee to discuss the allegations and to give him an opportunity to respond. Generally at such a meeting it is advisable to have more than one member of management present, so that there is a witness to anything that may be said, and it is also reasonable to allow the employee to be accompanied, although the statutory right only applies to disciplinary hearings, not to the preliminary investigation. You should make it clear that the meeting is to investigate the facts and that it is not a formal disciplinary hearing.

If new facts emerge during the meeting then it may be necessary to have an adjournment to investigate these. At the end of the meeting you should tell the employee what will happen next, which will usually be:

- no further action, or
- further consideration, or
- a disciplinary hearing.

If you decide to pursue the matter under the disciplinary procedure the employee then has the right to be notified in writing of the allegations against him.

Suspension with pay

For some more serious offences there may be a need to suspend the employee on full pay while the matter is investigated before taking any action. You should generally avoid this as it amounts to the imposition of a penalty before any disciplinary hearing has taken place. However, if you feel that such a sanction might be required then it should be provided for in the contract of employment. The company's disciplinary procedure should make it clear which level of manager has the authority to suspend an employee.

The situations in which you may have to suspend an employee include those where:

- the alleged offences are so serious that to allow the employee to remain at work might weaken your case for summary dismissal because of gross misconduct, if this is subsequently proven;
- the employee's continued presence at the workplace might undermine any effective investigation of the complaints made against him;

- attendance at the workplace by the employee might have a disruptive effect or might enable him to take actions to undermine the case against him, eg by removing records or files;
- the employee might be able to disrupt the business.

Any suspension for the above reasons should be described as 'precautionary' and it should be made clear that it is not a disciplinary sanction.

CONDUCTING A DISCIPLINARY HEARING

Preparing for a disciplinary hearing

To prepare for a disciplinary hearing you should:

- make sure that the circumstances have been fully investigated and that all the necessary facts and information are available at the hearing;
- arrange a suitable time, date and venue for the hearing;
- notify the employee concerned in writing of the precise nature of the complaint being made and of the arrangements for the hearing;
- notify any manager who may be required to attend of the arrangements for the hearing;
- inform the employee of his right to be accompanied by a fellow employee or a trade union representative;
- review the evidence being put forward and explore whether there are any other circumstances that might affect the position;
- ensure that the employee is notified in time to be able to prepare his case and to consult with any fellow employee or representative;
- where a trade union official is the subject of the disciplinary procedure, ensure that the relevant full-time trade union officer has been notified;
- ensure that all relevant information relating to the employee, including details of any previous disciplinary action, is available at the hearing;
- arrange for someone to take notes;
- if there are likely to be any communication difficulties, try to arrange for someone to be present who may be able to assist with these;
- where witnesses are being asked to attend ensure that they are aware of the arrangements for the hearing, or if they are unable to be present, get witness statements from them;
- ensure that the hearing is free from interruptions;
- ensure that some other manager is available to act as a witness.

An example of a letter asking an employee to attend a disciplinary hearing is set out below.

Example letter asking an employee to attend a disciplinary hearing

Dear ....

Disciplinary hearing

I have received a complaint from .... [insert name] that you .... [insert nature of complaint including dates and times of any alleged incident].

I have also been told that you made the following admissions: ....

To investigate this matter, a disciplinary hearing has been arranged in accordance with the company's disciplinary procedure. This will take place on .... [insert date] at .... [insert time] at .... [insert location] and you are required to attend, accompanied if you wish by your trade union representative or a colleague. Please let me know the name of any person who will be attending the hearing with you and the names of any witnesses you would like to be present. I will arrange for them to be released from their duties so that they can attend the hearing.

I have already arranged for the following persons to attend the hearing: .... [insert names].

Yours sincerely,

When conducting the disciplinary hearing you should adopt the following process:

- Introduce everyone present and state the reason for their attendance.
- Explain that the purpose of the hearing is to consider whether disciplinary action should be taken.
- Explain how the hearing will be conducted.
- State precisely the nature of the complaint and why the possibility of disciplinary action is being considered.
- Give the employee an opportunity to respond to the points made and to present any evidence on his behalf.
- Ensure that all the facts relating to the complaint emerge and that any special circumstances are noted.
- At the end of the hearing summarize the main points made by both parties and highlight any that may need to be checked further.

- If it is felt during the hearing that there is inadequate information to make a decision the hearing should be adjourned so that this can be checked.
- At the end of the hearing the employer's representatives should adjourn to consider their decision.
- Summarize the hearing's conclusions and ensure that the employee is clear about what is likely to happen next.

During the hearing:

- Both sides should be able to call witnesses.
- The employee and/or his representative must be able to ask questions of the manager presenting the employer's case and of any witnesses called by the manager.
- The manager must be able to ask questions of the employee and of any witnesses called by the employee.
- The employee and/or his representative can argue the employee's case.
- The arguments of both sides, including any pleas of mitigation, must be considered.

If it turns out that the employee has a satisfactory explanation then no further disciplinary action will be necessary. In all cases the burden of proof must be established 'on a balance of probabilities'.

If an employee refuses to attend a disciplinary hearing you can still hold it in his absence, provided he had been appropriately notified of it and has been told that the hearing will go ahead whether he attends or not. If, however, he is unable to attend because of absence through ill health, then you should postpone the meeting until he returns to work.

Any disciplinary hearing should comply with the rules of natural justice which, in essence, means that the accused person should know the nature of the accusation, should be given an opportunity to state his case, and the tribunal should act in good faith.

Notifying an employee of the result of a disciplinary hearing

Following a disciplinary hearing you should notify the employee in writing of:

- the result of the hearing;
- the reason for the decision taken;
- what specific improvement is required;

- the period over which such improvement must take place and how it will be assessed;
- the likely consequences if the required improvement does not occur;
- his right of appeal and how any such appeal should be made.

Records

You should keep a record of any disciplinary hearings and actions, which should include:

- the nature of the breach of discipline;
- the employee's defence of mitigation;
- the action taken;
- the reasons for the action;
- whether an appeal was made;
- the outcome of any appeal and subsequent developments.

This information is usually kept on the individual's personal file and it is common practice for these to be removed after a certain period, eg 12 months, if the employee commits no further offences. If such a provision is included in the disciplinary procedure it is important for you to remember that you cannot then subsequently refer to any such incidents that are out of time. The ACAS Code recommends that such records are treated as confidential and are kept no longer than necessary in accordance with the Data Protection Act 1998.

You should give the employee a copy of any notes held, although it would be legitimate to withhold information in certain cases, eg to protect a witness.

TAKING DISCIPLINARY ACTION

Generally, following a disciplinary hearing you will have three main options:

1. to drop the matter because there is no case to answer, or
2. to provide counselling or training which might help to resolve the matter, or
3. to take disciplinary action.

Before deciding what disciplinary action to take you should consider whether:

- there has been as much investigation as may be considered reasonable in the circumstances;
- the company has followed the requirements of its disciplinary procedure;
- sufficient account has been taken of any explanations given by the employee;
- you have a genuine belief in the guilt of the employee;
- on the balance of probabilities, it is more likely than not that the employee is guilty of the misconduct complained of;
- the misconduct is serious enough to warrant the disciplinary action being considered;
- any mitigating circumstances have been taken into account;
- the disciplinary sanction being considered is within the band of reasonable responses open to you.

You should also take into account the employee's employment and disciplinary record and the disciplinary action taken in any previous similar cases.

Disciplinary warnings

Once it has been decided that disciplinary action is necessary you will need to decide what type of action is appropriate. Generally, a staged approach should be adopted, as follows:

1. The first step should be an informal warning, or warnings, from the individual's line manager or supervisor. This is not part of the formal procedure and no record should be kept.
2. If the informal warning has no effect, or if the misconduct is more serious, you may need to give a formal warning, which is the first stage of the formal procedure. In this case, instead of just telling the employee about the improvements required you will need to put in writing the nature of the complaint, what needs to be done to remedy the situation, the timescale for improvement and the likely consequences of no such improvement taking place.
3. If the formal written warning has no effect, or you consider the misconduct to be sufficiently serious, you may need to issue a final written warning specifying that any further breaches will result in dismissal. For serious misconduct you may wish to proceed straight to this stage.

4.   If none of the previous steps has any effect you may need to proceed to the final stage of dismissal.

Although following the stages recommended above should help to ensure that you have handled the issue fairly, it does not necessarily mean that you have to go through all these stages for every offence. For more serious offences you may leapfrog a number of stages, and for gross misconduct you can go to the final stage immediately. The key test is what is reasonable in the circumstances.

Examples of written warning letters are set out below.

Example of a first written warning to an employee for unsatisfactory performance

Dear ....

This letter is to confirm the outcome of our meeting on .... [insert date] when you were told that your work performance was not satisfactory in the following respects .... [insert details of unsatisfactory work performance].

You were told at that meeting that to remedy the situation you must take the following actions: .... [describe actions to be taken].

You are expected to reach the standard of performance described above by .... [insert date], when the position will be reviewed. However, your performance will continue to be monitored until that date and we expect to see an improvement before that deadline.

If you do not reach the standard required by the date stated, further disciplinary action is likely to be taken under the company's disciplinary procedure.

In the meantime, the company will provide all necessary training and support to help you achieve the standard required, and you should ensure that you let me know of any support you feel you require.

Please let me know if you wish to appeal against this decision or if you wish to discuss any aspect of this letter.

Finally, please sign the enclosed copy of this warning and return it to me as acknowledgement of receipt.

Yours sincerely,

Example of a first written warning to an employee for misconduct

Dear ....

This letter is to confirm the outcome of our meeting on .... [insert date] when we discussed the complaint about your conduct.

You were told that, following a thorough investigation, the company had found that .... [insert details of complaint].

You are warned that any repetition of this misconduct, or similar misconduct, will result in further disciplinary action under the company's disciplinary procedure.

Please let me know if you wish to appeal against this decision or if you wish to discuss any aspect of this letter.

Finally, please sign the enclosed copy of this warning and return it to me as acknowledgement of receipt.

Yours sincerely,

Example of a final written warning to an employee

Dear ....

I write to confirm the outcome of our discussion on .... [insert date].

As you are aware, over the past .... [months/weeks] you have failed to meet the standards required by the company in the following respects: .... [list ways in which performance or conduct have fallen short of the required standard].

As discussed with you, we have agreed to give you until .... [insert date] to meet the standards required. This means that you are required to take the following actions by that date: .... [describe actions required].

I must warn you that, in view of previous warnings you have been given, if you fail to meet the standards required as described above by the above date, you will be dismissed.

Please let me know if you wish to appeal against this decision or if you wish to discuss any aspect of this letter.

In meantime, would you please sign the enclosed copy and return it to me as acknowledgement of receipt.

Yours sincerely,

Other disciplinary sanctions

Other sanctions you could consider include transferring the employee to another job, demotion, non-payment of increments or bonuses, etc. However, you need to be aware that any such sanction could be a breach of the employment contract unless specifically provided for in the contract. Withholding pay or bonuses, or imposing any penalty in which the employee suffers a financial loss, could result in action by the employee under the Employment Rights Act 1996 to recover any such loss, or possibly the employee resigning and pursuing a case for constructive dismissal. This is, in effect, a unilateral repudiation of the contract by the employer.

Dismissal

The ultimate sanction is dismissal. Usually this should be with the appropriate notice, but for gross misconduct you may dismiss without giving notice or pay in lieu of notice.

SPECIFIC DISCIPLINARY SITUATIONS

Failure to comply with a reasonable instruction

It is an implied term of an employee's contract that he will follow the reasonable instructions of an employer and you would therefore be justified in taking disciplinary action against anyone who failed to do so. The situation becomes more complicated if you wish to change an employee's duties or working pattern for business reasons. Although you may have no automatic contractual right to insist on any such change, if there are compelling business reasons for doing so, you may be within your rights to ask an employee to work under the new arrangements and to take disciplinary action if he fails to do so. The ultimate test is what is reasonable in the circumstances. Ideally, any such changes should be through discussion and agreement.

Breach of disciplinary rules

Disciplinary and work rules should be made known to all employees and it is completely legitimate for you to state that any breach of a particular rule could render the employee liable to dismissal. As stated earlier it is inadvisable to state that dismissal will be automatic, as this implies that the matter has been prejudged and that no account would be taken of any mitigating circumstances.

When considering disciplinary action for breach of any rules it is important to ensure that there is consistency. For example, if a rule has previously been ignored, it is likely to be unfair to make an example of a person by applying a disciplinary sanction automatically and without first drawing the attention of employees to the need to follow the rule in question.

Breach of health and safety regulations

Provided you take all necessary steps to alert employees to health and safety requirements, such as by placing appropriate notices near dangerous machinery, any disciplinary action for breach of health and safety rules is likely to be fair. It is important, however, that you carry out a full investigation of any alleged breach, that the employee is informed of any allegation against him and is given an opportunity to explain, and that any penalty is reasonable in the circumstances.

Drunkenness at work

Although drunkenness at work often crops up as an example of what consti-tutes gross misconduct, whether it is or not depends on the circumstances of the case. There are a number of factors that have to be taken into account, including for example:

- the nature of the work carried out and the degree of risk to the employee, his colleagues and others;
- whether there is a specific rule relating to drinking;
- the position and responsibilities of the employee in the organization;
- the general attitude of the organization to drinking;
- the evidence that the employee is under the influence of alcohol;
- any explanation provided by the employee about his conduct.

A common reaction by an employee accused of drunkenness is that this occurred because he was ill or on medication at the time. If this proves to be correct, following investigation, then disciplinary action might not be appropriate.

You also need to consider whether this is an isolated incident or the symptom of an underlying medical problem. If it is the latter then it might require counselling and possibly longer-term medical treatment. Any instance of drunkenness needs to be investigated carefully, taking into account the nature of the work carried out by the individual, his age, length of service, previous disciplinary record, personal circumstances, general conduct, etc.

Where drunkenness results in threatening or abusive behaviour, then a disciplinary process should take into account that behaviour. In these circumstances, and also where the employee may be working in a potentially dangerous industrial environment, it is often necessary to send the employee home on suspension.

Fighting at work

Fighting at work is frequently described in disciplinary procedures as gross misconduct. However, whether or not it is specifically mentioned, fighting would generally be regarded as very serious misconduct. You would still have to carry out an investigation, consider all the facts, give the employees concerned the opportunity to respond and to explain their actions, and finally to take action that is considered reasonable in the circumstances.

Unsatisfactory attendance

Unsatisfactory attendance can include a range of different behaviours such as:

- failure to comply with absence reporting procedures;
- reporting the wrong reasons for absence;
- being absent without authorization;
- prolonging an authorized absence without good reason;
- working while on sick or compassionate leave;
- carrying out other activities, eg participating in sports while on sick leave;
- being absent frequently, even though for genuine reasons;
- persistent lateness or generally poor time-keeping.

The procedure for dealing with an unacceptably high level of absence is set out in Chapter 6.

It is sometimes the case that an employee tries to avoid a disciplinary meeting by claiming sickness. In these circumstances you should usually rearrange the meeting to accommodate this sickness absence, but should notify the employee that the rearranged hearing will go ahead anyway on the new date whether or not the employee can attend, and that the employee can put forward his case through a representative, or in writing, if he is unable to attend at the rescheduled time. Although it is difficult to be totally prescriptive about the actions to be taken, as this will depend on the circumstances, you cannot be expected to keep postponing hearings until the employee is available.

Unsatisfactory performance

Disciplinary action will normally be taken because of misconduct or capability, such as failing to conform to the required standards. If you are considering taking disciplinary action because of the employee's poor performance, you should ensure that:

- the employee has been given all necessary training and instructions about the work;
- an explanation has been given of the standards required;
- the employee has been made aware of any shortcomings;
- the consequence of failing to meet the required standards has been explained;
- there is clear evidence of failure to achieve the standards required.

Before taking any disciplinary action for poor performance you must ensure that the employee has been given all necessary training and counselling and has been given an opportunity to improve. Of course, where the consequences of an error are extremely serious, there may be a need instead to take immediate action.

Criminal proceedings

If an employee has been found guilty of a criminal offence outside work and which bears no direct relationship to his work in the company, you should not treat this as an automatic reason for dismissal. There is a need to consider the impact on his work and the company before taking any decision. Equally, if a criminal case is pending, there is no reason for you to wait for the outcome before making a decision. The issue is not whether the employee is guilty of the offence he is charged with, but whether you, the employer, acted reasonably in the circumstances. This means that if you dismissed the employee in the belief that he was going to be convicted, even if no conviction resulted, a dismissal would be fair if this was considered to be a reasonable response in the circumstances.

APPEALS AGAINST DISCIPLINARY ACTION

You are legally required to provide a procedure that enables employees to appeal against any disciplinary action. The procedure should:

- specify time limits for lodging and hearing the appeal;
- provide for the appeal to be dealt with swiftly;
- if possible, provide for the appeal to be heard by a more senior manager not previously involved in the process;
- notify the appellant of the arrangements for the hearing and of his right to be accompanied;
- describe what will happen during the appeal hearing;
- give the employee an opportunity to comment on any new evidence arising before the appeal hearing.

You should write to the employee with the results of the appeal and the reason for the decision as soon as possible after the hearing.

Those hearing the appeal should consider the following questions:

- Has there been a sufficient investigation to establish the facts?
- Has the organization's own disciplinary procedure been correctly followed?
- Was the employee given sufficient information about the allegations against him?
- Was the employee given sufficient opportunity to respond to those allegations?
- Has sufficient attention being given to explanations put forward by the employee?
- Do they genuinely believe that the employee has committed the alleged misconduct?
- Can this belief be sustained on the balance of probabilities?
- Is the misconduct sufficient to justify the disciplinary penalty imposed?
- Have all mitigating circumstances being considered?
- Is the penalty imposed reasonable?

If the managers hearing the appeal can satisfy themselves on all the above issues, this will prove a strong response to any case brought against the company by the employee.

In small companies it may not be possible to find a manager who has not been previously involved, in which case the person or persons hearing the appeal should try to be as neutral as possible, or the organization could consider appointing an external arbitrator, which should be included in any agreed procedure.

FURTHER INFORMATION

ACAS Code of Practice on Disciplinary and Grievance Procedures, 2004
Employment Act 2002
Employment Rights Act 1996
Essential Facts – Employment (2006) Gee Publishing Ltd, London

13

Dealing with grievances

GRIEVANCE PROCEDURE

As an employer you have a legal obligation under the Employment Rights Act 1996 to provide, in the written statement of terms and conditions of employment, details of the person to whom any employee who has a grievance should apply. A grievance procedure sets out how such an application should be made and how it will be dealt with.

Principles

The procedure should aim to settle the grievance as quickly, fairly and as near to the point of origin as possible. In practice this means that the issue should, more often than not, be settled by the employee's immediate supervisor or line manager. However, the procedure should describe what will happen if the grievance cannot be resolved at this level. Any such procedure should:

- be in writing;
- be made known to all employees;
- allow for the employee to be accompanied by a fellow employee or trade union representative, if desired;
- ensure a speedy resolution of the problem.

An example of a grievance procedure is set out below.

Example grievance procedure

Principles

1. The company realizes that there will be occasions when our employees may wish to raise formally issues or complaints about the company or other employees. While we would hope that in most cases these could be resolved informally, we will try to deal speedily and effectively with any that remain unresolved, through the following procedure.
2. This procedure applies to all employees, but does not confer any contractual rights.
3. Any employee pursuing a grievance should continue to work normally while the grievance is being investigated. Generally the status quo will be maintained during this investigation, unless doing so could result in serious problems for the employee or the company.
4. You may be accompanied or represented by a fellow employee or a trade union representative at any stage of the procedure.
5. If your grievance relates to disciplinary action it should be raised under the company's disciplinary procedure.
6. Where a grievance is against your immediate supervisor or line manager, the matter should be raised with the next manager above that person.
7. In any collective disputes or grievances a spokesperson should be appointed to represent the group of employees affected.

Procedure

Stage 1

Any grievance should be raised initially with your immediate supervisor or line manager. The supervisor or manager should normally respond in writing within five working days.

Stage 2

If the matter is not resolved at Stage 1 or within five working days you should refer the grievance in writing to the next senior manager, who should normally arrange a meeting to consider it within five working days of your request. You should clearly set out the reason for referring the grievance to the second stage of the procedure.

Stage 3

If the matter still remains unresolved after Stage 2 you may refer the grievance in writing to .... [insert job title], who should normally arrange a meeting to consider it within 10 working days. You should clearly set out the reason for referring the grievance to the third stage of the procedure. The decision of the .... [insert job title] will be given in writing and will be final.

HANDLING A GRIEVANCE

In handling a grievance you should take the following actions:

- ensure that you are familiar with the procedure and that you apply it correctly;
- listen carefully to the points being made by the employee and try to gauge whether the specific grievance may be symptomatic of more deep-rooted problems;
- listen to any opposing points of view;
- having considered all the evidence, try to conclude whether there is an issue to be addressed;
- decide what action to take, trying to be fair to the individual, but without setting a precedent for the company;
- notify all those concerned of the decision reached, and of the appeal process;
- where a grievance has raised issues relating to policies, procedures or behaviour ensure that action is taken to remedy any problems.

It is common for employees who are being subjected to disciplinary action to raise a grievance as a sort of counterclaim. You should, as far as possible, treat the two issues separately, handling each under its respective procedure. If there is a disciplinary decision to dismiss the employee you should still ensure that you deal with any outstanding grievance.

Recent court cases have made it important that you consider any written complaint made by an employee as a potential grievance. If you receive any such complaint, even in a letter of resignation, you should ask the employee if he or she wants it treated as Stage 1 of the Grievance Procedure.

BULLYING AND HARASSMENT

Bullying and harassment in the workplace are serious matters for the employer and you should immediately investigate any such claims made by your employees. There are complexities in investigating these kinds of issue because there is a need to consider when what might be described as a 'robust management style', such as that demonstrated by certain television chefs, tips over into overt bullying.

The BERR states that bullying includes:

- offensive or insulting behaviour by another employee which makes an individual feel threatened, or taken advantage of;
- Humiliation of an employee, but not necessarily on the grounds of age, sex, race, disability, sexual orientation, religion or other belief;
- Less obvious ways of making an employee feel frightened or demoralized.

The kinds of actions that are usually described as bullying include where the individual is:

- constantly picked on;
- humiliated in front of colleagues;
- regularly unfairly treated;
- physically or verbally abused;
- blamed for problems caused by others;
- given too much to do so that failure is inevitable;
- regularly threatened with dismissal;
- unfairly passed over for promotion or training opportunities;
- subject to inconsistent changes in working conditions and duties;
- excluded from social events;
- subject to malicious rumours and gossip.

Harassment occurs where:

- There is unwanted conduct in any of the protected areas covered by anti-discrimination law – sex, sexual orientation, race, religion or belief, age, or disability.
- It has the purpose or effect of violating the dignity of an individual.
- It creates an intimidating, hostile, degrading, humiliating or offensive atmosphere.

Examples of harassment include:

- embarrassing or otherwise offensive jokes;
- unwelcome physical contact or sexual advances;
- racial or sexual abuse or abuse relating to sexual orientation, religion or other belief, age, or disability.

One of the main problems in dealing with claims of harassment and/or bullying is that such claims might be malicious, and they are frequently used as a defence mechanism when an employer seeks to discipline or dimiss an employee. However, you must thoroughly investigate any such claim and should:

- if possible use an impartial, trained investigator;
- consider suspension of the alleged bully or harasser on full pay;
- allow both parties to be accompanied to a hearing by a colleague or trade union officer;
- make it clear that both parties have the right of appeal.

When you are dealing with a case of bullying or harassment, decide carefully what action you are going to take. This could range from counselling or training to a disciplinary penalty. Such penalties can include a written warning, suspension, transfer or dismissal of the bully, harasser or malicious claimant. Where bullying or harassment are found to have occurred, make sure that the solution does not penalise the victim.

One of the ways of preventing bullying or harassment is to have a bullying and harassment policy that is widely publicised among staff and managers. An example of a policy of this kind is set out in Chapter 9.

APPEALS AGAINST GRADING

You should have a separate appeal process for appeals against grading, especially where a job evaluation scheme is used. Such a procedure might need to provide for the re-evaluation of a job by a different job evaluation panel if such panels are used to establish job sizes.

FURTHER INFORMATION

Essential Facts – Employment (2006) Gee Publishing Ltd, London
Personnel Manager's Factbook (2001) Gee Publishing Ltd, London

14

Terminating employment

There are various ways that the employment relationship can come to an end, the most common being that the employee resigns, or retires, or is dismissed. It is critical to distinguish between a voluntary resignation and a dismissal because it is only if there has been a dismissal that an employee can pursue a claim for unfair or wrongful dismissal, or redundancy.

MEANING OF DISMISSAL

A dismissal occurs when:

- the contract is ended by the employer with or without notice;
- a fixed-term contract expires without being renewed;
- the employee ends the contract with or without notice and is entitled to do so because of the employer's unreasonable conduct (known as 'constructive dismissal').

DISMISSAL WITH NOTICE

When you dismiss someone that person is entitled either to the period of notice set out in the contract of employment, or to the statutory minimum period of notice set out in the Employment Rights Act 1996, whichever is the more favourable.

The statutory periods of notice are:

- less than one month's employment – no statutory entitlement;
- one month' to two years' employment – one week;
- two years' to 12 years' employment – one week for each complete year of employment;
- twelve years' employment or more – 12 weeks.

For senior staff the contractual periods of notice are very often much longer than the statutory rights to notice, six months to one year being typical for directors.

An exception to these notice provisions is any employee engaged for a specific task that is not expected to last more than three months, unless he has continuous employment that takes over that limit.

When you give notice it should be in writing and should clearly state the last day of employment.

NOTICE BY THE EMPLOYEE

An employee is legally required to give you one week's notice after one month's service, but this does not increase with length of service, unless provided for in the contract. Subject to this statutory minimum, notice is otherwise that which is set out in the contract of employment.

While you have the right to insist that the employee give you the full notice set out in the contract, in writing if required, the only recourse open to you if he fails to do so is to sue for breach of contract. This may not be a practical solution as you would need to establish that the business had been damaged in some way. What you cannot do, however, is to withhold pay for all or part of the notice period, as this would be an illegal deduction.

COUNTER NOTICE

If an employee is dismissed with notice but gives counter notice, indicating a leaving date earlier than that proposed by you, the original notice will still stand and the employee will be treated as having been dismissed by you.

WITHDRAWING NOTICE

Sometimes an employee, having resigned, has second thoughts and seeks to withdraw his notice. However, once the notice has been given you are under no obligation to allow the employee to withdraw it.

PAY DURING NOTICE

You will normally have to pay an employee full salary during any notice period (subject to deduction of any sick pay, statutory sick pay, or any maternity pay being received), regardless of whether it is you or the employee who gives notice.

An exception to this is where the contract of employment provides for a notice period that is at least one week longer than the statutory notice to which the employee is entitled. For example, an employee with two years' service is entitled to two weeks' statutory notice, but if the contract gives one month's notice, then there is no legal obligation to pay the full salary during the notice period, unless the contract gives a specific right to the entitlement.

However, it is unlikely that you will be able to use the above provision to avoid paying salary during the notice period because it would generally be assumed by any court that an entitlement to notice in the contract means paid notice, even where this is not specifically stated.

PAY IN LIEU OF NOTICE

It is common practice, when an employee leaves, for the employer not to require that person to work his full notice period but to give pay in lieu of notice. As the employee has a contractual right to work during the notice period you should ensure that a clause giving you the option of payment in lieu of notice is inserted into the employment contract. You should also include any conditions attaching to the notice period. For example, you may not wish the employee to come into the office because of the danger of gaining access to commercially sensitive information. Conditions of this kind are generally known as 'garden leave' clauses.

OTHER PAYMENTS ON TERMINATION OF EMPLOYMENT

When an employee leaves the company the payments you will normally have to make are:

- any outstanding pay up to the last day of employment;
- payment for any holiday not taken;
- any outstanding bonuses to which the employee is entitled;
- any statutory sick pay (SSP) the employee is entitled to up to the last day of employment;
- any statutory maternity pay (or statutory paternity pay) to which the employee is entitled;
- a refund of pension contributions.

You may sometimes also wish to make an ex gratia payment, commonly known as a 'golden handshake', but this is entirely optional. Sometimes these are made subject to the employee agreeing to sign a compromise agreement. If the employee was dismissed because of redundancy there might also be an entitlement to redundancy pay.

The employee has the right to retain all benefits during the notice period but these can be bought out by agreement.

TERMINATION WITHOUT NOTICE

There may be occasions when you have to dismiss an employee without giving the full notice entitlement. This usually arises when there has been gross misconduct by the employee or where continued employment might pose a serious risk to others. In these circumstances the employee would not be entitled to any pay in lieu of notice.

Before taking such drastic action you should:

- investigate the circumstances;
- interview the employee concerned and any others who can shed light on the situation;
- notify the employee of the charge being brought against him;
- give the employee an opportunity to state his case.

If, having heard all the facts, you consider that:

- you have reasonable grounds for concluding that the employee committed the offence in question, and
- this falls within the definition of what you would regard as gross misconduct, and
- there are no mitigating circumstances,

then you can dismiss with immediate effect.

You should then send a letter confirming your decision (and giving a right of appeal).

The key points to bear in mind are whether it is reasonable to conclude that the incident in question amounts to gross misconduct and whether dismissal is the appropriate sanction in the circumstances.

Apart from dismissal for gross misconduct, termination of employment without notice is likely to be a breach of the employment contract that could allow the employee to bring a claim of wrongful (as opposed to 'unfair') dismissal.

WRITTEN REASON FOR DISMISSAL

You should provide a written reason for dismissal, although you are not legally required to do so unless the dismissed employee asks for one and had been continuously employed for at least one year.

DATE OF TERMINATION OF EMPLOYMENT

The actual date of termination of employment is important because this affects the employee's length of service and consequent entitlement to various employment rights.

Where notice has been given, the termination date will be the last day of the notice period. So, for example, if an employee has 10 months' service and is given three months' notice, this would bring the total length of service to over one year, thereby giving that person the right to bring an unfair dismissal claim if he wished to do so.

Where employment is terminated without notice, the termination date is the date on which the employee is told of the dismissal.

AVOIDING UNFAIR DISMISSAL

For a dismissal to be fair it must be for one of six reasons, and your decision to dismiss the employee for one of those reasons must have been reasonable in the circumstances. The six potentially fair reasons for dismissing an employee are:

- a lack of capability or qualifications for carrying out the work required;
- unsatisfactory conduct;
- redundancy;
- where continued employment would break the law;
- some other substantial reason;
- retirement.

In dismissing an employee for any one of the above reasons you must also ensure that:

- you follow the statutory disputes procedure;
- you follow your own disciplinary procedure, where applicable;
- except in the case of gross misconduct, the employee has been given an opportunity to improve;
- in the case of misconduct the employee has been given the opportunity to explain the behaviour complained of;
- any appeal by the employee has been heard.

A potentially fair reason for dismissal is retirement. For this to be fair, retirement must be at the contractually agreed age and you must follow the procedure set out later in this chapter.

Automatically unfair dismissal

Some reasons for dismissal are considered to be automatically unfair. These are decisions where the main reason is because of:

- pregnancy, or the taking of parental, paternity or adoption leave or time off for dependants;
- trade union membership or activities, or non-membership;
- the employee requesting a flexible working arrangement;
- the employee trying to exercise or exercising the right to be accompanied at a disciplinary or grievance hearing;

- statutory dismissal and disciplinary procedures not having been followed;
- reasons relating to jury service;
- reasons relating to the Information and Consultation of Employees Regulations 2004 for undertakings with 100 or more employees;
- failure to give correct notification of the right to continue working beyond the normal retirement age;
- the employee's duties as an employee representative in relation to redundancy consultation, business transfer or the Working Time Regulations 1998 or the Maternity and Parental Leave Regulations 1999;
- the employee's duties as a safety representative;
- an employee leaving the workplace because of some serious or imminent danger;
- an employee's responsibilities as a trustee of an occupational pension scheme;
- a protected or opting-out shop or betting office worker refusing to work on a Sunday;
- a shop or betting office worker giving or proposing to give an opting-out notice;
- the assertion of certain statutory rights, for example in relation to payment of wages and notice periods;
- the employee asserting rights under the Working Time Regulations;
- the employee making a protected disclosure under the Public Interest Disclosure Act 1998 ('whistle-blowing');
- the employee enforcing or proposing to enforce entitlement to the National Minimum Wage.

In all of the above situations there is no qualifying period of employment and no upper age limit for claiming unfair dismissal. Other reasons that are likely to make the dismissal unfair are where it:

- was for a reason that is discriminatory in relation to sex, race, age or disability;
- was because a business transfer was the main reason;
- related to a spent conviction under the Rehabilitation of Offenders Act 1974 (see Chapter 1);
- occurred during the first 12 weeks of industrial action.

Compromise agreements

When terminating employment you can ask the employee to sign a compromise agreement that will prevent that person making a later claim to an employment tribunal. This will be legally binding provided that:

- the agreement is in writing;
- it relates to the particular complaint or dispute (which might give rise to proceedings);
- the employee has received legal advice from a relevant independent adviser;
- an insurance policy or professional indemnity covering the risk or claim is held by the independent adviser;
- the agreement states that it satisfies the conditions regulating compromise agreements under the Act relating to the complaint.

Compromise agreements can only be used in relation to claims that can be made under the Sex Discrimination Act 1975, the Race Relations Act 1976, the Disability Discrimination Act 1995, the Trade Union and Labour Relations Consolidation Act 1992 and the Employment Rights Act 1996 (which incorporates the Wages Act 1986).

WRONGFUL DISMISSAL

Wrongful dismissal arises when an employee has been dismissed in breach of the contract of employment. This could arise, for example, if you failed to follow the stages in a disciplinary procedure that was part of the employee's contract, or if you failed to give the employee the contractual notice to which he was entitled.

The significance of wrongful dismissal is that the employee can bring a claim to an employment tribunal or through the courts without having to have the one-year's continuous employment necessary for bringing a claim of unfair dismissal.

Damages can potentially be quite high in these cases but the employee would be expected to 'mitigate his loss' by finding a new job and this would be taken into account in assessing the amount payable.

CONSTRUCTIVE DISMISSAL

Constructive dismissal arises when the employee resigns but feels that he has no option but to do so because of the employer's unreasonable behaviour. Generally, for such a claim to succeed against you as an employer your behaviour would have to be so unreasonable as to fundamentally breach the contract. However, this requirement is likely to be slightly less stringent in business transfers.

To avoid potential claims for constructive dismissal you should therefore avoid actions that might be construed as destroying the employment relationship. The kinds of actions that might give rise to such claims include:

- lowering the employee's status through demotion or a pay reduction without good reason;
- displaying a lack of confidence or trust in a subordinate;
- undermining a manager's or supervisor's authority by cutting him out of the loop and dealing instead directly with his staff;
- failing to give contractually agreed pay and benefits;
- changing someone's job responsibilities without consulting him;
- changing someone's working environment by moving him to inadequate office accommodation.

TYPES OF DISMISSAL

You can dismiss employees on the grounds of:

- inability to do the job to the required standard;
- illness or injury leading to an unacceptably high level of absence;
- a lack of qualifications;
- misconduct;
- redundancy;
- where continued employment would break the law (for example, where a driver loses his driving licence);
- for some other substantial reason.

Dismissal for inability to perform to the required standard

If you are considering dismissing an employee because of his inability to achieve the work standards required you need first to satisfy yourself that the individual cannot perform to the required standard. In doing so you need to ask yourself the following questions:

- What is the standard of performance required?
- In what way does the employee fail to meet the standard?
- What evidence do you have to support your belief?
- Has the employee received all necessary training and instruction?
- Does the employee know what standard of performance is required?
- Has the employee been warned about his poor performance?
- Has the employee been given a sufficient opportunity to improve?
- Have you considered transferring the employee to other work or redesigning the job?
- Has the employee been given an opportunity to put his point of view?
- Having regard to all the circumstances is dismissal a reasonable option?

Before taking the decision to dismiss for poor performance you need to go through the following process:

- consider whether the employee's performance is reasonable in relation to the standards laid down for the job;
- consider whether there are any changes that could be made, or training that should be given, to improve performance;
- produce evidence in support of your contention that performance is not up to the required standard;
- discuss the matter with the employee, informally at first, stating what improvements are required and the likely consequences if they do not arise;
- if the informal discussion does not produce improvement then a formal written warning may be necessary, in which you should tell the employee of the standards required, the ways in which he has fallen short of these standards, what he needs to do to remedy the situation and the likely consequences of him not doing so;
- following the first written warning it may be appropriate to give a final written warning, which should emphasize that if no improvement is forthcoming the result might be dismissal;
- dismissal is the final step if nothing else works and provided you have given every opportunity for improvement.

The process is summarized in Figure 14.1.

An example of the kind of letter you may need to write when dismissing for an inability to perform the job to the required standard is set out below.

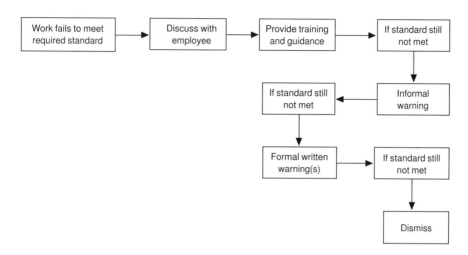

Figure 14.1   _Dismissal for poor performance_

Example letter terminating employment on grounds of capability

Dear .....

I write to confirm the outcome of our meeting on .... [insert date].

I regret that, because you are unable to carry out your work to the standard required by the company, we have no alternative but to terminate your employment with effect from .... [insert date].

As you know, we have made every effort to try and ensure that you met the standards required by providing all appropriate training and support, but without success. We have also looked into possible alternative employment in the company, but, as you know, there are currently no other jobs available appropriate to your skills and experience.

You are entitled to .... [insert notice entitlement] weeks' notice and [although you will not be required to attend work] you will continue to receive full pay and benefits during this period. You will also be entitled to any outstanding holiday pay up to your last day of service and I will arrange for these payments to be made to you as soon as possible.

If you disagree with this decision, or feel that you have been treated unfairly by the company, you have the right to appeal through the company's disciplinary procedure. If you wish to do so, please let me know by .... [insert date].

The company will be prepared to provide you with a fair and accurate reference.

I regret that we have had to take this step and would like to wish you every success in finding a new job.

Yours sincerely,

Absence through illness or injury

You need to exercise extra care when considering the dismissal of someone because of absence caused by illness or injury. It is quite legitimate to dismiss someone for such a reason if it is causing an unacceptable level of disruption to the business, but tribunals naturally tend to be more sympathetic to someone in this position than they might be to those dismissed for other reasons.

Long-term absence

The procedure to be followed in these cases is as follows:

- discuss the position with the employee to try to find out when he is likely to return to work;
- if there is some doubt about the date of return ask the employee if you could contact his doctor for an opinion about a likely return date;
- if the employee is unwilling for you to contact his doctor, or that doctor is unwilling to give an opinion, ask if the employee would be prepared to be examined by the company's medical adviser or other suitable specialist (see example letter below);
- if any medical opinion confirms that the employee is unlikely to return in the near future you will need to discuss the situation with him, indicating how long you would be prepared to keep the job open but making it clear that you might have to dismiss the employee if the absence continued beyond that date;
- consider whether there are any conditions inherent in the job that could have contributed to the employee's illness;
- if the employee is disabled consider if there are any reasonable adjustments that could be made to overcome the disability;
- consider whether there are other jobs in the company that the employee could carry out despite the illness or injury;
- ask yourself whether you have reached the point where you can no longer manage without the employee's job being carried out;
- if all options have been explored and you have no alternative to dismissal, you should give the employee notice (see example letter below).

The final step is to arrange for the appropriate termination payment to be made. Generally, the employee will be entitled to full pay during the notice period, even if his entitlement to sick pay or SSP has expired.

The process is summarized in Figure 14.2.

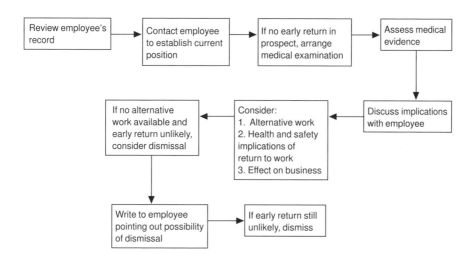

Figure 14.2 *Dismissal following long-term ill health*

Example letter to employee on long-term absence where termination of employment is being considered

Dear .....

I refer to my previous letter of .... [insert date] on this matter.

As you know, we have, with your permission, consulted your doctor about your illness and resulting absence from work, which has now been continuous since .... [insert date]. However, your doctor was unable to indicate when you might be able to return to work.

You will appreciate that we are unable to keep your job open indefinitely as this causes us operational difficulties. We therefore need to know whether you can give us a definite date when you are likely to return to work. If you feel that you are unable to return to your old job, but could carry out some other job in the company, could you please let us have your suggestions about any alternative job you feel would be suited to your skills and experience. We will give any such suggestion full consideration.

If you are unable to return to work in any capacity, we will reluctantly have to consider terminating your employment. However, before we take any final decision we would like you to have a medical examination, which we will pay for, so that we can obtain a second opinion.

If you do not agree to this medical examination, could you please let us know of any reasons why you consider that we should not take steps to terminate your employment.

I enclose a stamped, addressed envelope for your reply.

Yours sincerely,

Example letter terminating employment because of employee's long-term ill health

Dear .....

I'm sorry to hear that your health has not improved and that you will not, therefore, be able to return to your job as a .... [insert job title].

As you know, we have discussed this with you and although we have considered alternative work within the company, you are aware that we have been unable to find anything suitable.

We have also consulted our medical adviser about the likely prospect of a return to work, but he has confirmed that you are unlikely to be able to return to your job in the foreseeable future. In the circumstances, I regret that I have little choice but to give you notice in accordance with your contract of employment.

Your employment with the company will therefore cease on .... [insert date]. You will be entitled to payment for your notice period of .... [insert number of weeks] and we have also decided to pay you a further .... [insert number] weeks' pay, as an ex gratia payment in recognition of your past service with the company.

You will need to contact .... [insert name] to discuss any outstanding matters, such as your pension entitlement, and to get any other advice that you might require.

I am sorry that we have had to terminate your employment with the company and I hope that your health improves in the future. If it improves sufficiently for you to return to work at any time please do not hesitate to contact me.

Yours sincerely,

Frequent short-term absences

Frequent short unplanned absences can often be more disruptive than one long-term absence. Where such absences occur, and particularly where they follow a clear pattern, such as extra days being taken after bank holidays, you will need to take action that could lead to dismissal. What constitutes an unsatisfactory level of attendance is for you to decide.

When you have an employee whose absences have reached an unacceptable level you should take the following action:

- consider whether the absences are higher than those for comparable employees;
- consider the reasons for the absences and the employee's overall attendance record;
- discuss the absences with the employee, warn him that the attendance record is unacceptable, and tell him about the likely consequences if the record does not improve;

- consider whether there may be any factors in the job which could be contributing to the absences;
- give the employee an opportunity to improve;
- consider whether the problem could be resolved by changing the job, or by transferring the employee to other duties;
- if the position does not improve then you will have to issue a disciplinary warning;
- if the disciplinary warning has no effect, and you have followed your disciplinary procedure, then you may have no alternative but to dismiss the employee.

Dismissal for misconduct

There are a number of sanctions that might be appropriate in cases of misconduct. This depends on the seriousness of the misconduct. Some actions, such as lateness, for example, should be dealt with by giving the employee the appropriate warnings under the disciplinary procedure, with dismissal being the last resort if everything else has failed. In cases of serious misconduct you may instead go straight to a final written warning and, where this misconduct falls within the definition of gross misconduct, you may be justified in the summary dismissal of the individual concerned, ie dismissal without notice or payment in lieu of notice.

The kinds of actions that have been classified as gross misconduct are described in Chapter 12.

Before taking the step of dismissing someone you should:

- thoroughly investigate the circumstances;
- give the employee an opportunity to explain his conduct;
- consider the employee's previous record and particularly any prior disciplinary warnings;
- ensure that the employee had been made aware that the conduct in question could lead to dismissal, or that the conduct was such that any reasonable employee might expect dismissal to result from it (you cannot be expected to spell out every possible action that might be regarded as serious misconduct);
- consider whether, where appropriate, the employee had been given time to improve;
- ensure that you have followed the three-stage statutory procedure (see Chapter 12);
- ensure that you have followed your disciplinary procedure.

Finally, if all the above conditions have been complied with, and you have reasonable grounds for believing that the employee is guilty of the conduct complained of, and that dismissal is a reasonable response in the circumstances, then you may take action to dismiss the employee.

In taking this action the key points to bear in mind are that your action must be considered reasonable and it should be consistent with penalties that may have been imposed in the past for similar offences. You must also give the employee the right to appeal against the decision.

An example letter terminating employment for misconduct is set out below.

Example letter terminating employment on grounds of misconduct

Dear .....

I write to confirm the outcome of our meeting held on .... [insert date].

I regret that it has been decided to terminate your employment with effect from .... [insert date] for the following reason(s) .... [describe reason(s) for dismissal].

You are entitled to .... [insert notice entitlement] weeks' notice and you will continue to receive full pay and benefits during this period. You will also be entitled to any outstanding holiday pay up to your last day of service and I will arrange for these payments to be made to you as soon as possible.

If you disagree with this decision, or feel that you have been treated unfairly by the company, you have the right to appeal through the company's disciplinary procedure. If you wish to do so, please let me know by .... [insert date].

The company will be prepared to provide you with a fair and accurate reference.

I regret that we have had to take this step and would like to wish you every success in finding a new job.

Yours sincerely,

Redundancy

A redundancy occurs when you dismiss someone because your requirement for the work that person was doing has ceased or reduced in that location.

Avoiding redundancies

When faced with the prospect of making staff redundant your first step should always be to consider other possible options. These might include:

- putting a freeze on recruitment;
- bringing contracted-out work back into the company;

- reducing or removing overtime working;
- reducing working hours or asking staff to work part time, or share jobs;
- work reorganization, and so forth.

Selecting staff for redundancy

The first step in any redundancy programme is usually to ask for volunteers. The problem with this is that those who volunteer may not be the ones you wish to lose, and also employees might feel that by volunteering they might be undermining their future prospects with the company. However, a voluntary redundancy programme might help to reduce the overall number who may be subject to compulsory redundancy.

If compulsory redundancy is inevitable you will have to consider the selection criteria. In choosing the criteria you must ensure that they are objective and are not seen to be biased against any particular individual or group within the company.

Common redundancy criteria are:

- on the basis of performance – in which case you need to ensure that any decisions can be supported by concrete evidence, such as ratings in the company's performance appraisal scheme;
- attendance or disciplinary record – which again must be supported by accurate records.

A common approach in past years has been selection on the basis of age, eg selecting those over the age of 50. From October 2006 the Employee Equality (Age) Regulations 2006 have ruled out this approach. Whatever redundancy criteria are applied you must ensure that you do not select employees because of their sex, race, age, pregnancy, disability or for any reasons connected with trade union membership or carrying out duties as a safety representative. Also any selection made because the employee attempted to assert any of his legal rights is likely to be unfair.

An example letter of compulsory redundancy is set out below.

Example letter making an employee compulsorily redundant

Dear .....

I refer to our recent meeting when I indicated that because of a reduction in demand for the company's services I had to consider making your job redundant.

I regret that I now have to confirm that your job will become redundant with effect from .... [insert date].

We have fully discussed the possibility of you taking alternative employment with the company, but, as you know, there are at present no jobs available that are appropriate to your skills and experience. If this situation changes in the future we would be happy to re-employ you, should you still be available.

The redundancy payments you are entitled to are set out below:

- statutory redundancy pay: [. . . weeks × £ . . . per week] = £ . . . ;
- additional severance pay: [. . . weeks × £ . . . per week] = £ . . . ;
- pay in lieu of notice: [. . . weeks × £ . . . per week] = £ . . . ;
- outstanding holiday pay: [. . . weeks × £ . . . per week] = £ . . . .

The company secretary will write to you separately about your pension entitlement.

I would like to take this opportunity to thank you for your past service with the company and to wish you every success for the future. If you wish to appeal against this selection or if you would like to discuss any aspect of this letter please do not hesitate to contact me.

Yours sincerely,

The redundancy process

Consultation with trade unions and/or employee representatives

If you are proposing to make 20 or more employees redundant you are legally required to consult any trade unions and employee representatives about ways of avoiding or reducing the redundancies, and of ameliorating the consequences. You must tell them:

- the reasons for the redundancies;
- the numbers and descriptions of jobs it is proposed to make redundant;
- the total number of employees in the company or establishment where the redundancies are occurring;
- the method of carrying out the redundancies, including selection criteria;
- how redundancy pay will be calculated;

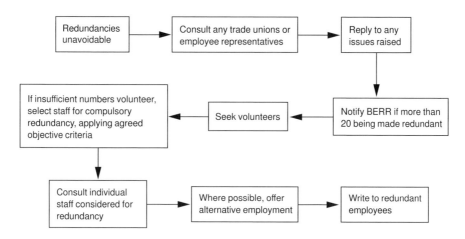

Figure 14.3 *The redundancy process*

- any proposals for reducing or avoiding the redundancies and for ameliorating the consequences.

There is also a strict timescale for consultation, depending on the numbers being made redundant, and if you intend to make 20 or more people redundant within 90 days or less you must also notify the Department for Business, Enterprise and Regulatory Reform (BERR).

The overall process is set out in Figure 14.3.

Following consultation with the employee representatives or trade unions you must also ensure that you consult with each individual that you propose to make redundant. You should indicate that you are considering making the employee's job redundant, explain the criteria to be used in selecting staff for redundancy, and give him the opportunity to put forward other options. You should consider these other options before making a final decision and make sure that you have set aside an appropriate length of time to do so.

Rights of redundant employees

Any employee made redundant has a right to:

- paid time off work to look for another job;
- redundancy pay if that person has completed at least two years' continuous service;
- the contractual or statutory notice period, or pay in lieu of notice;

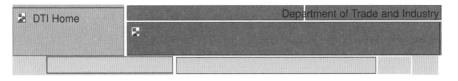

EMPLOYMENT LEGISLATION

Ready Reckoner for calculating the number of week's pay due

Read off your age and number of complete years' service. The table will then show how many weeks' pay you are entitled to. For the definition of a week's pay, see <u>Redundancy Payments</u>

Age	2	3	4	5	6	7	8	9	10	11	12	13	14	15	16	17	18	19	20
18*[1]	1																		
19	1	1½																	
20	1	1½	2																
21	1	1½	2	2½															
22	1	1½	2	2½	3														
23	1½	2	2½	3	3½	4													
24	2	2½	3	3½	4	4½	5												
25	2	3	3½	4	4½	5	5½	6											
26	2	3	4	4½	5	5½	6	6½	7										
27	2	3	4	5	5½	6	6½	7	7½	8									
28	2	3	4	5	6	6½	7	7½	8	8½	9								
29	2	3	4	5	6	7	7½	8	8½	9	9½	10							
30	2	3	4	5	6	7	8	8½	9	9½	10	10½	11						
31	2	3	4	5	6	7	8	9	9½	10	10½	11	11½	12					
32	2	3	4	5	6	7	8	9	10	10½	11	11½	12	12½	13				
33	2	3	4	5	6	7	8	9	10	11	11½	12	12½	13	13½	14			
34	2	3	4	5	6	7	8	9	10	11	12	12½	13	13½	14	14½	15		
35	2	3	4	5	6	7	8	9	10	11	12	13	13½	14	14½	15	15½	16	
36	2	3	4	5	6	7	8	9	10	11	12	13	14	14½	15	15½	16	16½	17
37	2	3	4	5	6	7	8	9	10	11	12	13	14	15	15½	16	16½	17	17½
38	2	3	4	5	6	7	8	9	10	11	12	13	14	15	16	16½	17	17½	18
39	2	3	4	5	6	7	8	9	10	11	12	13	14	15	16	17	17½	18	18½
40	2	3	4	5	6	7	8	9	10	11	12	13	14	15	16	17	18	18½	19
41	2	3	4	5	6	7	8	9	10	11	12	13	14	15	16	17	18	19	19½
42	2½	3½	4½	5½	6½	7½	8½	9½	10½	11½	12½	13½	14½	15½	16½	17½	18½	19½	20½
43	3	4	5	6	7	8	9	10	11	12	13	14	15	16	17	18	19	20	21
44	3	4½	5½	6½	7½	8½	9½	10½	11½	12½	13½	14½	15½	16½	17½	18½	19½	20½	21½
45	3	4½	6	7	8	9	10	11	12	13	14	15	16	17	18	19	20	21	22
46	3	4½	6	7½	8½	9½	10½	11½	12½	13½	14½	15½	16½	17½	18½	19½	20½	21½	22½
47	3	4½	6	7½	9	10	11	12	13	14	15	16	17	18	19	20	21	22	23

Figure 14.4 *Ready reckoner*

48	3	4½	6	7½	9	10½	11½	12½	13½	14½	15½	16½	17½	18½	19½	20½	21½	22½	23½
49	3	4½	6	7½	9	10½	12	13	14	15	16	17	18	19	20	21	22	23	24
50	3	4½	6	7½	9	10½	12	13½	14½	15½	16½	17½	18½	19½	20½	21½	22½	23½	24½
51	3	4½	6	7½	9	10½	12	13½	15	16	17	18	19	20	21	22	23	24	25
52	3	4½	6	7½	9	10½	12	13½	15	16½	17½	18½	19½	20½	21½	22½	23½	24½	25½
53	3	4½	6	7½	9	10½	12	13½	15	16½	18	19	20	21	22	23	24	25	26
54	3	4½	6	7½	9	10½	12	13½	15	16½	18	19½	20½	21½	22½	23½	24½	25½	26½
55	3	4½	6	7½	9	10½	12	13½	15	16½	18	19½	21	22	23	24	25	26	27
56	3	4½	6	7½	9	10½	12	13½	15	16½	18	19½	21	22½	23½	24½	25½	26½	27½
57	3	4½	6	7½	9	10½	12	13½	15	16½	18	19½	21	22½	24	25	26	27	28
58	3	4½	6	7½	9	10½	12	13½	15	16½	18	19½	21	22½	24	25½	26½	27½	28½
59	3	4½	6	7½	9	10½	12	13½	15	16½	18	19½	21	22½	24	25½	27	28	29
60	3	4½	6	7½	9	10½	12	13½	15	16½	18	19½	21	22½	24	25½	27	28½	29½
61*[2]	3	4½	6	7½	9	10½	12	13½	15	16½	18	19½	21	22½	24	25½	27	28½	30

18* [1] - It is possible that an individual could start to build up continuous service before age 16, but this is likely to be rare, and therefore we have started Table 2 from age 18.
61* [2] – The same figures should be used when calculating the redundancy payment for a person aged 61 and above.

Figure 14.4   *(Continued)*

- a four-week trial period (which can be extended by agreement) in a suitable alternative job without losing the right to redundancy pay if the job proves unsuitable – this can be ended by either party.

Redundancy pay is calculated on the basis of age and length of service as set out in Figure 14.4. The number of weeks' pay is multiplied by the current statutory rate, which is periodically reviewed. You should note that the upper age limit has been removed by the Employment Equality (Age) Regulations 2006 from 1 October 2006.

If you make an offer of alternative employment you should ensure that any such offer is made in writing. An example letter is set out below.

Example letter offering alternative employment

Dear .....

Following our recent discussion, I write to confirm that your previous job has become redundant with effect from .... [insert date] but that the company is able to offer you alternative employment as a .... [insert job title] from that date.

Your terms and conditions of employment will remain unchanged.

As explained to you, you have the right to a trial period of four weeks, beginning with the date you start the new job, for both you and the company to decide whether the job is a suitable one for you. If either party decides that the job is not suitable, this will not affect your entitlement to a redundancy payment.

I would be grateful if you would confirm your acceptance of this offer.

Yours sincerely,

Redundancy policy

You may wish to introduce a redundancy policy and an example is set out below.

Example redundancy policy

Introduction

The aim of this policy is to clarify what procedures will be followed in the event of redundancies becoming unavoidable in the company. Every effort will be made to ensure that redundancies will be avoided, but we have to accept that there could be circumstances beyond the company's control that could result in a reduced demand for our services.

Avoidance of redundancies

In the event of a reduction in demand serious enough to require a commensurate reduction in working hours, our first step will be to consider organizational ways of adjusting to the reduction. This will include:

- reducing costs where possible;
- cutting back on overtime;
- reducing the number of short-term temporary or agency staff;
- bringing work in-house, rather than using contractors, where this is possible;
- redesigning jobs and reorganizing work;

- asking for volunteers to work part time or job-share;
- considering any other proposals put forward.

If we are unable to achieve the required savings by reorganizing we would ask for volunteers for redundancy. However, the company reserves the right to refuse to agree to make someone redundant if it is not in our interests to do so.

Consultation

In the event of compulsory redundancies being unavoidable the company will consult trade union and employee representatives about:

- redundancies proposed;
- reasons for the proposals;
- number and descriptions of employees who it is proposed to make redundant;
- total number of employees of that type employed in the company;
- proposed method of selecting the employees for redundancy;
- how the redundancies will be carried out;
- how any redundancy payments will be calculated.

The consultation will be carried out for the purpose of considering ways of:

- avoiding the dismissals;
- reducing the number of employees to be dismissed; and
- mitigating the consequences of the dismissals.

In addition to any collective discussions, any individual employee whose job is considered for redundancy will also be consulted to consider alternative suggestions.

Selection of staff for redundancy

The criteria for the selection of staff to be made redundant will be discussed as part of the consultation process.

We will ensure that any criteria selected are fair and objective.

Any employee selected for redundancy will be notified in writing, following individual consultation.

Notice period

The employee's contractual or statutory period of notice, whichever is the greater, will apply.

Redundancy pay

Redundancy pay will be calculated in accordance with the relevant statutory provisions, which are based on the employee's age, length of continuous employment, and the current statutory weekly rate or the actual weekly wage.

Right of appeal

Any employee who feels that the selection criteria were unfair or incorrectly applied can appeal to the Managing Director. Any such appeal must be made in writing within 10 working days of receiving the redundancy notification. The Managing Director will arrange an interview within five days with the employee, who has the right to be accompanied by a trade union representative or colleague. The Managing Director will give a decision on the issue within 10 working days of the interview.

Time off to seek alternative employment

Any employee made redundant will be considered for other suitable jobs in the company. If no such jobs are available appropriate time off will be given to look for alternative employment.

Retirement

The retirement age should be made clear in the contract of employment and should be the same for men and women. You should write to the employee before the retirement date, reminding him of the date, giving the appropriate period of notice and notifying him that he has the right to request to work beyond that date. Where an employee requests such an extension you should arrange a meeting to discuss this and give the employee the right to appeal against your decision if the request is refused.

GIVING REFERENCES

You are not legally required to give a reference, although it is likely to be illegal if you withhold a reference for someone because of having previously taken legal action against you.

Any reference you do give must be fair and accurate, otherwise you could be liable to an action for defamation or negligence.

To avoid any possible legal action employers often opt to give a neutral reference, which merely states the facts about the job held by the employee but avoids any judgements about the employee's performance or personality.

Employees do not have an automatic right to see any reference you give, but under the Data Protection Act 1998 they do have access to any references given to you by another employer. However, you can refuse to give access if doing so would give information about another person who could be identified as the source of the information. Information about a third party cannot be disclosed unless that person has consented to the disclosure. Therefore, if you do not want a reference you give to be disclosed you should state that the reference is given in confidence.

The key points concerning references are:

- there is no legal obligation to provide a reference apart from jobs subject to FSA (Financial Services Authority) rules;
- most employers provide references for reasons of reciprocity and because not to do so could be to the detriment of the employee;
- when references are given it is important that they are accurate, as otherwise legal action could be taken against the giver; the recipient of an inaccurate reference could also have a claim for any loss incurred through acting on that reference;
- givers of references are not liable for any inaccurate statements if made in good faith;
- there are a number of ways in which the subject of a reference may gain access to it, and under the provisions of the Data Protection Act 1998 there is a right to such access – you should therefore work on the assumption that the reference may be seen by the person to whom it refers;
- you should be wary of giving a good reference to an unsatisfactory employee who is dismissed, as this could severely weaken your case if that person brings a charge of unfair dismissal; similarly, misleading a prospective employer could leave you open to a claim from that employer;
- references may be obtained in writing or by telephone, but a written note should be kept of any telephone reference.

EXIT INTERVIEWS

When an employee resigns you might find it useful to discuss the reasons for his departure. This may not only help to correct any perceived deficiencies, but can sometimes have the effect of persuading the employee not to leave, by addressing his concerns. The main drawback is that you cannot be sure that the reasons given for leaving are the true ones. Often, if an employee has decided to leave anyway he may see little point in criticizing the company or its management and possibly jeopardizing the content of any reference or future relationships.

Examples of the kinds of questions that you might want to ask at an exit interview are as follows:

- Why are you leaving the company?
- Which company are you going to?
- What sort of job are you going to do?
- What advantages does the new job offer over your old one?
- How will your reward package differ from your old one?
- Was your job with us what you expected?
- Could your qualifications, experience and skills have been better used?
- Did you receive all the support you required?
- Did you get all the training you needed?
- How did you view your prospects in the company?
- What did you think of the working environment?
- Are there any changes that we should make to our employment practices?
- Are there any other issues you think we should know about?

FURTHER INFORMATION

Data Protection Act 1998
Disability Discrimination Act 1995
Employment Rights Act 1996
Essential Facts – Employment (2001) Gee Publishing Ltd, London
Maternity and Parental Leave Regulations 1999
National Minimum Wage Regulations
Personnel Manager's Factbook (2001) Gee Publishing Ltd, London
Public Interest Disclosure Act 1998
Race Relations Act 1976
Rehabilitation of Offenders Act 1974
Sex Discrimination Act 1975
The Redundancy Payments Scheme – A guide for employees, employers and others, PL808, BERR
Trade Union and Labour Relations Consolidation Act 1992
Working Time Regulations 1998

15

Dealing with tribunal cases

The number of employment tribunal cases in 2006/07 was 132,500, an increase from 115,000 in 2005/06 (although much of this increase arose from multiple equal pay claims). There are a large number of employees who feel that they have nothing to lose by pursuing a tribunal case, and even where there is little chance of success at a tribunal, pressure can be brought to bear on the employer to settle before the hearing. Many are prepared to do so to avoid the time and effort involved in fighting a case, even where they feel that there is no justification for the claim. However, when deciding how to respond to a tribunal claim it should be remembered that only 12 per cent of claimants in 2006/07 were successful and the average award was £3,800 for unfair dismissal, with the median being £7,974.

The government has taken steps to try to reduce the number of employment tribunal claims by:

- asking ACAS to take a more active role in the arbitration of unfair dismissal cases, where both parties have voluntarily agreed to this approach;
- increasing the maximum deposit that can be asked for, following a pre-hearing review (see below), from £150 to £500;
- awarding costs where proceedings that have little prospect of success have been pursued;
- raising the maximum level of costs that can be awarded without a detailed assessment from £500 to £10,000.

The Employment Law team at Blake Lapthorn Tarlo Lyons have been listening to employers. What they told us is that they feel overwhelmed by the rising tide of employment legislation and are nervous about seeking legal advice and support because of the uncertainty of hourly rate costs.

So we have come up with the solution to make employers happy – a professionally delivered employment law support service charged at a fixed monthly rate for:

- advice and guidance on day-to-day employment law issues by telephone, email or in person from an employment solicitor at Blake Lapthorn Tarlo Lyons, one of the UK's leading law firms with an outstanding reputation in employment law

- professional review and redrafting of standard employment law documentation together with password access to our electronic database of HR documentation including policies, precedents and handbooks

- optional insurance indemnity against employment tribunal legal costs and compensatory awards including tribunal representation from one of our experienced advocates

Vigil removes the uncertainty of employment law litigation costs and provides you with a review, assurance and support services from a team of expert employment law solicitors.

We have teams based in London, Oxford and on the South Coast. For further information please call us on **0870 240 8096** or email us at: **vigil@bllaw.co.uk** Alternatively you can find information on our website **www.bllaw.co.uk**

Blake Lapthorn Tarlo Lyons

Generally each side pays their own costs and it is only in about 1 per cent of cases that costs are awarded. The average costs awarded in 2006/07 were just over £2,000.

THE ROLE OF EMPLOYMENT TRIBUNALS

Employment tribunals are legally constituted bodies set up to hear complaints about matters connected with employment. They are like informal courts with three members, including a legally qualified chairman.

How a claim arises

Any employee wishing to make a claim to an employment tribunal must do so within three months of the date of termination of employment, or of the event to which the complaint relates. The applicant has to complete a form ET1 (see below), which sets out the grounds of the complaint and this is then sent to the employer.

If you, as an employer receive a form ET1 you will need to respond by completing form ET3 (see below), generally within 21 days, a process known as entering an appearance.

HOW TO DEFEND A CLAIM

The process for defending a claim is as follows:

- you will receive a copy of the employee's claim, which will set out the grounds of her complaint in form ET1;
- you should read the form carefully to ensure that all the details are correct;
- you are asked whether you intend to contest the claim, and if you do you should set out the grounds for resisting it and address any errors in the employee's application;
- if insufficient information has been provided by the applicant for you to be clear about the exact nature of the claim you can ask the local tribunal office for a delay in responding – entering an appearance – until you have received further and better particulars;
- the defence you put forward will depend of course on the nature of the claim;

- following the receipt of the ET1 you are likely to be contacted by a conciliation officer of ACAS, whose role is to try to negotiate a settlement between the parties.

Preparing for a tribunal hearing

You should be notified about a tribunal hearing 14 days in advance. When preparing for a hearing you should:

- make sure that your witnesses are able to attend the hearing;
- brief any witnesses to ensure that they are aware of what they may be asked and are clear about their responses;
- arrange your documents into a bundle and number them consecutively;
- send large bundles of documents to the tribunal office well in advance to give everyone time to read them;
- prepare thoroughly and try to anticipate likely questions;
- consider whether you need to be represented at the tribunal.

Procedure at the hearing

The procedure to be followed at the hearing is:

- arrive early and let the receptionist know who is attending the hearing;
- contact the other party in case there is the possibility of a last-minute settlement;
- confirm with your witnesses the tribunal procedure and the evidence they are to give;
- the party with the burden of proof will be asked to present their case;
- the other party will then be asked to present her case;
- witnesses will next be questioned by both parties and tribunal members;
- after the presentation of the evidence both parties will have the opportunity to make a closing statement;
- the tribunal will then make a decision on the evidence presented.

COMPENSATION FOR UNFAIR DISMISSAL

Tribunals can award:

- Reinstatement or re-engagement.

- A minimum basic award calculated on a similar basis as the redundancy payment subject to a maximum of 30 weeks' pay at the current statutory rate (£330 per week in 2008).
- A compensatory award designed to compensate for loss of earnings up to a maximum of £63,000 in 2008 (reviewed annually). This limit may be disregarded in certain cases, such as those relating to race, sex or disability discrimination or where the dismissal relates to health and safety or whistle-blowing issues.

UNREASONABLE CLAIMS

Rules have been introduced to try to discourage employees from pursuing claims that are frivolous or unreasonable:

- Where such cases arise tribunals have always been able to ask for a pre-hearing review. If following this review the applicant still wishes to proceed with the case a deposit of up to £500 may be required.
- A tribunal can now take into account the unreasonable behaviour of a party's representative when awarding costs against that party.
- The tribunal now has to consider an award of costs where proceedings that have no reasonable prospect of success have been pursued.

REVIEW OF A TRIBUNAL'S DECISION

You can ask a tribunal to review a decision on the grounds that:

- the decision was wrongly made because of an error by the tribunal staff;
- a party did not receive notice of the proceedings leading to the decision;
- the decision was made in the absence of a party;
- new evidence has become available since the conclusion of the hearing to which the decision relates, providing its existence could not have reasonably been known of or foreseen at the time of the hearing; or
- the interests of justice require such a review.

It is up to the chairman of the tribunal to decide whether to allow any such review. An appeal to the Employment Appeal Tribunal can take place on a point of law.

Better practice. Smarter policies. Fewer headaches.

EEF is a trusted partner to thousands of businesses across Britain. We work on behalf of over 6000 companies. On any given day you'll find us helping our members tackle a whole range of employment challenges.

Working with our team of HR and legal experts means that EEF's complete suite of services for the HR professional is at your disposal:

- Preparation, negotiation and representation at employment tribunals
- Vetting of all your employment-related documents
- Expert advice delivered either on-site or by telephone and through regular briefings, seminars and web briefings
- An exclusive employment guide in print and online
- Comprehensive guides on new and existing legislation such as family-friendly policy, information and consultation and dispute resolution
- Advice on all aspects of trade union liaison

We'll help you implement and maintain best practice throughout your organisation, enabling you to manage your business, and your people, more effectively. Should a problem arise, we'll be there to help you work through it, whether it's an employment relations issue or a tribunal case.

EEF tribunal figures show continued success

With over 85 experienced advisers, including 50 qualified employment lawyers across the country, we are one of the largest and most highly qualified providers of employment law advice and employment tribunal representation. We consistently achieve excellent results for members.

Last year EEF companies won 82% of their tribunal claims

EEF results show that only 2% of all claims handled by EEF were upheld at a tribunal hearing. Of the claims that did proceed to a hearing, the employer was successful in 82% of them, demonstrating that EEF is achieving excellent results for member companies. This is well above the national average.

Our close relationship with government means that we create a direct link between your business and the policy makers

We stay closely involved in the legislative process to benefit companies like yours. This kind of work isn't always about the quick turnaround, but its effects are long-lasting.

For example in 2004, the Dispute Resolution Regulations were introduced in an attempt to tackle workplace disputes, improve conciliation and address the rising number of employment tribunals.

We have always argued that the initial regulations were too complicated a tool for ensuring workplace disputes were dealt with efficiently and proportionately. As a result, government appointed a review panel which included EEF and was led by Michael Gibbons.

The government accepted our recommendations and the new scheme is expected to become law in April 2009.

A successful outcome for our members

"The fact that EEF's solicitor had such in-depth knowledge of our company was hugely beneficial".

Amy Bonner, HR Officer at Dewhurst

As soon as Hounslow-based company Dewhurst received a tribunal claim form for constructive dismissal and race discrimination, they contacted EEF.

As an organisation which takes its employee commitments seriously, Dewhurst had not been faced with an employment tribunal for some 10 years and for the HR officer leading the case it was a first experience of tribunal. Fortunately, attendance at one of our mock tribunal sessions weeks before meant she knew what to expect.

We sent a solicitor on site straight away to gather evidence and prepare statements. By spending time in the business our solicitor was able to gain a detailed knowledge of the working environment. By the time we successfully represented Dewhurst at tribunal, everyone involved was fully briefed and knew what to expect.

Even though Dewhurst won, the tribunal prompted it to review its equal opportunity policies and to ensure that managers were confident in applying them. Our solicitor reviewed the policies to ensure best practice was being applied and carried out a development programme for staff, thereby ensuring that training was both practical and relevant.

Our services

We can also provide your company with a full range of business services including Health & Safety, Information & Research, Environmental Services, Training & Development and Policy & Representation.

If you want to be kept up-to-date on important legislation changes and find out more about how our services can help you and your organisation visit **www.eef.org.uk** or call **0800 458 1500**.

Claim to an Employment Tribunal

Please read the **guidance notes** and the notes on this page carefully **before** filling in this form.

By law, you **must** provide the information marked with ✳ and, if it is relevant, the information marked with ⬤ (see guidance on Pre-acceptance procedure).

You may find it helpful to take advice **before** filling in the form, particularly if your claim involves discrimination.

How to fill in this form

All claimants **must** fill in **sections 1, 2 and 3**. You then only need to fill in those sections of the form that apply to your case. For example:

For **unpaid wages**, fill in **sections 4 and 8**.

For **unfair dismissal**, fill in **sections 4 and 5**.

For **discrimination**, fill in **sections 4 and 6**.

For a **redundancy payment**, fill in **sections 4 and 7**.

For **unfair dismissal** and **discrimination**, fill in **sections 4, 5 and 6**.

For **unfair dismissal** and **unpaid wages**, fill in **sections 4, 5 and 8**.

Fill in **section 10** only if there is some information you wish to draw to the tribunal's attention and **section 11** only if you have appointed a representative to act on your behalf in dealing with your claim.

If this form sets out a claim by more than one claimant arising from the same set of facts, please give the names and addresses of additional claimants on a separate sheet or sheets of paper.

Please make sure that all the information you give is as accurate as possible.

Where there are tick boxes, please tick the one that applies.

If you fax the form, do not send a copy in the post.

ET1

Form ET1

1 Your details

1.1 Title: Mr ☐   Mrs ☐   Miss ☐   Ms ☐   Other

1.2* First name (or names):

1.3* Surname or family name:

1.4 Date of birth (date/month/year):   /   /   Are you: male? ☐   female? ☐

1.5* Address:

Postcode

You do not need to answer 1.6 and 1.7 if you have appointed a representative (see section 11).

1.6 Phone number **(where we can contact you during normal working hours):**

1.7 How would you prefer us to communicate with you?

Post ☐   Fax ☐   E-mail ☐

Fax:

E-mail address:

2 Respondent's details

2.1* Give the name of your employer or the organisation or person you are complaining about (the respondent).

2.2* Address:

Postcode

2.3 If you worked at an address different from the one you have given at 2.2, please give the full address.

Postcode

2.4● If your complaint is against more than one respondent please give the names, addresses and postcodes of additional respondents.

Form ET1   *(Continued)*

3 Action before making a claim

3.1* Are you, or were you, an employee of the respondent?   Yes ☐   No ☐
If 'Yes', please now go straight to section 3.3.

3.2 Are you, or were you, a worker providing services to the respondent?   Yes ☐   No ☐
If 'Yes', please now go straight to section 4.
If 'No', please now go straight to section 6.

3.3● Is your claim, or part of it, about a dismissal by the respondent?   Yes ☐   No ☐
If 'No', please now go straight to section 3.5.

3.4● Is your claim about anything else, in addition to the dismissal?   Yes ☐   No ☐
If 'No', please now go straight to section 4.
If 'Yes', please answer questions 3.5 to 3.7 about the
non-dismissal aspects of your claim.

3.5● Have you put your complaint in writing to the respondent?

Yes ☐   Please give the date you put it to them in writing.   /   /
No ☐

If 'No', please now go straight to section 3.7.

3.6● Did you allow at least 28 days between the date you put your   Yes ☐   No ☐
complaint to the respondent and the date you sent us this claim?
If 'Yes', please now go straight to section 4.

3.7● Please explain why you did not put your complaint in writing to the respondent or,
if you did, why you did not allow at least 28 days before sending us your claim.
(In most cases, it is a legal requirement to take these procedural steps. Your claim
will not be accepted unless you give a valid reason why you did not have to meet
the requirement in your case. If you are not sure, you may want to get legal advice.)

Form ET1   *(Continued)*

4 Employment details

4.1 Please give the following dates if possible.

When your employment started   /   /

When your employment ended or will end   /   /

Is your employment continuing?   Yes ☐   No ☐

4.2 Please say what job you do or did.

4.3 How many hours do or did you work each week?   ....hours each week

4.4 How much are or were you paid?

Pay before tax   £   each

Normal take-home pay (including overtime, commission, bonuses and so on)   £   each

4.5 If your employment has ended, did you work (or were you paid for) a period of notice?   Yes ☐   No ☐

If 'Yes', how many weeks or months did you work or were you paid for?   ....weeks ....months

5 Unfair dismissal or constructive dismissal

Please fill in this section only if you believe you have been unfairly or constructively dismissed.

5.1 ● If you were dismissed by your employer, you should explain why you think your dismissal was unfair. If you resigned because of something your employer did or failed to do which made you feel you could no longer continue to work for them (constructive dismissal) you should explain what happened.

Form ET1 *(Continued)*

5 Unfair dismissal or constructive dismissal continued

5.1 continued

5.2 Were you in your employer's pension scheme? Yes ☐ No ☐

5.3 If you received any other benefits from your employer, please give details.

5.4 Since leaving your employment have you got another job? Yes ☐ No ☐
If 'No', please now go straight to section 5.7.

5.5 Please say when you started (or will start) work.

5.6 Please say how much you are now earning (or will earn). £   each

5.7 Please tick the box to say what you want if your case is successful:
    a To get your old job back and compensation (reinstatement)   ☐
    b To get another job with the same employer and compensation (re-engagement)   ☐
    c Compensation only   ☐

Form ET1 *(Continued)*

6 Discrimination

Please fill in this section only if you believe you have been discriminated against.

6.1 • Please tick the box or boxes to indicate what discrimination (including victimisation) you are complaining about:

Sex (including equal pay)	☐	Race	☐
Disability	☐	Religion or belief	☐
Sexual orientation	☐		

6.2 • Please describe the incidents which you believe amounted to discrimination, the dates of these incidents and the people involved.

Form ET1 *(Continued)*

7 Redundancy payments

Please fill in this section only if you believe you are owed a redundancy payment.

7.1● Please explain why you believe you are entitled to this payment and set out the steps you have taken to get it.

8 Other payments you are owed

Please fill in this section only if you believe you are owed other payments.

8.1● Please tick the box or boxes to indicate that money is owed to you for:

unpaid wages? ☐
holiday pay? ☐
notice pay? ☐
other unpaid amounts? ☐

8.2 How much are you claiming?

Is this: before tax? ☐　　　after tax? ☐

8.3● Please explain why you believe you are entitled to this payment. If you have specified an amount, please set out how you have worked this out.

Form ET1　*(Continued)*

9 Other complaints

Please fill in this section only if you believe you have a complaint that is not covered elsewhere.

9.1 ● Please explain what you are complaining about and why.
Please include any relevant dates.

Form ET1 *(Continued)*

10 Other information

10.1 Please do not send a covering letter with this form.
You should add any extra information you want us to know here.

11 Your representative

Please fill in this section only if you have appointed a representative. If you do fill this section in, we will in future only send correspondence to your representative and not to you.

11.1 Representative's name:

11.2 Name of the representative's organisation:

11.3 Address:

Postcode

11.4 Phone number:

11.5 Reference:

11.6 How would they prefer us to communicate with them?

Post ☐   Fax ☐   E-mail ☐
Fax:
E-mail address:

Please sign and date here

Signature: Date: /   /

Data Protection Act 1998. We will send a copy of this form to the respondent(s) and Acas. We will put some of the information you give us on this form onto a computer. This helps us to monitor progress and produce statistics.

Form ET1   *(Continued)*

Case number:

1 Name of respondent company or organisation

1.1* Name of your organisation:

Contact name:

1.2* Address   Number or Name

Street

Town/City

+   County

Postcode

1.3 Phone number:

1.4 How would you prefer us to   E-mail   Post   Fax
communicate with you? (Please tick only one box)
E-mail address:

@

Fax number:

1.5 What does this organisation mainly make or do?

1.6 How many people does this organisation employ in Great Britain?

1.7 Does this organisation have more than one site in Great Britain?   Yes   No

1.8 If 'Yes', how many people are employed at the place where the
claimant worked?

2 Action before a claim

2.1 Is, or was, the claimant an employee?   Yes   No
If 'Yes', please now go straight to section 2.3.

2.2 Is, or was, the claimant a worker providing services to you?   Yes   No
If 'Yes', please now go straight to section 3.
If 'No', please now go straight to section 5.

2.3 If the claim, or part of it, is about a dismissal,   Yes   No
do you agree that the claimant was dismissed?
If 'Yes', please now go straight to section 2.6.

2.4 If the claim includes something **other than** dismissal,   Yes   No
does it relate to an action you took on
grounds of the claimant's conduct or capability?
If 'Yes', please now go straight to section 2.6.

2.5 Has the substance of this claim been raised by the claimant   Yes   No
in writing under a grievance procedure?

2.6 If 'Yes', please explain below what stage you have reached in the dismissal and disciplinary
procedure or grievance procedure (whichever is applicable).
If 'No' and the claimant says they have raised a grievance with you in writing, please say
whether you received it and explain why you did not accept this as a grievance.

Form ET3

3 Employment details

3.1 Are the dates of employment given by the claimant correct? Yes No
   If 'Yes', please now go straight to section 3.3.

3.2 If 'No', please give dates and say why you disagree with the dates given by the claimant.

   When their employment started

   When their employment ended or will end

   Is their employment continuing? Yes No

   I disagree with the dates for the following reasons.

3.3 Is the claimant's description of their job or job title correct? Yes No
   If 'Yes', please now go straight to section 3.5.

3.4 If 'No', please give the details you believe to be correct below.

3.5 Is the information given by the claimant correct about being Yes No
   paid for, or working, a period of notice?
   If 'Yes', please now go straight to section 3.7.

3.6 If 'No', please give the details you believe to be correct below. If you gave them no notice or
   didn't pay them instead of letting them work their notice, please explain what happened and why.

3.7 Are the claimant's hours of work correct? Yes No
   If 'Yes', please now go straight to section 3.9.

3.8 If 'No', please enter the details you believe to be correct. hours each week

3.9 Are the earnings details given by the claimant correct? Yes No
   If 'Yes', please now go straight to section 4.

3.10 If 'No', please give the details you believe to be correct below.

			Hourly
Pay before tax	£ ,	.00	Weekly
			Monthly
Normal take-home pay (including overtime, commission, bonuses and so on)	£ ,	.00	Yearly

Form ET3   *(Continued)*

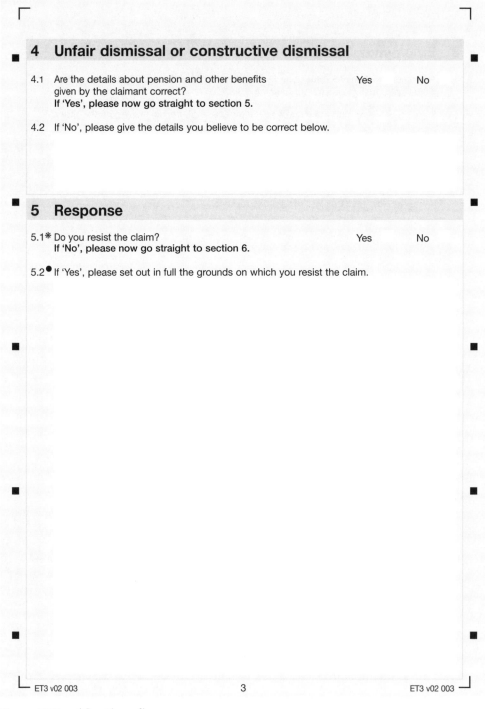

4 Unfair dismissal or constructive dismissal

4.1 Are the details about pension and other benefits given by the claimant correct? Yes No
If 'Yes', please now go straight to section 5.

4.2 If 'No', please give the details you believe to be correct below.

5 Response

5.1* Do you resist the claim? Yes No
If 'No', please now go straight to section 6.

5.2● If 'Yes', please set out in full the grounds on which you resist the claim.

Form ET3   *(Continued)*

6 Other information

6.1 Please do not send a covering letter with this form. You should add any extra information you want us to know here.

7 Your representative If you have a representative, please fill in the following.

7.1 Representative's name:

7.2 Name of the representative's organisation:

7.3 Address   Number or Name

                     Street

                  + Town/City

                     County

                     Postcode

7.4 Phone number:

7.5 Reference:

7.6 How would you prefer us to   E-mail   Post   Fax
    communicate with them? (Please tick only one box)
         E-mail address:
                                          @
         Fax number:

Please sign and date here

Signature: Date:

Data Protection Act 1998. We will send a copy of this form to the claimant and Acas. We will put some of the information you give us on this form onto a computer. This helps us to monitor progress and produce statistics. Information provided on this form is passed to the Department for Business Enterprise and Regulatory Reform to assist research into the use and effectiveness of Employment Tribunals.

Form ET3 *(Continued)*

FURTHER INFORMATION

Employment Tribunals Act 1996

Employment Tribunal enquiry line: telephone 0845 795 9775

Industrial tribunals procedures for those concerned in tribunal proceedings – ITL1

16

Ensuring the health, safety and welfare of employees

GENERAL RESPONSIBILITY

Duties of employers to employees

As an employer you have a general responsibility to ensure the health and safety of your employees. This requirement is given legal force through the Health and Safety at Work etc Act 1974. This requires that you must take all reasonably practicable steps to provide:

- a safe working environment, including safe access to and from your premises;
- a safe system of work;
- safe tools, appliances and equipment;
- protection from hazards;
- any necessary training and instruction to your staff.

In addition, if you employ five or more people you must:

- publish a written health and safety policy (see example below);

- form a safety committee if asked to do so in writing by at least two safety representatives;
- consult all employees on health and safety matters.

Duty to general public

In addition to your duties to employees, you also have a duty to ensure the health and safety of any visitors to your premises.

Duties of employees

At work your employees have a duty to take reasonable care of their own health and safety at work and of other persons who may be affected by their acts or omissions, and to cooperate with you and others to ensure that your legal obligations are met.

ENFORCEMENT OF THE HEALTH AND SAFETY AT WORK ETC ACT 1974

The Health and Safety at Work etc Act is enforced by inspectors appointed by the Health and Safety Executive. They have the power to:

- enter and inspect premises;
- collect information, including measurements, photographs, recordings and so forth;
- take samples;
- issue prohibition notices which have the effect of immediately halting the machinery or process in question;
- issue improvement notices requiring you to remedy specific defects;
- bring proceedings before a magistrates' court.

In practice an inspector will not institute criminal proceedings unless you have persistently flouted the law or the breach is a very serious one.

SAFETY REPRESENTATIVES

Safety representatives can be appointed by recognized independent trade unions, and, where appointed, you have a duty to consult them on safety issues.

Any safety representative should, as far as is reasonably practicable, have been employed continuously for two years or more, or have at least two years' experience in a similar environment. It is common for unions to appoint shop stewards as safety representatives, but this can lead to a conflict of interest where, for example, the shop steward has to represent employees who have been accused of breaching safety procedures. However, you have no choice but to accept the union's nominated representative.

The role of a safety representative is to:

- investigate potential hazards and dangerous occurrences at work and examine the causes of accidents;
- investigate complaints by any employee represented about that employee's health, safety or welfare;
- make representations about general health, safety and welfare matters;
- carry out inspections;
- represent employees in consultations with the Health and Safety Executive;
- receive information from inspectors;
- attend meetings of safety committees.

You must give all reasonable assistance and facilities to enable safety inspections to take place.

In addition, the Health and Safety (Consultation with Employees) Regulations 1996 require you to consult employees, where there are no recognized trade unions, on a range of health and safety issues that are likely to affect employees. Consultation can be with the employees directly or with elected 'representatives of employee safety' (RoES).

Whether you deal with safety representatives appointed by recognized independent trade unions or with RoES elected by employees, you must let them have reasonable paid time off to carry out their functions and to receive training.

Protection for health and safety representatives

You may not dismiss, or take action short of dismissal (such as downgrading, or disciplinary action) against safety representatives and employees for taking what may be regarded as appropriate action in relation to health and safety issues.

This protection is for:

- any employee to whom you give specific health and safety responsibilities;
- a recognized workers' representative on health and safety matters or a member of a safety committee;
- any employee who draws your attention to circumstances connected with his work that he believes to be harmful or potentially harmful (generally this will apply only where there is no appointed safety representative);
- any employee who leaves or proposes to leave his place of work because he reasonably believes that there is a serious and imminent danger that he could not have been expected to avert, and who refuses to return to the place of work while the danger persists;
- any employee who, in dangerous circumstances, takes or proposes to take appropriate steps to protect himself or other people from danger.

Whether or not any action you take against an employee is justified will depend on the circumstances. If the employee is negligent and you can demonstrate that the action you took would have been taken by any reasonable employer in the same circumstances, the protection will not apply to the employee. If the employee considers that the action is not justified, he may complain to an employment tribunal, regardless of his length of service.

SAFETY COMMITTEES

Safety representatives can require you to set up a safety committee and this must be done within three months of receiving a written request from two or more safety representatives. Before setting up the safety committee, however, you should consult both the safety representatives and any recognized trade union.

Membership

Where a safety committee is set up you can decide the membership, although it clearly makes sense to have regard to the views of the trade union representatives. The relationship of the safety committee to other committees, and the general working arrangements, will depend on how your company is organized. For example, where you have a number of different plants or workplaces it might be necessary to have separate committees at each of these, perhaps with a coordinating committee at the group or company level.

The membership of the committee should be limited to a reasonable size with an equal number of management and employees' representatives.

Management representatives should include those who have the necessary knowledge and experience to provide accurate information on technical issues relating to health and safety, and should include not just line managers, but also functional specialists such as engineers. They should have the necessary authority to be able to make decisions. Other specialists may be co-opted onto the committee or can be asked to attend meetings in relation to items about which they have particular knowledge.

Role and objectives

The main role of the safety committee is to keep under review health and safety measures taken by the company. Specific functions are likely to include:

- the study of accidents and notifiable diseases, statistics and trends, to enable reports and recommendations to be made to the company's management;
- examination of safety audits, to report on problems and recommend any necessary changes;
- the consideration of reports and information provided by health and safety inspectors;
- the consideration of reports from safety representatives;
- assistance in the development of works safety rules and safe systems of work;
- monitoring the effectiveness of safety training for employees;
- monitoring the effectiveness of health and safety communication in the workplace;
- providing a link with the various government inspectorates and agencies.

MANAGEMENT OF HEALTH AND SAFETY

The Management of Health and Safety at Work Regulations 1999 require you to:

- assess the risk to health and safety of your employees and anyone else affected by your work activities, and if you have more than five employees, to record any significant findings;

- make arrangements for putting into practice the preventive and protective measures arising from the risk assessments, and to put these in writing if you have more than five employees;
- carry out health and safety surveillance of employees where appropriate;
- appoint competent persons to carry out health and safety measures, preferably from within your company;
- arrange any necessary contacts with emergency services;
- provide information and training to employees;
- cooperate with other occupants of your premises to coordinate safety measures;
- ensure that temporary employees are also given the appropriate information.

FIRST AID

You are required to make first-aid arrangements for your employees. The extent of these facilities will depend on the:

- number of employees;
- type of work carried out;
- size of the working premises and the location of employees;
- location of the working premises.

The number of first-aid staff to be provided will depend on all of the above factors, plus whether there is shift working, and the distance from medical services. As a general rule there should be one first-aider for every 50 to 100 employees. Where hazards are greater there should be one for every 50 employees and at least one for 20 or more employees. If you feel that there is no need for a first-aider you should appoint someone to take action in the event of an injury or illness.

REPORTING OF INJURIES, DISEASES AND DANGEROUS OCCURRENCES

The Reporting of Injuries, Diseases and Dangerous Occurrences Regulations 1995 (RIDDOR) require you to report to the HSE any of the following types of incident:

- a death at work or within one year as a result of an injury or condition incurred at work;
- certain specified injuries such as fractures, amputation, loss of sight, electric shock, loss of consciousness, poisoning, injury caused by violence at work and so forth;
- lost time where the person is unfit for work for more than three consecutive days excluding the day of the accident;
- any of the dangerous occurrences specified in the Regulations, including those relating to lifting machinery, pressure systems, dangerous substances, breathing apparatus, explosives and so forth;
- where a person suffers from any of the diseases listed and works in one of the specified activities.

Generally, these must be reported immediately, followed by a written report within seven days.

Health and safety policy

If you have more than five employees you are required to have a health and safety policy, which would normally be incorporated into the staff handbook. An example policy is set out below.

Example health and safety policy

It is the company's policy to establish and maintain safe and healthy working conditions for all staff in accordance with current health and safety legislation.

It is also your responsibility, along with all of our employees, to take reasonable care to ensure the health, safety and welfare of yourself, your colleagues and any visitors to our offices. You should cooperate with any measures introduced to promote health and safety and should bring to the attention of the appropriate supervisor or line manager anything which you feel is, or may become, a safety hazard.

Any infringement of the health and safety policy and rules could lead to disciplinary action and, in certain circumstances, to criminal proceedings.

The director of operations is the main person responsible for ensuring the overall health and safety of our premises.

Fire and bomb alerts

Instructions on what to do in the event of the fire alarm sounding or a bomb alert, and the instructions for evacuating the building are displayed throughout the building. You should make sure that you have read and understood these instructions and know the location of all emergency exits. In the event of an alarm you should leave the building immediately without attempting to retrieve papers, files, personal possessions and so forth.

Security

You are issued with instructions relating to security and the wearing of security passes on joining the company. These must be complied with at all times. In the interests of security the company reserves the right to search staff and their baggage on entering or leaving the premises.

First aid

Some members of staff are trained in first aid and their names are displayed on the notice board. First-aid boxes are located at . . .

Accidents

Any accident or injury on our premises must be reported to your line manager immediately, so that the matter can be properly investigated, recorded, and if appropriate, reported to the proper authorities.

Risk assessments

The company will carry out regular risk assessments relating to the work environment and the equipment used to ensure that these pose no health hazards. Any concerns you might have in this respect should be reported to your line manager.

SMOKING AT WORK

Legislation has now been introduced to ban smoking in public places and offices. A policy document on smoking is set out in Chapter 9.

HEALTH AND SAFETY REGULATIONS

Some of the main health and safety regulations you may need to be aware of, depending on the nature of your business, are as follows:

- Safety Representatives and Safety Committees Regulations 1977
- Control of Asbestos at Work Regulations 1987

- Control of Lead at Work Regulations 1998
- Noise at Work Regulations 1989
- Control of Substances Hazardous to Health Regulations (COSSH) 2002
- Electricity at Work Regulations 1989
- Personal Protective Equipment at Work Regulations 1992
- Manual Handling Operations Regulations 1992
- Health and Safety (Display Screen Equipment) Regulations 1992
- Provision and use of Work Equipment Regulations 1998
- Supply of Machinery (Safety) Regulations 1998
- Workplace (Health, Safety and Welfare) Regulations 1992
- Chemicals (Hazard Information & Packaging for Supply) Regulations 1996
- Fire Precautions (Workplace) Regulations 1997
- Lifting Operations and Lifting Equipment Regulations 1998
- Construction (Design and Management) Regulations 1994
- Confined Spaces Regulations 1987
- Pressure Systems and Transportable Gas Containers Regulations 1989
- Health and Safety (Safety Signs and Signals) Regulations 1996
- Highly Flammable Liquids and Liquefied Petroleum Gases Regulations 1972

FURTHER INFORMATION

Health and Safety at Work etc Act 1974
Health and Safety (Consultation with Employees) Regulations 1996
Management of Health and Safety at Work Regulations 1999
Stranks, J (2007) *Health and Safety at Work,* revised 8th edition, Kogan Page, London

17

Working with trade unions

The majority of small and medium-sized businesses in the United Kingdom, do not have trade unions and this chapter will not therefore apply to them. However, where trade unions do exist, and particularly where they are recognized by the employer, they do make a difference to the way in which the company is run.

The degree of difference between an organization with a union or unions and one without depends on the attitude of management and whether or not there is union recognition. The key difference in a company where unions are recognized is that changes to terms and conditions of employment, and perhaps to working methods and arrangements, will be discussed and negotiated collectively with those unions, rather than with individual employees or their non-union representatives.

The rest of this chapter highlights some of the other key implications for employers and managers.

THE ROLE OF A TRADE UNION

The primary role of a trade union is to protect the interests of its members. This entails negotiating the best possible deals in terms of pay, conditions of service and working arrangements generally. Many unions also have political objectives but these are generally a secondary consideration.

RECOGNIZING A TRADE UNION

Why recognize a trade union?

If you have not previously recognized a union the thought of having to consult one and possibly negotiate with it on a range of issues can be alarming. However, there are a number of advantages:

- it can provide a focal point for consultation and communication;
- it can help to convince the employees of the need for change or for new ways of working;
- the involvement of a union in the change process can help to legitimize the actions of management in the eyes of the workforce;
- it can improve communications between management and the workforce;
- one of the main advantages is that if you wish to introduce changes to working practices, or contract terms, you need only reach agreement with the elected representatives and not with every individual employee, provided they are all members of the union.

The right of recognition

You can voluntarily agree to recognize a trade union. However, following the Employment Relations Act 1999, if you have 21 or more workers, you are legally required to recognize an independent trade union (or unions) for a group of workers (described as a 'bargaining unit') if a majority of the workforce vote for such recognition. A 'majority' in this case means a simple majority of those voting and at least 40 per cent in that bargaining unit.

The meaning of a bargaining unit

Any group or groups of workers at a particular workplace can constitute a 'bargaining unit'. This is one of the issues that you will need to resolve in discussion with the union.

The meaning of union independence

Many trade union rights depend on the trade union being recognized as independent – not under the control of the employer. Being independent has the advantages that:

- the right not to be dismissed or suffer action short of dismissal on the grounds of trade union membership or activities only applies where the union is independent;
- only an independent union can negotiate an unfair dismissal procedure to take the place of the statutory scheme;
- only an independent union can negotiate away the right to strike in a collective agreement.

If an independent union is recognized by you it then acquires additional rights. These are:

- the right to information for collective bargaining purposes;
- the right (in certain circumstances) to be consulted about proposed collective redundancies and transfers;
- the right to paid time off for union officials and for unpaid time off for union members to carry out trade union activities;
- the right to be consulted on health and safety matters.

Recognition procedure

An application by a union for recognition must satisfy the following criteria:

- the request must be received by the employer;
- the trade union must be independent and have a certificate to that effect;
- the employer must have at least 21 workers on the day the request is received or have employed an average of at least 21 workers in the 13 weeks preceding the date of the request;
- the request must be in writing, identify the union(s) involved and state that it is a request under the provisions of schedule 1 of the Trade Union and Labour Relations (Consolidation) Act 1992.

If you accept the union's request and agree with the identification of the bargaining unit within 10 working days of receiving the request from the union, then the union becomes recognized for collective bargaining purposes and no further action is required. If, however, you wish to negotiate, there is a procedure to be followed, which is summarized in Figure 17.1.

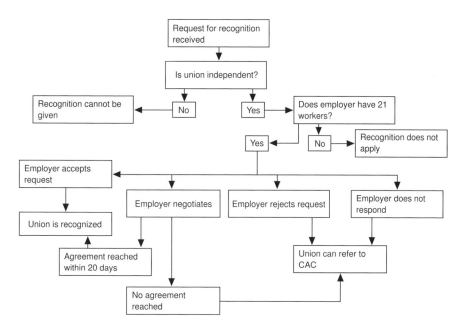

Figure 17.1 *Union recognition process (simplified)*

From Cushway, B (2000) *Working with Unions – The new skills required to deal with union recognition* (reproduced with permission from Pearson Education Ltd)

Voluntary recognition

If you are considering the voluntary recognition of a union you should take into account:

- the degree of support for the union among the workforce;
- the ability of the union to represent those employees effectively;
- whether any other union is recognized for the workforce in question;
- the costs and benefits to you as employer;
- the status and reputation of the union;
- the effects of union recognition on existing collective agreements and other terms and conditions of employment.

Action to be taken on receiving a request for recognition

When a request for recognition is received you have to consider:

- whether to recognize that union;

- whether to enter into a single-union agreement;
- the issues about which recognition should be given and whether they should be limited to specific issues such as disciplinary and grievance procedures;
- whether recognition is in the interests of the company and workforce;
- whether recognition has been given to any other union(s) representing any of those workers.

The scope and content of any recognition policy

Drafting a recognition agreement

Once a union has been recognized a recognition agreement will need to be drawn up.

A recognition agreement provides a framework for collective bargaining and sets out those issues about which bargaining will take place. The agreement should include:

- the names of the parties to the agreement;
- the workers covered by the agreement;
- the purposes for which the trade union is recognized;
- the numbers of shop stewards the organization is prepared to deal with and the process for their election;
- the facilities that they will be given;
- the way in which the agreement will operate;
- provisions for terminating the agreement.

You should try to get a single-union agreement as this is likely to simplify administration, save time and money, and reduce the potential for inter-union disputes.

De-recognizing a trade union

Once a recognition agreement has been entered into you cannot end it within three years of the agreement being made. After that period you can end the agreement with or without the consent of the union. On the other hand, the union can end the agreement at any time with or without your consent.

You can withdraw from recognition agreements if the number of workers falls below the minimum required number of 21 in any 13-week period. To withdraw from the agreement in these circumstances you must give a notice to this effect to the union(s) involved and notify the Central Arbitration Committee. The information given must:

- identify the bargaining arrangements;
- set out the 13-week period;
- state the date on which notice is given;
- be given within a period of five working days following the 13-week period;
- state that you and any associated employer employed fewer than 21 workers on average during that 13-week period;
- state the date on which the bargaining arrangements are to cease, and this must be at least 35 working days after the date of the notice.

EMPLOYEES' UNION RIGHTS

Trade union membership

All employees have the right either to belong to, or refuse to belong to, a trade union.

You must not penalize or in any other way discourage trade union membership, for example by failing to provide training or promotion opportunities, by selecting union members first in the event of redundancy, and so forth. Similarly, it is unlawful to dismiss someone either because she is a member of a union or because she refuses to join one.

Where an employee feels that she has been penalized for belonging to a trade union she can bring a complaint to an employment tribunal. The onus is then on the employer to prove that the behaviour complained of, or the penalty imposed, is not because of the employee's membership or non-membership of a trade union.

Time off rights for trade union officers and members

Both members and officials of recognized independent trade unions have the right to a reasonable amount of time off from work to take part in various trade union duties and activities. Trade union officials have the right to *paid* time off to carry out trade union duties and to undertake training.

Any official should be paid at the normal rate, just as if she had not had any time off, or where earnings are variable, such as in piece work, at the average hourly rate.

LOCAL TRADE UNION REPRESENTATIVES OR SHOP STEWARDS

Role

Most trade unions have local unpaid representatives, commonly known as shop stewards, although there are number of other descriptions. The role of these representatives will vary according to the organization but is likely to include some or all of the following:

- representing their members locally, particularly at grievance and disciplinary hearings;
- recruiting new members to the union;
- collecting trade union dues in the absence of any check-off agreement;
- acting as a conduit of information between the union and its members;
- representing the views of the local members to the full-time trade union officer;
- consulting with the management;
- negotiating certain issues at a local level, although the extent and range of this will depend on the structure of the union;
- safeguarding employees' health and safety in the workplace, where the steward is also the safety representative.

Appointment of shop stewards

You should agree the appointment of shop stewards with the union and you should reserve the right to impose conditions or veto particular appointments. The kinds of conditions that it would be reasonable to impose are those relating to the employee's length of service, experience of the jobs being represented, disciplinary record, attendance and so forth. There should also be an agreement about the number of shop stewards.

Facilities for shop stewards

The facilities you will normally be expected to give to shop stewards include:

- reasonable time off with pay to carry out trade union duties such as attending meetings and representing employees;
- reasonable time off with pay to receive training in trade union duties;
- office facilities.

Working with shop stewards

The nature of the working relationship with shop stewards will often depend more on the personalities involved than on any organizational factors. If you or your management experience difficulty in working with any particular local representative the matter should be raised with the full-time union officer at the next higher tier in the union, before taking action such as withdrawing time-off facilities. Generally the union will be interested in maintaining good relations, so will try to resolve any problems.

When working with shop stewards or any other trade union representatives on a day-to-day basis it is wise to confirm any agreement in writing (unless it is 'off the record'). Any such letter should also relate to one subject only, so if several subjects are discussed there will need to be several letters. This is to avoid any possibility of ambiguity, or of certain points being accidentally or deliberately overlooked

PROVIDING INFORMATION TO TRADE UNIONS

You are legally required to disclose to representatives of recognized independent trade unions information that they might need for collective bargaining, and to maintain good industrial relations.

Although the information to be given is not specified in the legislation, it is likely to cover at least the following:

- pay and benefits;
- conditions of service and employment policies;
- manpower data;
- performance, productivity and efficiency data;
- financial data.

The above is the kind of information which should be disclosed according to an ACAS Code of Practice. It is, therefore, advisory rather than obligatory. Listed, recognized unions also have the statutory right to information relating to redundancies, transfers of undertakings (mergers and takeovers), occupational pensions, and the company's policy on training.

Restrictions on disclosure

You can refuse to disclose information that:

- would be against the interests of national security;

- cannot be disclosed because doing so would be illegal;
- has been given to you in confidence;
- relates specifically to an individual and she has not consented to its disclosure;
- would cause substantial damage to your business;
- has been obtained by you to bring, or to defend against, any legal proceedings.

Information and Consultation Directive

The Information and Consultation Directive gives employees the right to be informed about an undertaking's economic situation, informed and consulted about employment prospects, and informed and consulted about decisions likely to lead to substantial changes in work organization or contractual relations, including redundancies and transfers. It applies to undertakings employing 50 or more people and must be implemented in the United Kingdom by March 2005. However, there are transitional provisions that mean that the legislation applies to:

- undertakings with 150 or more employees from 6 April 2005;
- undertakings with 100 or more employees from 6 April 2007;
- undertakings with 50 or more employees from 6 April 2008.

The number of employees in an undertaking is averaged out over a 12-month period.

You are free to agree different procedures to those set out in the Directive and can meet your obligations through existing agreements. You may also withhold information where disclosure would seriously harm the undertaking or be prejudicial to it. Alternatively, you can require that the information be kept confidential by any employee representatives to whom it is disclosed.

The requirement to inform and consult employees is triggered either by a formal request from employees for an information and consultation (I&C) agreement, or it can be initiated by the employer. An employee request to negotiate an agreement must be made by at least 10 per cent of the employees in the undertaking, subject to a minimum of 15 employees and a maximum of 2,500. Where you have a pre-existing agreement you can ballot the workforce to ascertain whether it endorses the request by employees, provided that fewer than 40 per cent of your employees make the request.

HANDLING DISPUTES

A trade dispute is any dispute about work issues either between you and your workers, or between different groups of workers.

Industrial action

Industrial action includes:

- strikes;
- a ban on overtime;
- working to rule;
- refusal to undertake voluntary or non-contractual activities;
- withdrawing cooperation from the employer, for example by not sitting on joint committees;
- refusal to work at a location or operate certain plant or equipment or processes.

There is no right to strike in UK employment law but there is immunity from civil liability for actions in tort provided certain conditions are met.

Legal immunity of unions

A trade union will only be immune from legal action where:

- there is a trade dispute and the action is called wholly or mainly in support of that dispute;
- the trade union has held a properly conducted secret ballot;
- the trade union has given notice of official industrial action to employers likely to be affected;
- the action is not secondary action (action against another employer who is not the main party to the dispute);
- the action is not intended to promote union closed shop practices or to prevent employers using non-union firms as suppliers;
- the action is not in support of any employee dismissed while taking unofficial industrial action;
- the action does not involve unlawful picketing.

Dismissing employees for taking unofficial industrial action

You can dismiss all or some of your employees if they take unofficial action and can re-engage some or none of them without facing claims for unfair dismissal.

Picketing

Although the official reason for picketing is to give information, the real aims of picketing are to:

- try to persuade others to join the strike;
- prevent goods or supplies from reaching the employer; and
- ensure that those already on strike do not return.

Picketing is only lawful if it is:

- undertaken in relation to a trade dispute;
- carried out by a person attending near her own place of work, or a trade union official accompanying a member;
- for the purpose of peacefully obtaining or communicating information or peacefully persuading a person to work or not to work;
- an unemployed person picketing by or near her last place of work in relation to a trade dispute connected with the dismissal;
- a person who does not have a fixed place of work, or for whom it is not practicable to picket at her place of work, who may picket at any premises of her employer from which her work is administered.

You can sue any pickets not complying with these rules, take out an injunction to stop any unlawful picketing, and start an action for damages.

There is no statutory limit on the number of pickets.

Handling industrial action

How you respond to any industrial action will depend on the nature and scale of that action. However, there are a number of responses that might generally apply in a range of situations. These are:

- consider voluntary conciliation, possibly through ACAS, or alternatively through an independent arbitrator;

- take no action and continue to pay the employees normally, if it is felt that the business can be continued without too much disruption during the dispute;
- where there is a breach of contract consider taking individual disciplinary action against those taking part in the action;
- where any actions are unofficial and do not have immunity seek a court injunction;
- use any agreed collective disputes procedure to settle the dispute;
- call upon support from the relevant employer's association or ACAS;
- consider writing to any employees taking part, threatening to suspend them, possibly even terminating their employment if the industrial action persists;
- where industrial action takes the form of non-performance of certain activities notify the employees that they will only be paid for those activities they do undertake;
- if the industrial action is unofficial, consider dismissing those taking part;
- consider withholding all or part of the pay of any employee taking part in a strike or other industrial action;
- refuse to let employees work normally unless they sign an undertaking not to take part in industrial action;
- close down the place of work and reopen it after a period of, say, three months, selectively re-engaging dismissed employees;
- terminate existing contracts and offer new ones calculated on the basis of the work the employees are prepared to do;
- consider notifying the union and the individuals involved in the action that you will be seeking to make deductions from employees' wages to make up for lost revenue arising from the industrial action.

FURTHER INFORMATION

Cushway, B (2000) *Working with Unions – The new skills required to deal with union recognition*, Pearson Education, London
Employment Relations Act 1999
Trade Union and Labour Relations (Consolidation) Act 1992

Glossary

ACAS – Advisory Conciliation and Arbitration Service.
AML – Additional Maternity Leave.
Assessment centre – range of tests used for staff selection.

Balanced scorecard – a technique for setting objectives in performance management.
BEI – behavioural event interview.
BERR – Department for Business, Enterprise and Regulatory Reform (formerly DTI – Department of Trade and Industry).

Check-off agreement – an agreement between the employer and trade union or unions in which trade union subscriptions are automatically deducted from pay.
Competency or competence – a trait or behaviour required for effective job performance.
Compromise agreement – an agreement made between the employer and an employee in which the employee agrees not to pursue a specific complaint against the employer.
Constructive dismissal – a situation in which an employee resigns because he or she considers the behaviour of the employer to be so unreasonable that he or she has no other option.
CV – curriculum vitae.

Data controller – a term under the Data Protection Act 1988 for a person who is responsible for managing data in the company.
Data subject – a term under the Data Protection Act 1988 for a person about whom personal data is held.

ET1 – the claim form completed by an applicant to an employment tribunal.

ET3 – the form completed by an employer in response to a claim received on form ET1.
ETO – 'economic, technical and organizational', legitimate reasons for altering contracts of employment following the transfer of an undertaking.
EWC – expected week of childbirth.

Garden leave – leave an employee may be required to take during any notice period to prevent that person attending the workplace.
GOQ – genuine occupational qualification.
Gross misconduct – misconduct that is so serious that it justifies instant dismissal without notice.
Guarantee payment – a payment made to compensate for short-time working.

HSE – Health and Safety Executive.

I&C – information and consultation.
IPRP – individual performance-related pay (as distinct from group schemes).

Job evaluation – a systematic process for establishing the relative size of jobs in an organization.

KRA – key result area.

LIFO – last in, first out (basis for redundancy selection).
Lower Earnings Limit (LEL) – the earnings point at which an employee begins to pay National Insurance.

Mat B1 – evidence of pregnancy.

NI – National Insurance.
NIC – National Insurance contribution(s).

OML – Ordinary Maternity Leave.

PAYE – Pay As You Earn.
PILON – pay in lieu of notice.
PIW – period of interruption of work (in relation to statutory sick pay).
POVA – protection of vulnerable adults
PRP – performance-related pay.

RIDDOR – the Reporting of Injuries Diseases and Dangerous Occurrences Regulations 1995.
RoEs – representatives of employee safety.

SAP – Statutory Adoption Pay.
SMART objectives – performance objectives that are specific, measurable, achievable, realistic and time-related.
SMP – Statutory Maternity Pay.
SPP – Statutory Paternity Pay.
SSP – Statutory Sick Pay.

TUPE – Transfer of Undertakings and Protection of Employment Regulations 1981.

ULRs – Union Learning Representatives – union members appointed to advise other members about their training, development and educational needs.

Wrongful dismissal – dismissal in breach of the contract of employment, as distinct from 'unfair dismissal'.

Useful addresses

Advisory Conciliation and Arbitration Service (ACAS)

Head Office
Brandon House
180 Borough High Street
London
SE1 1LW
Tel: 020 7210 3000
Website: www.acas.org.uk

London
Euston Tower
286 Euston Road
London
NW1 3JJ
Tel: 020 7396 0022

East of England
Acas House
Kempson Way
Suffolk Business Park
Bury St Edmunds
Suffolk
IP32 7AR
Tel: 01284 774500

East Midlands
Lancaster House
10 Sherwood Rise
Nottingham
NG7 6JE
Tel: 0115 985 8253

West Midlands
Warwick House
6 Highfield Road
Edgbaston
Birmingham
B15 3ED
Tel: 0121 456 5434

North West
Commercial Union House
2–10 Albert Square
Manchester
M60 8AD
Tel: 0161 833 8500

North West
Pavillion 1
The Matchworks
Speke Road
Speke
Liverpool
L19 2PH
Tel: 0151 728 5600

North East
Cross House
Westgate Road
Newcastle upon Tyne
NE1 4XX
Tel: 0191 269 6000

Scotland
151 West George Street
Glasgow
G2 2JJ
Tel: 0141 248 1400

South West
The Waterfront
Welshback
Bristol
BS1 4SB
Tel: 0117 906 5200

South East
Suites 3–5
Business Centre
1–7 Commercial Road
Paddock Wood
Kent
TN12 6EN
Tel: 01892 837273

South East
Cygnus House
Ground Floor
Waterfront Business Park
Fleet
Hampshire
GU51 3QT
Tel: 01252 816650

Wales
3 Purbeck House
Lambourne Crescent
Llanishen
Cardiff
CF14 5GJ
Tel: 029 2076 2636

Yorkshire and Humber
The Cube
123 Albion Street
Leeds
LS2 8ER
Tel: 0113 205 3800

Central Office of the Employment Tribunals
England and Wales
Southgate Street
Bury St Edmunds
Suffolk
IP33 2AQ
Tel: 0122 459 3137

Scotland
Eagle Buildings
215 Bothwell Street
Glasgow
G2 7TS

Chartered Institute of Personnel and Development
IPD House
151 The Broadway
London
SW19 1JQ
Tel: 020 8612 6200

Department for Business, Enterprise and Regulatory Reform (BERR)
151 Buckingham Palace Road
London
SW1V 9SS
Tel: 020 7215 5000
Website: www.berr.gov.uk

Employment Publishers
Gee
100 Avenue Road
Swiss Cottage
London
NW3 3PG
Tel: 020 7393 7400

Equality and Human Rights Commission Disability Helpline (England)
FREEPOST MID02164
Stratford upon Avon
CV37 9BR
Tel: 08457 622 633
Textphone: 08457 622 644
Fax: 08457 778 878

Equality and Human Rights Commission Helpline Wales
Freepost RRLR-UEYB-UYZL
1st Floor
3 Callaghan Square
Cardiff
CF10 5BT
Tel: 0845 604 8810
Textphone: 0845 604 8820
Fax: 0845 604 8830
9am to 5pm, Monday to Friday (an out-of hours service will start running soon)

Equality and Human Rights Commission Helpline Scotland
Freepost RRLL-GYLB-UJTA
The Optima Building
58 Robertson Street
Glasgow
G2 8DU
Tel: 0845 604 5510
Textphone: 0845 604 5520
Fax: 0845 604 5530

Health and Safety Executive
HSE Information Centre
Broad Lane
Sheffield
S3 7HQ
Tel: 0870 154 5500

For health and safety publications:
HSE Books
PO Box 1999
Sudbury
Suffolk
CO10 6FS
Tel: 01787 881165
Fax: 01787 313995
Website: www.hse.gov.uk

Information Commissioner
Wycliffe House
Water Lane
Wilmslow
Cheshire
SK9 5AE
Tel: 01625 545700

Institute of Directors
116 Pall Mall
London
SW1Y 5ED
Tel: 020 7839 1233
Website: www.iod.com

Overseas Labour Service
Department for Education and
Employment
Moorfoot
Sheffield
S1 4PQ
Tel: 0114 259 4074

Index

NB *italics* indicate a figure in the text

Index of advertisers

The sharpest minds need the finest advice

visit
www.koganpage.com
today